תפלת הלב
שבת/חג
Tefilat HaLev
Shabbat/Festivals

Prayers of the Heart

Shabbat and Festival Services
including Havdalah

with graphics

Compiled and Edited by Rabbi Shafir Lobb

Copyright © 2015 Rabbi Shafir Lobb

Artists retain their own Copyrights for works in this book.

·

All other rights reserved.

ISBN: 1505814650X
ISBN-13: 978-1505814651

Foreword / Acknowledgements

This book is the outgrowth of a number of different books. It is intended to serve those congregations using Reform liturgy in an inclusive style. It is modeled from the latest series of Reform prayer books, the Mishkan series. The liturgy in this prayer book has been further developed by lessons learned from the custom prayer books in a number of congregations throughout the United States and Canada.

The opening prayer (Nishmati) for both evening and morning is based on a teaching of Rabbi Sholom Silver z"l and these lyrics were developed with Rev Gabai Eli Shirim Lester at the second Cactus Kallah.

A very special thank you goes to Rabbi Zalman Shachter-Shalomi, z"tl, Rabbi Marcia Prager, Rabbi Shawn Zevit, and Rabbi Daniel Siegel for teaching about the need and ways to caress the words of liturgy.

All non-attributed original text is the work of Rabbi Shafir Lobb. Song lyrics are attributed to the artists in the body of the Siddur. Special thanks to Rabbi Hanna Tiferet Siegel, Rabbi Shefa Gold and Debbie Friedman z"l for their liturgical lyrics throughout. Art work is thanks to Rabbi Ayla Grafstein, Carol S Kestler, Rabbi Shafir Lobb, Rabbi Marcia Prager, Diane Schiff (Photography) and others whose names have become detached from their work through the Public Domain, but whose effort and vision is appreciated.

Efforts were made to use clear and large fonts, both for Hebrew and English. All Hebrew liturgy is translated using Times New Roman if the translation is not part of the liturgy read aloud or Book Antiqua if it is used as a reading or song, even if only some of the time. Transliteration of all of the Hebrew liturgy (to allow non-Hebrew readers to join in with the Hebrew liturgy) that is normally read aloud, chanted or sung is done using Arial, with the accented syllable in **bold**. We follow the convention that what the reader reads alone is in regular font and what the congregation reads in unison (whether responsive or not) *is in italics*. Each prayer has multiple ways of being included (or not) in any given service. The English translations for prayers and a selection of interpretive readings are included for each prayer and are marked by a graphic to facilitate indicating the service leader's choice for a given service.

Color is used to indicate special readings: Winter or Summer. Torah troph are included on the Shema as traditional troph melody is used for chanting these prayers.

Our siddur offers several alternative amidah choices: the traditional amidah, an English Amidah to be read or chanted (the option with the 🍃 is designed to be chanted if you include the final prayer, the chatima), as well as an amidah in guided imagery (pp. 73-76).

There is also an appendix with expanded explanations of different elements in the liturgy to enhance the user's understanding. This section is based in large part on work done with Rabbi Ed Stafman in the preparation of prayer books for his congregation. Other significant contributors include Rabbi Joseph Weizenbaum, z"l, who created a congregation specific prayer book for his congregation and encouraged me to expand on his book for others, always reminding me that the most important aspect of any book is that it be inviting and accessible to those who will use it in their congregations.

It with that sense in mind that this prayer book is offered in a variety of styles. The dark blue cover includes graphics on each page with the prayer. The light blue cover has white space without the graphics. The dark lavendar cover has a color interior (with graphics); the light lavender has no transliteration for student use. A special Tot Shabbat Siddur is also available.

If you know of any work that has been misattributed or is unattributed and you know the correct artist/author, please advise us at rebshafir@earthlink.net

This book is dedicated
to those who work actively
to build community.

אל תקרא בניך

Our children are our builders

אלא בוניך

"Do not call them your children,
call them your builders"

Our tradition invites us
to remember our community
and those in need through Tzedakah.

TABLE OF CONTENTS

Kabbalat Shabbat / Shabbat Evening..........1
Shabbat Morning..................79
Hallel..................189
Yizkor..................201
Havdalah..................222

Special Features
Amidah in Guided Imagery..................73
Weekday Amidah..................183
Appendix - Some background on Prayers..................228
Songs..................254
Birkat Hamazon..................266

Tefilat HaLev - Shabbat/Festivals — שבת/חג - תפלת הלב

Kabbalat Shabbat — קבלת שבת

SHABBAT SHALOM!

Nishma**ti** ahu**vah**
lehitcha**reit** hakli**pah**
letshu-**vah** usli**chah**
le**to**dah uvra**chah**
Halelluh**Yahh**,
Halelluh**Yahh**

נִשְׁמָתִי אֲהוּבָה
לְהִתְחָרֵט הַקְלִיפָּה
לִתְשׁוּבָה וּסְלִיחָה
לְתוֹדָה וּבְרָכָה
הַלְלוּיָהּ הַלְלוּיָהּ

O my Soul, I Love You,
Pain and Sorrow from my life
Repenting and Releasing
Thanks to You, Blessings come HalelluhYahh
HalelluhYahh

הִנֵנִי מוּכָן וּמְזוּמָן לְקַבֵּל עָלַי מִצְוַת עֲשֵׂה
וְאָהַבְתָּ לְרֵעֲךָ כָּמוֹךָ.

Hine**niy** mu**chan** umezu**man** leka**beil** alai mitz**vat** asei
Ve-a**hav**ta le**rei**-acha kamo**cha**.
I am prepared completely to take upon myself the
mitzvah of doing:
"And you will love each person as you love yourself."

Lechi Lach — לכי לך

Lechi Lach, to a land that I will show you,
Lech Lecha, to a place you do not know.
Lechi Lach, on your journey I will bless you.
And you shall be a blessing, *Lechi Lach*.
Lechi Lach, and I shall make your name great,
Lech Lecha, and all shall praise your name.
Lechi Lach, to the place that I will show you.
Lesimchat Chayim, Lechi Lach.
© Debbie Friedman

Tefilat HaLev - Shabbat/Festivals — שבת/חג – תפלת הלב

We pray, with the power of Your Great Love,
please release all those who are bound.
Blessed be the glorious realm of God's presence,
forever and ever, through all time and space.

Ana Becho-ach - Please, with Strength — אנא בכח

אָנָּא בְּכֹחַ גְּדֻלַּת יְמִינְךָ תַּתִּיר צְרוּרָה:...
בָּרוּךְ שֵׁם כְּבוֹד מַלְכוּתוֹ לְעוֹלָם וָעֶד:

Ana be**cho**-ach gedu**lat** yemin**cha**
tatir tzerura.
Baruch sheim **kavod** malchu**to**
le-o**lam** va-**ed**.

Source of Life, Blessing, Hope and Love, on this Shabbat, calm our lives and still our spirits that we might greet the ministering angels of Shalom, wholeness and peace. Bring them into our lives, let them bless us, and may they depart in peace when this Shabbat is concluded.

Amen.

If we but close our eyes for just a moment and breathe in the Shalom of Shabbat, we might even catch a glimpse of these angels as they surround us in all directions as we enter Shabbat.

O Source of Healing, Healer of the broken hearted, we think now of those who have experienced the tragedy of loss through the power of nature and those whose souls have been torn by the individual losses or challenges they have faced in recent days. Gathered in the security of this Sanctuary, we are yet touched by those who are victims of earthquakes, hurricanes, tsunami, mud slides, and many other natural or

Tefilat HaLev - Shabbat/Festivals שבת/חג - תפלת הלב

otherwise tragic events. For some, the pain of life altered threatens the ability to see the good in others and in ourselves. For some of us, even our easy confidence in the coming of tomorrow is shaken.

Strengthen our confidence that even in the uncertainty of the moment, the power of faith in Your unconditional and boundless love sustains us. Strengthen our capacity for compassion for others that look to us to be there in their moments of uncertainty. The very gift of Shabbat, a time to catch our breath and just BE for a point in time, is part of Your love. Let our footsteps not falter nor our hands and hearts be closed as we respond to the needs of our brothers and sisters.

❃ God, help us now to make this new *Shabbat*.
After noise, we seek quiet;
After crowds of indifferent strangers,
we seek to touch those we love;
After concentration on work and responsibility,
We seek freedom to meditate,
to listen to our inward selves.
We open our eyes to the hidden beauties
and the infinite possibilities in the world
You are creating;
We break open the gates
to the wells of goodness and kindness
in ourselves and in others;
We reach toward one holy perfect moment of *Shabbat*.
    © Ruth F. Brin, adapted

Tefilat HaLev - Shabbat/Festivals — שבת/חג – תפלת הלב

✡ Mighty One, Source of All Life, we have come together to pray as a community and as a congregation; yet each of us is strangely alone in Your Presence. Each of us comes before You with special hopes and dreams; each of us has personal worries and concerns.

Each of us has a prayer which no one else can utter.
Each of us brings praise which no one else can offer.
Each of us feels a joy no one else can share.
Each of us has regrets which others cannot know.

And so we pray together, each of us in our own way:
If we are weary, give us strength.
If we are discouraged, give us hope.
If we have forgotten how to pray, remind us;
If our hearts have been chilled by indifference,
Warm them with Your love
and inspire us with the glowing spirit of Shabbat.

הִנֵּה מַה טּוֹב וּמַה נָּעִים שֶׁבֶת אַחִים גַּם יָחַד.

Hinei ma tov umah na'**im** she**vet** achi**ym** gam yachad.
Behold how good it is and how pleasant it is, when brethren dwell together in unity.

Either you will go through this door or you will not go through. If you go through there is always the risk of remembering your name. Things look at you doubly and you must look back and let them happen. If you do not go through	it is possible to live worthily to maintain your attitudes to hold your position to die bravely but much will blind you, much will evade you, at what cost who knows? The door itself makes no promises. It is only a door. © Adrienne Rich

4

Tefilat HaLev - Shabbat/Festivals — שבת/חג — תפלת הלב

בְּשֵׁם יהוה אֱלֹהֵי יִשְׂרָאֵל, מִימִינִי מִיכָאֵל, וּמִשְּׂמֹאלִי גַּבְרִיאֵל, וּמִלְּפָנַי אוּרִיאֵל, וּמֵאֲחוֹרַי רְפָאֵל, וְעַל רֹאשִׁי שְׁכִינַת אֵל.

Besheim A**do**nai El**ohei** Yisra-**eil** mi**mini** Micha-**eil** umis**mo**li Gavri-**eil,** umil**fa**nai Uri-**eil,** umei-acho**rai** Rafa-**eil** ve'**al** ro**shi,** Shechi**nat** Eil.

In the name of God, Elohai Yisra-eil: May Micha-el be on my right and on my left, Gavri-el, Uri-el before me, behind me Rafa-el. And o'er my head, surrounding me, Shechinat El.

Prayer, termed "Service of the Heart", at once both intimate or personal, and yet public and communal.

One time the Baal Shem Tov was about to step into an abandoned shul when he stopped. He explained "I can't go in because there is no room for us; it is too crowded."

Seeing their astonishment, since the shul was of course empty, he explained: "A prayer, when uttered sincerely and wholeheartedly, sprouts wings and soars upwards to the Throne of Glory. But those who once prayed here, had no kavanah, their prayers had no wings and thus collapsed and fell upon one another. The shul is now densely packed with dead, wingless prayers."

In Judaism, an angel is a spiritual entity in the service of God. When we serve God, we become God's angels. The Hebrew for angel is "messenger." When we pray or sing for angels to surround us, we are praying to God for "messengers" of God's presence. We do not pray to the angel. When someone does something we need "just in time," they are an "angel" for us. When we do the same thing for others, we are angels. It is the help and companionship of community that we welcome when we welcome the angels of Shabbat into our midst.

Tefilat HaLev - Shabbat/Festivals — שבת/חג - תפלת הלב

שלום עליכם / Shalom Aleichem

שָׁלוֹם עֲלֵיכֶם, מַלְאֲכֵי הַשָּׁרֵת, מַלְאֲכֵי עֶלְיוֹן,
מִמֶּלֶךְ מַלְכֵי הַמְּלָכִים, הַקָּדוֹשׁ בָּרוּךְ הוּא:
בּוֹאֲכֶם לְשָׁלוֹם, מַלְאֲכֵי הַשָּׁלוֹם, מַלְאֲכֵי עֶלְיוֹן,
מִמֶּלֶךְ מַלְכֵי הַמְּלָכִים, הַקָּדוֹשׁ בָּרוּךְ הוּא:
בָּרְכוּנִי לְשָׁלוֹם, מַלְאֲכֵי הַשָּׁלוֹם, מַלְאֲכֵי עֶלְיוֹן,
מִמֶּלֶךְ מַלְכֵי הַמְּלָכִים, הַקָּדוֹשׁ בָּרוּךְ הוּא:
צֵאתְכֶם לְשָׁלוֹם, מַלְאֲכֵי הַשָּׁלוֹם, מַלְאֲכֵי עֶלְיוֹן,
מִמֶּלֶךְ מַלְכֵי הַמְּלָכִים, הַקָּדוֹשׁ בָּרוּךְ הוּא:

Shalom alei**chem,** male**chei** hasha**reit,** male**chei** El**yon,**
Mi**melech** male**chei** hamla**chiym,** haKa**dosh** Ba**ruch** Hu.
Bo-a**chem** lesha**lom,** male**chei** hasha**lom,**
male**chei** El**yon,**
Mi**melech** male**chei** hamla**chiym,** haKa**dosh** Ba**ruch** Hu.
Bar**chu**ni lesha**lom,** male**chei** hasha**lom,**
male**chei** El**yon,**
Mi**melech** male**chei** hamla**chiym,** haKa**dosh** Ba**ruch** Hu.
Tzeit**chem** lesha**lom,** male**chei** hasha**lom,**
male**chei** El**yon,**
Mi**melech** male**chei** hamla**chiym,** haKa**dosh** Ba**ruch** Hu.

Peace be to you, O ministering angels, messengers of the Most High,
the supreme Sovereign of Sovereigns, the Holy One, blessed be.
Enter in peace, O messengers of peace, messengers of the Most High,
the supreme Sovereign of Sovereigns, the Holy One, blessed be.
Bless me with peace, O messengers of peace, messengers of the Most High,
the supreme Sovereign of Sovereigns, the Holy One, blessed be.
Leave in peace, O messengers of peace, messengers of the Most High,
the supreme Sovereign of Sovereigns, the Holy One, blessed be.

Tefilat HaLev - Shabbat/Festivals — שבת/חג - תפלת הלב

Ma Tovu — מה טבו

מַה טֹּבוּ אֹהָלֶיךָ יַעֲקֹב, מִשְׁכְּנֹתֶיךָ יִשְׂרָאֵל.
וַאֲנִי בְּרֹב חַסְדְּךָ אָבוֹא בֵיתֶךָ,
אֶשְׁתַּחֲוֶה אֶל הֵיכַל קָדְשְׁךָ בְּיִרְאָתֶךָ.

Mah **tov**u oha**le**cha Ya-a**kov**, Mishkeno**te**cha Yisra-**eil**.
Va-**ani** be**rov** chasde**cha** avo vei**te**cha, eshtacha**veh** el
hei**chal** kodshe**cha** beyira**te**cha.

Blessings flow into the world from the Source of Life.
Be a vessel for the lovesong of God
© R. Hanna Tiferet Siegel

O how good are your tents, Jacob, your dwelling-places, Israel. And I, through Your abundant loving kindness, now enter Your House, drawing near, seeking You, in the house of Your holiness.

※※※ ※※※

וַאֲנִי תְפִלָּתִי לְךָ יהוה, עֵת רָצוֹן,
אֱלֹהִים בְּרָב חַסְדֶּךָ,
עֲנֵנִי בֶּאֱמֶת יִשְׁעֶךָ.

Va-**ani** tefi**la**ti le**cha** Adonai eit ra**tzon**
Elo**hiym** be**rov** hasde**cha** a**nei**ni be-**emet** yish'**e**cha.

I am hope and my prayer to You, through You Adonai,
blending in with Your desire and Your great mercy.
Answer me with Your truth, O great One.
Psalm 69:14 Rev Maya Kashtelyan and Rabbi Shafir Lobb

※※※ ※※※

Tefilat HaLev - Shabbat/Festivals   שבת/חג - תפלת הלב

Candlelighting

Shabbat candles call us to come together as family and as community.

 As we gaze upon the light of the candles, may we remember that it is better to light one candle than to complain about the darkness. It is more rewarding to be part of the light to the world than to release negativity into it through anger or bitterness. May this light enter our souls and our beings and may we see its light reflected in our loved ones' eyes as we enter Shabbat. Let us turn to each other and greet a shining face that mirrors our own and the Source of Life. In Your light, we see light.

✡ On this day we would see the world in a new light.
On this day we would add new spirit to our lives.
 On this day we would taste a new time of peace.
 We would rest from our desire for gain
 and from our ambition for things.
We would raise our eyes to look
beyond time and space toward eternity.
O may we come to see the world in a new light.
 As it is written: "Let a new light shine upon Tzion,
 and may it be our blessing to see its splendor."

Shabbat is a special time for us and our families.
 For a short time, we can sit and imagine peace.
 We can imagine a world where everyone respects
 each other, where all can live in peace.

(Light the Shabbat candles)

8

Tefilat HaLev - Shabbat/Festivals שבת/חג - תפלת הלב

Come, let us light up our hearts.
Come, let us light up our homes.
Breathe in and breathe out, making circles of love.
Oh come, let us light up the world.

בְּרוּכָה אַתְּ שְׁכִינָה אֵם כָּל חַי, אֲשֶׁר קֵרַבְתָּנוּ אֶל לְבָבֵךְ וְהִזְמִנְתָּנוּ לְהַדְלִיק נֵר שֶׁל שַׁבָּת.

Brucha At Shechi**nah**, Eim kol chai **asher** keirav**ta**nu el lev**a**veich **ve**hizmin**ta**nu lehad**lik** ner shel Sha**bat**.

A source of Blessings are You, Divine Presence, Parent of all life. You bring us close to heart and invite us to kindle the light of Shabbat.
© R. Hanna Tiferet Siegel

בָּרוּךְ אַתָּה יהוה אֱלֹהֵינוּ מֶלֶךְ הָעוֹלָם, אֲשֶׁר קִדְּשָׁנוּ בְּמִצְוֹתָיו, וְצִוָּנוּ לְהַדְלִיק נֵר שֶׁל שַׁבָּת.

Baruch Ata Ado**nai** Elo**hei**nu **Me**lech ha-**o**lam, **asher** kid**sha**nu bemitzvo**tav**, Vetzi**va**nu, lehad**lik** ner, shel Sha**bat**.

A source of Blessings are You, Eternal Divine, Sovereign of all time and space. You make us special with Mitzvot and instruct us to kindle the light of Shabbat.

Candle meditation: When lighting the Sabbath candles, some wave their hands in a circular motion three times and bring their hands to their face when finished. A beautiful interpretation of this practice is that it helps us bring the light and peace of Shabbat into our neshamas (our souls), our homes, and our families. Most weeks, it is easy to appreciate this personal practice, sometimes it is not. Especially on those Fridays when it is not, it is important to remember the teaching of Yehuda Amichai: "Let [peace] come like wildflowers, suddenly, because the field must have it: wildpeace."

Each household is instructed to light Shabbat candles - so it is not only a woman's requirement. Single or separated males are also expected to light Shabbat candles in their homes (or even hotel rooms).

Tefilat HaLev - Shabbat/Festivals   שבת/חג – תפלת הלב

✡ I am a Jew because, born of Israel
and having lost her,
I have felt her live again in me, more living than myself.
> *I am a Jew because, born of Israel and having regained her,*
> *I wish her to live after me, more living than in myself.*

I am a Jew because the faith of Israel demands of me
no abdication of the mind.
> *I am a Jew because the faith of Israel requires of me*
> *all the devotion of my heart.*

I am a Jew because in every place
where suffering weeps, the Jew weeps.
> *I am a Jew because at every time when despair cries out,*
> *the Jew hopes.*

I am a Jew because the word of Israel
is the oldest and the newest.

> *I am a Jew because the promise of Israel*
> *is the universal promise.*

I am a Jew because, for Israel,
the world is not yet completed; we are completing it.
> *I am a Jew because, above the nations and Israel,*
> *Israel places humanity and its Unity.*

I am a Jew because above humanity,
image of the divine Unity,
Israel places the divine Unity, and its divinity.

© *1927* From *"A Letter to my Grandson"* Edmond Fleg (adapted)

For us, Israel is a country in the Middle East,
   Our people,   And a special place in our hearts.
   Most of us are not Israelis,
   for they are the citizens of the country Israel.
Yet we are Benei Yisrael, *members of Israel.*
May all of the Israels to which we connect
find peace and joy this Shabbat.
May the peace we seek reach all of the world.

Tefilat HaLev - Shabbat/Festivals שבת/חג - תפלת הלב

LECHAH DODI -
We greet the Shabbat Bride

✡ The mystics of Israel conceived of the Shabbat as entering the world as Israel's bride, and they welcomed her with ecstatic joy. They saw Shabbat, especially hallowed by God, as the day when Israel may unite with God in love.
They would gather in the fields all dressed in white to watch the Shabbat enter the world and accompany her.
They sang the Song of Songs as a love song of God and Israel, and they sang Lechah Dodi:

🕊 When we sing Lechah Dodi, we are saying, "Come my Beloved, let us greet Shabbat," and we are indicating that we will also receive our *pnei Shabbat*, "Shabbat faces," faces that glow with a promise of fulfillment, faces that reflect our joy for the time to spend with family and friends.

🌴 Lechah Dodi is our call to each other
to greet Shabbat,
to make time and space
for the soft and gentle Shabbat Bride
within our lives and within our Self.
In accepting that call, we find our own "face" of Shabbat.

✍ Welcoming the Bride of Shabbat helps us recognize That Shabbat is a time to be happy and to celebrate.
As we sing, we want joyous things more and more.
Shabbat, a time for peace, love, and joy.

Tefilat HaLev - Shabbat/Festivals   שבת/חג - תפלת הלב

❀ We no longer spend the entire day as the ancients did in preparing for Shabbat. In our hectic lives, there is still work to be done and errands to run to complete the week. For many of us, we can only prepare for Shabbat after a long and stressful day at work. In our hurrying and rushing, it is easy to forget what Shabbat is really all about. Our tradition teaches that we are gifted with a special Shabbat Soul for the brief hours of Shabbat to help us recognize Shabbat's gift.

May this special time of Greeting Shabbat
help us prepare ourselves for Shabbat
by shedding, even if just for a few brief hours,
the hecticness of our everyday lives.

✡ The practice of welcoming Shabbat as Israel's bride is mentioned in the Talmud, and that mention forms the basis of the sixteenth-century Kabbalistic ritual in Sfat of going out into the fields, dressed in white to welcome the Sabbath, identified with the Shechinah.

Rabbi Shelomo Ha-Levi Alkabetz, the author of the Lechah Dodi, composed the poem specifically for this ritual. Today we sing this song as part of our welcome to Shabbat, whether mystical or not, to open our own hearts to the joy of Shabbat.

🔔 The practice of observing Shabbat comes from multiple references in Torah, where we are instructed to cease our *maalachah,* traditionally translated as work. Yet the root of *maalachah* is the same root as the word *Maalach,* traditionally translated as angel. The *shoresh,* or root, invites us to consider how we and others act as angels for each other in our daily lives, and what does it mean to step back from that activity and celebrate.

Tefilat HaLev - Shabbat/Festivals — שבת/חג — תפלת הלב

Lechah Dodi - "Come, My Beloved" — לכה דודי

לְכָה דוֹדִי לִקְרַאת כַּלָּה. פְּנֵי שַׁבָּת נְקַבְּלָה:

<u>Chorus</u>: **Lechah** dodi li**krat** kalah, penei **Shabat** nekablah
Come, my Beloved, to greet the Bride; Let us greet our face of Shabbat.

*Set out, My Beloved, Divine Groom, to greet Divine Shechinah,
the Shabbat Bride.
Let us, as entourage for the Shabbat Bride,
usher Her under the wedding canopy.*

(Verses 1, 2, 5 & 9
are the most popular)

1 ✻

שָׁמוֹר וְזָכוֹר בְּדִבּוּר אֶחָד, הִשְׁמִיעָנוּ אֵל הַמְּיֻחָד.
יהוה אֶחָד וּשְׁמוֹ אֶחָד.
לְשֵׁם וּלְתִפְאֶרֶת וְלִתְהִלָּה: לכה דודי

✻ **1 Sha**mor veza**chor** bedi**bur echad** hishmi-anu eil hamyu**chad**. Ado**nai echad** ush**mo echad** le**sheim** ulti**feret** velit'hi**lah**. Lechah dodi

"Keep" (Deut 5:12) and "Remember" (Ex. 20:8) as one Divine word.
The unified God caused us to hear;
the Eternal is One, and God's Name is One.
Eternal and unified, for honor, splendor, and praise.

Although the Divine Groom uttered the Shabbat commandment at Sinai with one voice, some heard a feminine voice saying, "Nurture Shabbat" (Deut 5:12), while others heard a male voice saying, "Hold on to Shabbat" (Ex 20:8). These voices are only different ways that we perceive the One. Sometimes we know a genderless Godsense, sometimes, we know God as male or female. At other times, we know God only as Name, Splendor, or Reflection.

Lechah Dodi was written by Rabbi Shlomo HaLevi Alkabetz (1505-1584), one of the Kabbalists of Sfat. This song has been described as perhaps one of the finest pieces of religious poetry in existence.

The poem, called an acrostic, is arranged so that the first letters of each stanza spells out the name of the author, a practice quite common among liturgical poets. This poem is the only one that was adopted by Rabbi Issac Luria, the foremost authority among the Kabbalistic masters.

Tefilat HaLev - Shabbat/Festivals — שבת/חג

לְכָה דוֹדִי לִקְרַאת כַּלָּה. פְּנֵי שַׁבָּת נְקַבְּלָה:

Chorus: **Lechah** do**di** lik**rat** ka**lah**, pe**nei** Sha**bat** ne**kab**lah
Come, my Beloved, to greet the Bride; Let us greet our face of Shabbat.

2 *

לִקְרַאת שַׁבָּת לְכוּ וְנֵלְכָה. כִּי הִיא מְקוֹר הַבְּרָכָה.
מֵרֹאשׁ מִקֶּדֶם נְסוּכָה.
סוֹף מַעֲשֶׂה בְּמַחֲשָׁבָה תְּחִלָּה: לכה דודי

* 2 Lik**rat** Sha**bat** le**chu** venei**lchah** ki hi me**kor**
hab**ra**chah. Mei**rosh** mi**ke**dem nesu**chah**.
Sof ma'**a**seh bemacha**sha**vah techi**lah**. Lechah dodi
Come let us go now toward Shabbat. For She is always the source of blessing. Abundance flowing before the beginning of time. Last in creation, first in design.

Set out, let us go, entourage of the Shabbat Bride, to greet Her!
On the Shabbat, She opens the gates and lets the Divine blessings flow upon us from above.
She herself hails from the upper realms of the Hidden and Infinite, the last of the Sefirot and the most important of all.

3 מִקְדַּשׁ מֶלֶךְ עִיר מְלוּכָה. קוּמִי צְאִי מִתּוֹךְ
הַהֲפֵכָה. רַב לָךְ שֶׁבֶת בְּעֵמֶק הַבָּכָא.
וְהוּא יַחֲמוֹל עָלַיִךְ חֶמְלָה: לכה דודי

3 Mik**dash me**lech ir melu**cha**. **Ku**mi tze-i mi**toch**
hahafe**chah**. Rav lach **she**vet be'**e**mek haba**cha**.
Ve**hu** yacha**mol** a**la**yich chem**lah**. Lechah dodi
Shrine of the Sovereign, royal city, rise up from the midst of your ruins!
Too long have you dwelled in the valley of tears.
To you, God will show mercy and compassion.

Shechinah, Holy Bride, Heavenly Jerusalem, Sanctuary for the Divine - Rise up
from Your ruins! Just as Jerusalem has been too long in ruins, so you have been
for six days - too long apart from Your Spouse.
Let love shine upon You that You feel loved.

Tefilat HaLev - Shabbat/Festivals - שבת/חג

4 הִתְנַעֲרִי מֵעָפָר קוּמִי. לִבְשִׁי בִּגְדֵי תִפְאַרְתֵּךְ
עַמִּי: עַל יַד בֶּן יִשַׁי בֵּית הַלַּחְמִי.
קָרְבָה אֶל נַפְשִׁי גְאָלָהּ: לכה דודי

4 Hitna'ari me'afar kumi. Liv**shi** big**dei** tifar**teich** ami
Al yad ben yi**shai** beit halach**mi.**
Kor**vah** el naf**shi** ge-a**lahh**. Lechah dodi

Arise and shake off the dust.
Dress yourself in the clothes of your people's splendor.
With the help of David, son of Jesse, the Bethlehemite.
Come near to my soul - redeem it!

*Arise, Shechinah, Holy Bride, and shake off the dust.
Dress Yourself in the splendor of Your people for Your Divine
Groom. Then, the Annointed One, a descendant of King David,
son of Jesse, a Bethlehemite, will bring about Your holy wedding,
Your restoration, above and below.*

✱ 5 הִתְעוֹרְרִי הִתְעוֹרְרִי. כִּי בָא אוֹרֵךְ קוּמִי אוֹרִי.
עוּרִי עוּרִי שִׁיר דַּבֵּרִי. כְּבוֹד יהוה עָלַיִךְ נִגְלָה:
לכה דודי

✱ **5 Hit'oreri hit'oreri. Ki vah o**reich **ku**mi ori.
Uri uri shir dabei**ri.**
Kevod Adonai a**la**yich nig**lah**. Lechah dodi

Awake, Awake! For your light has come. Arise, my light!
Wake, Wake! Sing out in song!
The Holy One's glory on you will shine.

*Awake! Awake! Divine Shechinah, Sabbath Bride, Your light has come!
Arise my light! The Shabbat wedding is upon us.
Wake! Wake! Sing this song of redemption,
for the Divine Groom will shine gloriously upon You.*

Tefilat HaLev - Shabbat/Festivals — שבת/חג — תפלת הלב

לְכָה דוֹדִי לִקְרַאת כַּלָּה. פְּנֵי שַׁבָּת נְקַבְּלָה:

Chorus: **Lechah dodi likrat kalah, penei Shabat nekablah**
Come, my Beloved, to greet the Bride; Let us greet our face of Shabbat.

6 לֹא תֵבוֹשִׁי וְלֹא תִכָּלְמִי. מַה תִּשְׁתּוֹחֲחִי וּמַה תֶּהֱמִי. בָּךְ יֶחֱסוּ עֲנִיֵּי עַמִּי, וְנִבְנְתָה עִיר עַל תִּלָּהּ:
לכה דודי

**6 Lo teivoshi velo tikalmi. Mah tishtochachi umah tehemi. Bach yechesu aniyei ami,
venivnetah ir al tilahh.** Lechah dodi

Be not ashamed. Be not distressed! Why are you bowed and why do you yearn? My people's poor will find comfort in you.
And the city will be rebuilt upon its great hill.

Shechinah, be not ashamed. Be not distressed despite Your humble condition. Why are You bowed in exile and why do You yearn? The poorest among us will find their comfort in You. And Jerusalem will be rebuilt once again on its great hill.

7 וְהָיוּ לִמְשִׁסָּה שֹׁאסָיִךְ. וְרָחֲקוּ כָּל מְבַלְּעָיִךְ. יָשִׂישׂ עָלַיִךְ אֱלֹהָיִךְ. כִּמְשׂוֹשׂ חָתָן עַל כַּלָּה: לכה דודי

**7 Vehayu limshisah shosayich. Verachaku kol meval'ayich. Yasis alayich elohayich.
Kimsos chatan al kalah.** Lechah dodi

Those who plundered you will themselves be destroyed.
Your foes will be distanced. Your God will soon rejoice in you,
As a bridegroom rejoices in his bride.

Those who defiled You, Shechinah, will themselves be destroyed. Your foes will be distanced. Your Beloved will soon rejoice in You; as the bridegroom rejoices in his bride.

The mystics of Sfat, Israel, would go out into the fields shortly before sundown to await the arrival of Shabbat. Earlier in the day they had completed all of their preparations for Shabbat which included a trip to the Mikvah (ritual bath). Dressed all in white, the mystics would sing hymns and psalms and poem-prayers, such as this still popular L'chah Dodi. Our Kabbalat Shabbat services on Shabbat evenings are derived from these mystic practices.

Tefilat HaLev - Shabbat/Festivals — שבת/חג — **תפלת הלב**

8 יָמִין וּשְׂמֹאל תִּפְרֹצִי. וְאֶת־יהוה תַּעֲרִיצִי.
עַל יַד אִישׁ בֶּן פַּרְצִי. וְנִשְׂמְחָה וְנָגִילָה: לכה דודי

**8 Yamin usmol tifrotzi. Ve-et Adonai ta-aritzi.
Al yad ish ben partzi .Venismecha venagilah.** Lechah dodi

Spread out to the right and to the left. Revere God! Through the help of David, the descendant of Peretz, we will soon rejoice and celebrate.

Reach out in every direction, right and left, high and low, and revere יהוה, Your Beloved, the Divine Groom. Then, with the help of the Annointed One, a descendant of King David, great grandson of Ruth, descendant of Peretz. We will celebrate Your wedding for one day, and rejoice for all eternity.

The first two and last stanzas focus on Shabbat-specific themes, while the other six stanzas focus on stages of redemption and the restoration of Jerusalem using the wedding metaphor.

On one hand, Shabbat is called the queen, a reference to *Malchut*, the "lowest" of the *Sefirot*, and receives blessing from them. On the other hand, all the days of the week are blessed from the Shabbat. "In six days God created the heavens and the earth." The mystics understand the six days as referring to God's six emotional attributes, which were the active agents in creation. Shabbat then refers to *Malchut*. Through creation, *Malchut* descended to the worlds of *Briah* (Knowing), *Yetzirah* (Feeling/Formation), and *Asiah* (Doing). This is the service (the daily elevation of the instinctive soul and all material things) in the six days of the week. However, after and through the "work" of Shabbat, *Malchut* rises from the worlds of *Briah, Yetzirah,* and *Asiah* to its original source, where it transcends to the One. From this level, all the days of the week draw blessing.

Tefilat HaLev - Shabbat/Festivals שבת/חג – תפלת הלב

לְכָה דוֹדִי לִקְרַאת כַּלָּה. פְּנֵי שַׁבָּת נְקַבְּלָה:

<u>Chorus:</u> **Le**chah **do**di lik**rat** ka**lah, pe**nei Sha**bat** neka**blah**
Come, my Beloved, to greet the Bride; Let us greet our face of Shabbat.

Set out, My Beloved, Divine Groom, to greet Divine Shechinah,
the Shabbat Bride. Let us, as entourage for the Shabbat Bride,
usher Her under the wedding canopy.

(Please stand and face the door.)

٭ 9 בּוֹאִי בְשָׁלוֹם עֲטֶרֶת בַּעְלָהּ.
גַּם בְּשִׂמְחָה וּבְצָהֳלָה. תּוֹךְ אֱמוּנֵי עַם סְגֻלָּה.
בּוֹאִי כַלָּה, בּוֹאִי כַלָּה: לכה דודי

٭ 9 **Bo**-i vesha**lom** a**te**ret ba'e**lahh.**
Gam besim**cha** uvetzo**ho**lah. **Toch** emu**nei** am segu**lah.**
Bo-i Cha**lah**, bo-i Cha**lah**. Lechah dodi
Come in peace, crown of your mate. Come in joy and radiance.
To the faithful ones among the treasured people. Come, oh bride!
Come, oh bride!

Come, now in peace, in joy and radiance, crowning glory of your Spouse.
To the mystic participants in your Holy
Wedding, You are the entry to the
messianic age. You are the Bride!
You are the Bride! Enter the bridal
canopy, it is time. We turn and greet
you, arriving from the West. Come, oh
Bride! Come, oh Bride!

(Please be seated.)

Traditional choreography is to bend the knee and bow deeply from the waist at each *bo-i Chalah* to welcome the Queen Bride.

Tefilat HaLev - Shabbat/Festivals   שבת/חג - תפלת הלב

A Psalm for Shabbat   מזמור לשבת

🌴 I try hard to hold fast to the truth that a full and thankful heart cannot entertain great conceits. When brimming with gratitude, one's heartbeat must surely result in outgoing love, the finest emotion that we can ever know.   Bill W., *Grapevine* March 1962

🍃 To worship God does not mean to idolize God.
Rather it means to feel that nurturing Presence in our homes and on our ways or to see the beauty of creation in mountain, sea, and sky, and in the human form, or to hear God in the very silence of our own hearts, speaking the truths only the heart knows.

When we remember that feeling, then we arrive at a place where we say, "It is good to sing hymns to Your Name, and to tell of Your faithfulness in the night."

✡ God does not need our songs of praise, we do.
We feel good when we get outside ourselves
enough to acknowledge and praise
the One, who is the Source of All Life.
   We feel good when we pause long enough to see the beauty
   in the world around us or in life itself, whether we see it in
   the oceans or in the sunset or in a delicate flower.
We praise God because it helps us remember that there is something to be wondrous about, even during those times when we are troubled.
   Especially when we are troubled, we need to remember
   what the Psalmist said: "It is good to sing hymns to Your
   Name, and to tell of Your faithfulness in the night."

Tefilat HaLev - Shabbat/Festivals   שבת/חג – תפלת הלב

❋ There is something about us that is designed
to praise the One, the Source of Life.
We know that we are programmed that way
when we realize
that praising God is a way to feel better
about ourselves and our lives.
*May we experience the joy of life and living
by finding the words and the songs to Praise You,
O Source of All Life, the everliving and loving God.*
As the Psalmist learned so long ago, it is good to
acknowledge You as the Source of life and blessing and
to rejoice in Your love.

❋ All brachot, or blessings, are saying Thank You to
God. On Shabbat it is especially important to say
Thank You to God and to everyone else who has or will
help us in life.
*Thank You, God, for the wonderful things in my life.
Thank You, God, for being there to help me
when things are not so wonderful.
May I always remember that you are Tzur Yisrael,
my rock and my strength, whenever I need You.*

טוֹב לְהֹדוֹת לַיהוה וּלְזַמֵּר לְשִׁמְךָ עֶלְיוֹן:
לְהַגִּיד בַּבֹּקֶר חַסְדֶּךָ וֶאֱמוּנָתְךָ בַּלֵּילוֹת:

**Tov leho*dot* laAdo*nai*. Uleza*meir* leshim*cha* El*yon*,
Leha*gid* ba*bo*ker chas*de*cha Ve-emuna*te*cha balei*lot*,**
It is good to give thanks to Adonai and to sing of God's great Name, to tell of
God's mercy in the morning and faithfulness in the evening.

20

Tefilat HaLev - Shabbat/Festivals - שבת/חג - תפלת הלב

מַה גָּדְלוּ מַעֲשֶׂיךָ יהוה מְאֹד עָמְקוּ מַחְשְׁבֹתֶיךָ. הַלְלוּיָהּ.

Ma god**lu** ma-a**se**cha Yahh me-**od** am**ku** machshevo**te**cha. Hallelu**Yahh.**
How great are Your actions, Adonai; Your thoughts are very deep.

צַדִּיק כַּתָּמָר יִפְרָח
כְּאֶרֶז בַּלְּבָנוֹן יִשְׂגֶּה:
שְׁתוּלִים בְּבֵית יהוה
בְּחַצְרוֹת אֱלֹהֵינוּ יַפְרִיחוּ:
עוֹד יְנוּבוּן בְּשֵׂיבָה
דְּשֵׁנִים וְרַעֲנַנִּים יִהְיוּ:
לְהַגִּיד כִּי יָשָׁר יהוה
צוּרִי וְלֹא עַוְלָתָה בּוֹ.

Tza**dik** kata**mar** yif**rach** ke-**e**rez balva**non** yis**geh,**
Shetu**liym** be**veit** Ado**nai** bechatz**rot** Elo**hei**nu yaf**ri**chu.
Od yenu**vun** be**sei**vah deshei**niym**
vera'ana**niym** yih**yu,**
Leha**giyd** ki ya**shar** Ado**nai,** Tzu**ri,** ve**lo** av**la**tah bo.

Tefilat HaLev - Shabbat/Festivals — שבת/חג – תפלת הלב

❋ The righteous ones will flourish like the palm tree, thrive and grow tall, like a cedar in Lebanon.
They are rooted in the house of Adonai,
In God's own courtyards.
Even as they age, they will be fruitful, fresh and evergreen,
Proclaiming that Adonai is just, my Rock,
there is no hardship [coming from God].

When I sing the Name of God my spirit rises
From the depths she soars in the light

שַׁדַּי, שְׁכִינָה, יהוה צְבָאוֹת, הֲוָיָה, מְקוֹר חַיִּים,
צוּר, מָקוֹם, אֵל עֶלְיוֹן, יָהּ, רוּחַ, אֱלוֹהִים.

Shaddai, She**chi**na, Ado**nai** Tzeva'**ot**, Ha**vaya**,
Me**kor** Cha**yim**, Tzur, Ma**kom**, Eil El**yon**, Yahh,
Ruach, Elo**hiym**.   © R. Hanna Tiferet "A Voice Calls"

✡ Religion is essentially the act of holding fast to God. And that does not mean holding fast to an image that one has made of God, nor even holding fast to the faith in God that one has conceived. It means holding fast to the existing God. The earth would not hold fast to its conception of the sun (if it had one) nor to its connection with it, but to the sun itself.
Martin Buber

> Return again, return again,
> return to the Land of your Soul.
> Return to who you are,
> return to what you are,
> return to where you are, born and reborn again
> Rabbi Shlomo Carlebach

The Hebrew for "to pray" is *lehitpaleil* which is a reflexive verb meaning to make oneself hopeful or wondrous. We pray for ourselves, not because God needs our prayers. We are the ones who need prayer.

Tefilat HaLev - Shabbat/Festivals — שבת/חג

Powerful sun full of radiant light
Weave us the web that spins the night
Web of stars that holds the dark
Weave us the earth that feeds the spark
Strand by strand, hand over hand
Thread by thread, we weave the web.

שִׁירוּ לַיהוה שִׁיר חָדָשׁ שִׁירוּ לַיהוה כָּל הָאָרֶץ:
שִׁירוּ לַיהוה בָּרְכוּ שְׁמוֹ בַּשְּׂרוּ מִיוֹם לְיוֹם יְשׁוּעָתוֹ:

Shiru laAdonai shir chadash, Shiru laAdonai kol ha-aretz. Shiru laAdonai barchu shemo basru miyom leyom yeshuato.

Sing to Adonai a new song, Sing to Adonai all the earth! Sing to Adonai, acknowledge God's Essence, noble every day, source of salvation.

❁ The Talmud teaches that "If one reads [Scripture] without chant or studies [Mishnah] without melody, of that is it written, 'I gave them laws that were not good' (Ezekiel 20:25)." Melody adds not only to the beauty, but even to the quality of the words. When we sing, our prayers are not simply words, they are all of us in all ways. We are our prayers and music helps our prayers take wing to the heavens.

יִשְׂמְחוּ הַשָּׁמַיִם וְתָגֵל הָאָרֶץ יִרְעַם הַיָּם וּמְלֹאוֹ:

Yismechu hashamayim vetageil ha-aretz. Yir'am hayam umelo-o.

Rejoice O Heavens and unfurl O Earth; Roar O Seas, may all be fulfilled.

רוֹמְמוּ יהוה אֱלֹהֵינוּ וְהִשְׁתַּחֲווּ לְהַר קָדְשׁוֹ
כִּי־קָדוֹשׁ יהוה אֱלֹהֵינוּ:

Romemu Adonai Eloheinu vehishtachavu lehar kodsho. Ki Kadosh Adonai Eloheinu.

Exalt Adonai, our God and worship at God's holy mountain, for Adonai, our God is holy.

Tefilat HaLev - Shabbat/Festivals — תפלת הלב – שבת/חג

Chatzie Kaddish - Short Kaddish — חצי קדיש

יִתְגַּדַּל וְיִתְקַדַּשׁ שְׁמֵהּ רַבָּא. בְּעָלְמָא דִּי בְרָא כִרְעוּתֵיהּ, וְיַמְלִיךְ מַלְכוּתֵיהּ בְּחַיֵּיכוֹן וּבְיוֹמֵיכוֹן וּבְחַיֵּי דְכָל בֵּית יִשְׂרָאֵל. בַּעֲגָלָא וּבִזְמַן קָרִיב וְאִמְרוּ אָמֵן:

> On Shabbat Shuvah, drop the italicized words and say the bracketed gray.

Yitga**dal** veyitka**dash** shi**mei** raba be'alma di vra chiru**tei**, veyam**lich** malchu**tei** bechayei**chon** uveyomei**chon** uvcha**yei** dechol beit Yisra-**eil**, ba-aga**la**, uviz**man** ka**riv**, ve-im**ru**: A**mein**.

יְהֵא שְׁמֵהּ רַבָּא מְבָרַךְ לְעָלַם וּלְעָלְמֵי עָלְמַיָּא:

Ye**hei** sh**mei** raba meva**rach** le'**alam** ul'al**mei** al**maya**.

יִתְבָּרַךְ וְיִשְׁתַּבַּח וְיִתְפָּאַר וְיִתְרוֹמַם וְיִתְנַשֵּׂא וְיִתְהַדָּר וְיִתְעַלֶּה וְיִתְהַלָּל שְׁמֵהּ דְּקֻדְשָׁא בְּרִיךְ הוּא לְעֵלָּא מִן כָּל [לְעֵלָּא מִכָּל] בִּרְכָתָא וְשִׁירָתָא תֻּשְׁבְּחָתָא וְנֶחֱמָתָא, דַּאֲמִירָן בְּעָלְמָא, וְאִמְרוּ אָמֵן:

Yitba**rach**, veyishta**bach**, veyitpa-**ar**, veyitro**mam**, veyitna**sei**, veyit-ha**dar**, veyit-a**leh**, veyit-ha**lal** she**mei** dekud**sha**, brich hu. Le'**eila** *min kol* [l'ei**la** mi**kol**] bircha**ta** veshira**ta**, tushbecha**ta** venechema**ta** da-ami**ran** be'alma, ve-im**ru**: Amein.

God's gloriousness is to be extolled, God's great Name to be hallowed in the world whose creation God willed. And may God's reign be in our day, during our life, and the life of all Israel, let us say: Amen.
Let God's great Name be praised forever and ever.
Let the Name of the Holy One, the Blessing One, be glorified, exalted, and honored, though God is beyond all the praises, songs, and adorations that we can utter, and let us say: Amen.

Tefilat HaLev - Shabbat/Festivals   שבת/חג – תפלת הלב

🔔 Teach me, God, to pray, to bless, to acknowledge You as the Source of All Life.
Teach me, Adonai, to see the mystery in the sea, in a tree, in a fruit, sweet and ripe.
Help me to work for freedom of all peoples, for hope, for joy and delight.
Teach me, exalted One, to value life and time, morning and night.
Teach me, Source of Life to treasure life, lest one day become as any other, not holy.
Help me to live my life such that others can find You in my actions.
Help me to fulfill Your expectations as well as my own. Help me see the holy.

🔔 Ever evolving and increasing in holiness are the many names of God within this intentionally created world. May awareness of this governing principle be in effect for the days of each life and the lives of all our people in a time that is quickly approaching.
Let us affirm this faithful God.
May these many names be blessed in all the dimensions and even more dimensions.....
Blessed, praised, transcendently wondrous, ever trying harder and ever more glorious, going up to new levels, praiseful is this Holy Consciousness. Blessed be. Above and beyond all blessings and songs and praises and sweetness that could be spoken in any dimension.
Let us affirm this faithful God.
May there be increasing peace from cosmic intention and life for us and all our people.   Let us affirm this faithful God.
May the one who makes cosmic harmony make this for us, our people and all residents of this planet.   Let us affirm this faithful God.
© R. Goldie Milgram

Tefilat HaLev - Shabbat/Festivals   שבת/חג – תפלת הלב

These are interpretations of the Kaddish. Please feel free to read one of them as you listen to the Kaddish.
The Kaddish is largely an Aramaic prayer of praise about the Source of Life we call God. There are several variations. One variant is the *Chatzi Kaddish*, or Reader's Kaddish. This form is the short or half-Kaddish (*chatzi* means half). It is used to indicate sections of the service.
The central verse of the Kaddish is: Yehei shmei raba mevarach le'alam ul'almei almaya. "Let God's great name be praised forever and ever," which is an Aramaic translation of Psalm 113:2. The Kaddish is essentially a declaration of belief in the holiness and greatness of God, a prayer that God's name (Essence) be made Holy in this world. It is a recognition that even that which humankind cannot understand is a consequence of God's will.
To highlight this symbolism, the Kaddish is traditionally recited by the reader to the affirmation of the members of the congregation who answer Amen after each verse.
The full Kaddish is called Kaddish Shalem (shalem means complete).
There is also a special Kaddish d'Rabanan (Teacher's or Rabbi's Kaddish) which has a special section in it that talks about learning, teachers and their students and the students of their students.
Kaddish Yatom is known as the Mourner's Kaddish. It is the same as the full version; there is no reference to death or anything else to distinguish this Kaddish from the others. It is simply a matter of who is reciting the Kaddish. Persons who have lost a dear one or are marking a Yahrzeit are reciting this version. This Kaddish occurs at the end of services.
The Kaddish is recited in the presence of a Minyan, since, like the Kedusha prayer, it praises God's Name. There are several customs as to who stands for the Kaddish. When one recites the Kaddish, one traditionally stands. Therefore, mourners rise to recite the prayer. Some people will stand when they hear the Kaddish being recited. Thus, you may see several people stand when the Kaddish is recited, be it the half or full. Each community develops its traditions in this area. And even traditions change over time. And, while God does not change, our perceptions and understanding of God also change over time.

Tefilat HaLev - Shabbat/Festivals — תפלת הלב - שבת/חג

The Shema and Its Blessings — שמע וברכותיה

As we bless the Source of Life
So we are blessed.
And our blessings give us strength,
and make our visions clear,
and our blessings give us peace,
and the courage to dare,
As we bless the Source of Life,
So we are blessed.

© Faith Rogow

If you are comfortable doing so, please rise as we recite the Barchu

בָּרְכוּ אֶת יהוה הַמְבֹרָךְ:

Barchu et Adonai hamevorach.
Let us praise Adonai, the Source of Blessing, Who blesses all.

בָּרוּךְ יהוה הַמְבֹרָךְ לְעוֹלָם וָעֶד:

Baruch Adonai hamevorach leolam va'ed.
A Source of blessings is Adonai, through all time and space.

Praise the One to whom all praise is due.
Praised be the One to whom all praise is due,
Now and forever.
Praise the One to whom all praise is due.
Praised be the One to whom all praise is due
Now and forever, now and forever, now and forever,
praise the One.

Traditional choreography for the "*Barchu*" is that as the prayer leader says "*Barchu*" (the actual call to worship), he or she bends the knee and bows from the waist, becoming erect as "*Adonai*" is recited. The communal response of "*Baruch Adonai*" repeats the same choreography as the first line. The prayer leader then repeats the response to indicate that he or she is also a full participant.

Tefilat HaLev - Shabbat/Festivals — שבת/חג – תפלת הלב

🌴 By God's word was evening formed.
God, You distinguish day from night and light from darkness. All divisions are Your work. Therefore, we pray that You may guide our lives and actions.

✡ We praise You, Eternal One,
Sovereign of All, by Whose
word, evening settles with
wisdom opening our gates.
*Understanding shifts time
and cycles the seasons.*
Your will orders
the system of stars
dancing through the night skies.
*You are Creator of day and night,
rolling away the light
before the darkness
and the darkness before the light.*

🌸 You shift the day into nights
and You distinguish
between day and night.
Adonai Tzeva-ot
is one of Your names.
*May You be a Force in our lives
at all times and places.
A Source of Blessing are You, Adonai,
who settles the evening.*

> Out of deep center
> night passes through
> gates open
> seasons change
> stars swirl
> on their eternal pathways
> through the light.
> Light to dark to light
> spins the glorious
> heavenly array.
> This too is the name of
> יהוה
> living and eternal
> until the end of time.
> A Fountain of Blessing
> are You
> Endless One
> who blends
> the light of evening.
> © R. Lynn Gottlieb

🅢 Every evening, the day turns to night.
Every rising of the sun brings morning.

28

Tefilat HaLev - Shabbat/Festivals – שבת/חג – תפלת הלב

EVENING THE EVENINGS

Evening, the evenings; evening the frayed edges of our lives;

מַעֲרִיב עֲרָבִים, אָמֵן Ma-**ariyv** ara**viym**; a**mein** (2x)

Sacred words even the evenings;
Wisdom opens gates locked around our hearts.

אֲשֶׁר בִּדְבָרוֹ A**sher** bidva**ro**

מַעֲרִיב עֲרָבִים Ma-**ariyv** ara**viym**;

בְּחָכְמָה פּוֹתֵחַ שְׁעָרִים Bechoch**mah** potei-ach sh'a**riym**.

Understanding alters with the times;
Changing seasons, cycles divine

וּבִתְבוּנָה מְשַׁנֶּה עִתִּים Uvitvu**nah** mesha**neh** i**tiym**;

וּמַחֲלִיף אֶת הַזְּמַנִּים Uma**chalif** et haz'ma**niym**.

Paint diamonds on the canvas called sky;
Soothe our souls with a lilting lullaby.

וּמְסַדֵּר אֶת הַכּוֹכָבִים Umsa**deir** et hakocha**viym**;

בְּמִשְׁמְרוֹתֵיהֶם Bemishmerotei**hem**

בָּרָקִיעַ כִּרְצוֹנוֹ bara**ki**-a kirtzo**no**.

Rolling, rolling, into the night;
Rolling rolling away the light.

גּוֹלֵל אוֹר מִפְּנֵי חֹשֶׁךְ Go**leil** or mip**nei** cho**shech**;

גּוֹלֵל חֹשֶׁךְ מִפְּנֵי אוֹר goleil cho**shech** mip**nei** or.

Spirit of the Night we bless Your Name,
Eternal Light, Eternal flame.

אֵל חַי וְקַיָּם Eil chai veka**yam**

תָּמִיד יִמְלוֹךְ עָלֵינוּ ta**miyd** yim**loch** a**leinu**;

לְעוֹלָם וָעֶד Le'o**lam** va-ed. © Geela Rayzel Raphael

תפלת הלב - שבת/חג — Tefilat HaLev - Shabbat/Festivals

בָּרוּךְ אַתָּה יהוה, אֱלֹהֵינוּ מֶלֶךְ הָעוֹלָם,
אֲשֶׁר בִּדְבָרוֹ מַעֲרִיב עֲרָבִים,
בְּחָכְמָה פּוֹתֵחַ שְׁעָרִים, וּבִתְבוּנָה מְשַׁנֶּה עִתִּים,
וּמַחֲלִיף אֶת הַזְּמַנִּים, וּמְסַדֵּר אֶת הַכּוֹכָבִים,
בְּמִשְׁמְרוֹתֵיהֶם בָּרָקִיעַ כִּרְצוֹנוֹ.
בּוֹרֵא יוֹם וָלַיְלָה, גּוֹלֵל אוֹר מִפְּנֵי חֹשֶׁךְ,
וְחֹשֶׁךְ מִפְּנֵי אוֹר. וּמַעֲבִיר יוֹם וּמֵבִיא לַיְלָה,
וּמַבְדִּיל בֵּין יוֹם וּבֵין לַיְלָה, יהוה צְבָאוֹת שְׁמוֹ.
אֵל חַי וְקַיָּם, תָּמִיד יִמְלוֹךְ עָלֵינוּ לְעוֹלָם וָעֶד.
בָּרוּךְ אַתָּה יהוה, הַמַּעֲרִיב עֲרָבִים:

Baruch Ata, Adonai Eloheinu melech ha-Olam,
asher bidvaro ma-ariyv araviym, Bechochma
potei-ach she-ariym, Uvitvuna meshaneh itiym,
Umachaliyf et hazmaniym, Umsadeir et hakochaviym,
Bemishmeroteihem barakiya kirtzono. Borei yom
valaila, Goleil or mipnei choshech, Vechoshech
mipnei or. Uma-aviyr yom umayviy leila, Umavdiyl
bein yom uvein laila,   Adonai tz'va-ot shemo.
Eil chai vekayam, tamiyd yimloch Aleinu le-olam
va-ed. Baruch Ata Adonai, hama-ariyv araviym.

A Source of Blessing are You, Adonai, our God, Sovereign of the universe, who makes evening evening by Your word. With wisdom, You open the portals and with understanding You change the seasons and exchange the times, setting order among the stars, setting their orbits in the firmament according to Your will. You create day and night, rolling away the light before the darkness and the darkness before the light. You cause day to pass and bring night and You make a distinction between day and night, Adonai Tz'va-ot is Your Name. You are a living and established God, You will always reign over us forever and ever. A Source of Blessing are You, Adonai, our God, Sovereign of the universe, who makes evening, evening.

Tefilat HaLev - Shabbat/Festivals — שבת/חג — תפלת הלב

🌴 Your Love is felt
through the obligations toward people
and the environment that You place upon us.
With them, You teach lessons we do not always
want to learn nor do we always understand.
> *How can I learn that life is for living*
> *and love is for feeling?*

Teach us to engage with texts and with life.
Teach us to live life and feel love.

✡ Teach us Your way, that we may walk in Your truth;
Unite our hearts, that we may honor Your Name.
> *Then we will walk in liberty; mercy and truth will meet,*
> *justice and peace will embrace. And we will give*
> *thanks to You, O God, and honor Your name forever.*

A Source of blessing is Adonai, our God, who makes us
special with Mitzvot, and calls us to acclaim God's
kingdom with a whole heart, to serve with a willing
spirit, and to proclaim God's unity with a pure mind.

Ahavah is God's love, and our highest love.
Love should never hurt or cause pain.
Love is wanting the best for the one you love.
> *When we love God, we want to do and be the best we can,*
> *we show our love for God by treating others with respect,*
> *caring about them, and by being kind to all.*

Tefilat HaLev - Shabbat/Festivals שבת/חג – תפלת הלב

We are loved by an unending love.
We are embraced by arms that find us,
 even when we are hidden from ourselves.
We are touched by fingers that soothe us,
 even when we are too proud for soothing.
We are counseled by voices that guide us,
 even when we are too embittered to hear.
We are loved by an unending love.
 We are supported by hands that uplift us,
  even in the midst of a fall.
 We are urged on by eyes that meet us
  even when we are too weak for meeting.
 We are loved by an unending love.
Embraced, touched, soothed, and counseled;
Ours are the arms, the fingers, the voices;
Ours are the hands, the eyes, the smiles;
We are loved by an unending love.
 A Source of Blessings are You, Beloved One,
 who loves Your people Israel.   © Rabbi Rami M Shapiro

We are our stories and they are us.
They define who we are and they teach us about life
in ways that are sometimes so subtle,
and yet so ingrained.
 As a people, we choose our memories,
 and then, they choose us.
 The more we devote ourselves to this heritage,
 the more it grows and gives to us.
Wisdom and wonder, passion and instruction, symbol and story, mystery and depth. This is the holiness of Your love, the Torah implanted within us.

Your mizvot, Your statutes, Your teachings, Your mysteries.
As we meditate on them,
they make our lives full and our days fulfilled.

Tefilat HaLev - Shabbat/Festivals - שבת/חג

אַהֲבַת עוֹלָם בֵּית יִשְׂרָאֵל עַמְּךָ אָהָבְתָּ, תּוֹרָה
וּמִצְוֹת, חֻקִּים וּמִשְׁפָּטִים, אוֹתָנוּ לִמַּדְתָּ. עַל כֵּן
יהוה אֱלֹהֵינוּ, בְּשָׁכְבֵנוּ וּבְקוּמֵנוּ נָשִׂיחַ בְּחֻקֶּיךָ,
וְנִשְׂמַח בְּדִבְרֵי תוֹרָתֶךָ וּבְמִצְוֹתֶיךָ לְעוֹלָם וָעֶד.
כִּי הֵם חַיֵּינוּ וְאֹרֶךְ יָמֵינוּ, וּבָהֶם נֶהְגֶּה יוֹמָם
וָלַיְלָה, וְאַהֲבָתְךָ אַל תָּסִיר מִמֶּנּוּ לְעוֹלָמִים.
בָּרוּךְ אַתָּה יהוה, אוֹהֵב עַמּוֹ יִשְׂרָאֵל:

Ahavat olam beit Yisraeil amecha ahavta, tora
umitzvot, chukim umishpatiym, otanu limadeta. Al kein
Adonai Eloheinu, beshachbeinu uvekumeinu nasi-ach
bechukecha. Venismach bedivrei toratecha
uvemitzvotecha le'olam va'ed. Ki heim chaiyeinu
ve-orech yameinu. Uvahem negeh yomam valaila.
Ve-ahavatcha al tasir mimenu le-olamiym.
Baruch Ata Adonai, oheiv amo Yisraeil.

Open to me; open your (my) heart;
Let my (Your) Presence dwell in you (me).
I am (You are) within you (me), all around you (me),
I (You) fill the universe.

The *ayin* and *dalet* of the Shema (next page) are enlarged in the Torah. They spell *eid*, which means witness or testimony, evidence. Our recitation and understanding of the Shema is the evidence of God's oneness.

Tefilat HaLev - Shabbat/Festivals   שבת/חג – תפלת הלב

שְׁמַע יִשְׂרָאֵל, יהוה אֱלֹהֵינוּ, יהוה אֶחָד:

Shema Yisra-eil: Adonai Eloheinu, Adonai Echad!
Listen up, O Israel: Adonai is our God, Adonai is One!

(softly)
בָּרוּךְ שֵׁם כְּבוֹד מַלְכוּתוֹ לְעוֹלָם וָעֶד.

Baruch sheim kevod malechuto le-olam va-ed!
Blessings from God's glorious majesty extend through all time and space.

We are seated

וְאָהַבְתָּ אֵת יהוה אֱלֹהֶיךָ בְּכָל־לְבָבְךָ
וּבְכָל־נַפְשְׁךָ וּבְכָל־מְאֹדֶךָ: וְהָיוּ הַדְּבָרִים הָאֵלֶּה
אֲשֶׁר אָנֹכִי מְצַוְּךָ הַיּוֹם עַל־לְבָבֶךָ: וְשִׁנַּנְתָּם
לְבָנֶיךָ וְדִבַּרְתָּ בָּם בְּשִׁבְתְּךָ בְּבֵיתֶךָ וּבְלֶכְתְּךָ
בַדֶּרֶךְ וּבְשָׁכְבְּךָ וּבְקוּמֶךָ: וּקְשַׁרְתָּם לְאוֹת
עַל־יָדֶךָ וְהָיוּ לְטֹטָפֹת בֵּין עֵינֶיךָ: וּכְתַבְתָּם
עַל־מְזֻזוֹת בֵּיתֶךָ וּבִשְׁעָרֶיךָ:

Ve-ahavta eit Adonai Elohecha; bechol levavcha
uvechol nafshecha uvechol me-odecha. Vehayu
hadvariym ha-eileh asher Anochi metzavcha hayom
al levavecha. Veshinantam levanecha vedibarta bam;
beshivtecha beveitecha uvlechtecha vaderech
uvshochbecha uvkumecha. Ukshartam le-ot 'al
yadecha; vehayu letotafot bein 'einecha. Uchtavtam
'al-mezuzot beitecha uvish'arecha.   (Deut 6:4-9)

34

Tefilat HaLev - Shabbat/Festivals — שבת/חג — תפלת הלב

וְאָהַבְתָּ אֵת יהוה אֱלֹהֶיךָ בְּכָל לְבָבְךָ
וּבְכָל נַפְשְׁךָ וּבְכָל מְאֹדֶךָ:

Ve-ahavta eit Adonai Elohecha; bechol
levavcha uvchol nafshecha uvchol me-odecha.

And you shall teach your children as you live each day.
The path you walk. The way you talk,
And how you listen for the Good in each soul saying...

וְאָהַבְתָּ אֵת יהוה אֱלֹהֶיךָ

Plant seeds of lovingkindness in the fertile soil of faith,
The joy we sow will help us grow
A fragrant Garden of Truth embracing...

וְאָהַבְתָּ אֵת יהוה אֱלֹהֶיךָ

We inscribe these words on the door posts of our being
With heart and mind, we each can find
The precious Light that we are seeking...

וְאָהַבְתָּ אֵת יהוה אֱלֹהֶיךָ

We are all God's children, Living on Mother Earth.
Let hatred cease. Bless her with peace.
Become the Mountain, Witness, Holy Wonder birthing...

וְאָהַבְתָּ אֵת יהוה אֱלֹהֶיךָ © R. Hanna Tiferet

And thou shalt love the Lord thy God with all of thy heart, with all thy soul, and with all of thy might. And all these words which I command ye on this day shall be in thy heart. And thou shalt teach them diligently unto thy children. And thou shalt speak of them when thou sittest in thy house, when thou walkest by the way, and when you risest up and when thou liest down. And thou shalt bind them for a sign upon thy hand. And they shall be for frontlets between thine eyes. And thou shalt bind them on the door posts of thy house, and upon thy gates. That ye may remember and do all of my commandments and be holy unto thy God.

Tefilat HaLev - Shabbat/Festivals   שבת/חג - תפלת הלב

Shema Yisrael

Listen! you Yisrael person
יהוה who is, is our God.
יהוה who is, is One,
unique, all there is.

Through Time and Space
Your Glory Shines
Majestic One!

Love, that יהוה
who is your God,
in what your heart is in,
in what you aspire to,
in what you have made
your own.

May these values
which I connect
with your life
be implanted
in your feelings.

May they become
the norm for your children,
addressing them
in the privacy
of your home,
on the errands you run.

May they help you relax,
and activate you
to be productive.

Display them visibly
on your arm.
Let them focus
your attention.
See them in all transitions,
at home and in your
environment.

How good it will be
when you really listen
and hear My directions
which I give you today,
for loving יהוה
who is your God,
and acting Godly
with feeling and
inspiration.

Your earthly needs
will be met
at the right time,
appropriate to the season.
You will reap
what you have planted
for your delight and health.

And your animals
will have ample feed.
All of you will eat
and be content.

Be careful -- watch out!
Don't let your cravings
delude you.
Don't become alienated.
Don't let your cravings
become your gods.
Don't debase yourself
to them,
because the God-sense
within you
will become distorted.
Heaven will be shut to you.
Grace will not descend.
Earth will not produce.
Your rushing
will destroy you

36

Tefilat HaLev - Shabbat/Festivals — שבת/חג - תפלת הלב

and Earth will not be able
to recover her good balance
in which
God's gifts manifest.

May these values of Mine
reside in your aspirations
marking what you produce,
guiding what you perceive.

Teach them
to your children,
so that they
be addressed by them
in making their homes,
how they deal with traffic;
when you are depressed
when you are elated.

Mark your entrances
and exits
with them
so you are more aware.

Then you and your children
will live out on earth
that divine promise
given to your ancestors
to live heavenly days
right here on this earth.

יהוה, who is, said to Moshe
"Speak, telling
the Israel folks
to make tzitzit
on the corners

of their garments
so they will have
generations to follow them.

On each tzitzit-tassel
let them set a blue thread.
Glance at it,
and in your seeing,
remember
all the other directives
of יהוה who is,
and act on them.

This way
you will not be led astray,
craving to see and want,
and then prostitute yourself
for your cravings.

This way
you will be mindful
to actualize My directions
for becoming
dedicated to your God,
to be aware that
I AM
יהוה who is your God --
the One who freed you
from the oppression
in order to God you.

I am יהוה your God."
That is the truth.

Interpretive translation by
Rabbi Zalman Schachter-Shalomi

Adonai Elohei**chem. Emet..** ..אֱמֶת׃ אֱלֹהֵיכֶם יהוה

Tradition takes the *emet*, "true" from the prayer which follows (True and certain it is that there is One God) and appends it onto the Shema as an immediate affirmation of the Shema's truth for us.

Tefilat HaLev - Shabbat/Festivals — שבת/חג - תפלת הלב

וְהָיָה אִם־שָׁמֹעַ תִּשְׁמְעוּ אֶל־מִצְוֹתַי אֲשֶׁר אָנֹכִי מְצַוֶּה אֶתְכֶם הַיּוֹם לְאַהֲבָה אֶת־יְהוָה אֱלֹהֵיכֶם וּלְעָבְדוֹ בְּכָל־לְבַבְכֶם וּבְכָל־נַפְשְׁכֶם: וְנָתַתִּי מְטַר־אַרְצְכֶם בְּעִתּוֹ יוֹרֶה וּמַלְקוֹשׁ וְאָסַפְתָּ דְגָנֶךָ וְתִירֹשְׁךָ וְיִצְהָרֶךָ: וְנָתַתִּי עֵשֶׂב בְּשָׂדְךָ לִבְהֶמְתֶּךָ וְאָכַלְתָּ וְשָׂבָעְתָּ: הִשָּׁמְרוּ לָכֶם פֶּן־יִפְתֶּה לְבַבְכֶם וְסַרְתֶּם וַעֲבַדְתֶּם אֱלֹהִים אֲחֵרִים וְהִשְׁתַּחֲוִיתֶם לָהֶם: וְחָרָה אַף־יְהוָה בָּכֶם וְעָצַר אֶת־הַשָּׁמַיִם וְלֹא־יִהְיֶה מָטָר וְהָאֲדָמָה לֹא תִתֵּן אֶת־יְבוּלָהּ וַאֲבַדְתֶּם מְהֵרָה מֵעַל הָאָרֶץ הַטֹּבָה אֲשֶׁר יְהוָה נֹתֵן לָכֶם: וְשַׂמְתֶּם אֶת־דְּבָרַי אֵלֶּה עַל־לְבַבְכֶם וְעַל־נַפְשְׁכֶם וּקְשַׁרְתֶּם אֹתָם לְאוֹת עַל־יֶדְכֶם וְהָיוּ לְטוֹטָפֹת בֵּין עֵינֵיכֶם: וְלִמַּדְתֶּם אֹתָם אֶת־בְּנֵיכֶם לְדַבֵּר בָּם בְּשִׁבְתְּךָ בְּבֵיתֶךָ וּבְלֶכְתְּךָ בַדֶּרֶךְ וּבְשָׁכְבְּךָ וּבְקוּמֶךָ: וּכְתַבְתָּם עַל־מְזוּזוֹת בֵּיתֶךָ וּבִשְׁעָרֶיךָ: לְמַעַן יִרְבּוּ יְמֵיכֶם וִימֵי בְנֵיכֶם עַל הָאֲדָמָה אֲשֶׁר נִשְׁבַּע יְהוָה לַאֲבֹתֵיכֶם לָתֵת לָהֶם כִּימֵי הַשָּׁמַיִם עַל־הָאָרֶץ:

And it will be, if you really listen and hear My *mitzvot* which I instruct you today, to love Adonai your God and to serve with all your heart and with all your being, I [have designed the world so that there] will be rain for your land at the proper time, the early rain and the late rain, and you will gather in your grain, your wine and your oil. And I will see that there is grass in your fields for your cattle, and you will eat and be sated. Take care lest your heart be seduced by your cravings, and you turn astray and worship other things as gods and serve them. For then the fury of Adonai will flare up inside you, and the heavens will close so that there will be no rain and the earth will not yield its produce, and you will swiftly perish from the good land which Adonai gives you. Therefore, place these words of mine upon your heart and upon your being, and bind them for a sign on your hand, and they shall be *totafot* between your eyes. You shall teach them to your children, to speak of them when you sit in your home and when you go on your way, when you lie down and when you rise. And inscribe them on the doorposts of your house and on your gates - so that your days and the days of your children may be long and full on the land which Adonai swore to your fathers to give to them for heavenly days on the earth.

Tefilat HaLev - Shabbat/Festivals - שבת/חג

וַיֹּאמֶר יְהוָה אֶל־מֹשֶׁה לֵּאמֹר: דַּבֵּר אֶל־בְּנֵי יִשְׂרָאֵל וְאָמַרְתָּ אֲלֵהֶם וְעָשׂוּ לָהֶם צִיצִת עַל־כַּנְפֵי בִגְדֵיהֶם לְדֹרֹתָם וְנָתְנוּ עַל־צִיצִת הַכָּנָף פְּתִיל תְּכֵלֶת: וְהָיָה לָכֶם לְצִיצִת וּרְאִיתֶם אֹתוֹ וּזְכַרְתֶּם אֶת־כָּל־מִצְוֺת יְהֹוָה וַעֲשִׂיתֶם אֹתָם וְלֹא תָתוּרוּ אַחֲרֵי לְבַבְכֶם וְאַחֲרֵי עֵינֵיכֶם אֲשֶׁר־אַתֶּם זֹנִים אַחֲרֵיהֶם:

Vayo**mer** Ado**nai** el Mo**she** lei**mor**: Da**beir** el be**nei** Yisra-**eil** ve-amar**ta** alei**hem** v'a**su** la**hem** tzi**tzit** al kan**fei** bigdei**hem** ledo**ro**tam venat**nu** al tzi**tzit** haka**naf** pe**til** te**chei**let. Veha**ya** la**chem** letzi**tzit** ur'iy**tem** oto uzchar**tem** et kol mitz**vot** Ado**nai** va-asi**tem** o**tam** velo tatu**ru** acha**rei** lev**av**chem ve-acha**rei** ei**nei**chem a**sher** a**tem** zo**niym** acharei**hem**.

Adonai spoke to Moshe, saying: "Speak to the children of Israel and tell them to make for themselves reminder fringes on the corners of their garments for the sake of their generations, and to put a thread of *techelet* blue on the reminder fringe of each corner. They are to be to you as tzizit, reminder fringes, and when you look at them, remember all the mitzvot of Adonai and do them, and you will not wander after your heart and after your eyes, lest you hunger after cravings;

לְמַעַן תִּזְכְּרוּ וַעֲשִׂיתֶם אֶת־כָּל־מִצְוֺתָי וִהְיִיתֶם קְדֹשִׁים לֵאלֹהֵיכֶם: אֲנִי יְהוָה אֱלֹהֵיכֶם אֲשֶׁר הוֹצֵאתִי אֶתְכֶם מֵאֶרֶץ מִצְרַיִם לִהְיוֹת לָכֶם לֵאלֹהִים אֲנִי יְהוָה אֱלֹהֵיכֶם:

Lema-an tizke**ru**, va-asi**tem** et kol mitzvo**tai** vihey**item** kedo**shiym** l'Eilo**hei**chem. Ani Adonai Elo**hei**chem, a**sher** hotzeiti et**chem** mei-eretz Mitz**ra**yim, lihi**yot** la**chem** l'Eilo**hiym**. Ani Ado**nai** Elo**hei**chem.
(Numb 15:40-41)

So that you may remember and do all of My *mizvot* and be holy to your God. I am Adonai, your God, who brought you out of the land of Egypt to be your God; I, Adonai, am your God." [It is True.]

Tefilat HaLev - Shabbat/Festivals　שבת/חג – תפלת הלב

אֶמֶת אֱמֶת אֱמֶת אֱמֶת **אֱמֶת** אֱמֶת אֱמֶת אֱמֶת

Emet ve-emu**nah** kol zot,　אֱמֶת וֶאֱמוּנָה כָּל זֹאת,

All this is true and certain, ...

✡ All this we hold to be true and trustworthy for us.
You alone are our God, and we are Israel Your people.
  You give us life and steady our footsteps.
  You performed miracles for us before Pharaoh,
  signs and wonders in the land of Egypt;
When Your children witnessed Your strength,
gratefully they praised Your Name.
Accepting Your sovereignty upon themselves,
Moses, Miriam and all Israel
sang to You together, lifting their voices joyously:

 Standing at the shores of history, we see what we
were taught: Turn around and see the miracle.
  Every place is Mitzrayim, the narrow or tight place
  Until we look for the path through the walls of high water.
There is always a promise of redemption, a place
better to reach, only when we join together with
each other and with our history.
From there, we can join together in song:

 Moshe and Miryam taught us to sing
when we saw Your mighty acts.
They taught us to see You, even in *Mitzrayim*.

May we learn that through You, we can come out
of the darkest places with strength and courage.

May we work together for the day
when all nations will live together in peace
so that we can rejoice together,
just as Israel did at the shores of the Sea of Reeds:

Tefilat HaLev - Shabbat/Festivals שבת/חג - תפלת הלב

❋ This is a world torn by violence and pain,
far from peace and wholeness.
Yet when we look out at the world,
there are miracles and wonders all around.
How do we hold the truth of You
with the truth of pain and suffering?
> *In joining with You in coming out of Egypt,*
> *we learn to feel suffering and oppression,*
> *wherever it might be.*
> *In looking to the miracles that You performed for us,*
> *we learned that miracles are possible and that there is hope,*
> *even in Mitzrayim, the tight place.*

Adonai, help us to do what needs to be done.
Help us to see the miracles before us every day.
Help us see Your strong right arm
as we sing the song Moshe and Miriam
and Your children sang at the Sea of Reeds:

Sometimes, life is hard, and it feels like everything I do is wrong.
There is trouble, no matter where I turn.
> *At such times it is important to remember that You care.*
> *God, please give me the courage to find the path I need.*
> *Help me join with our people in singing this prayer:*

🔔 God does not cause our problems. They are part of life.
God is there for us when we take the initiative to seek a
solution, rather than stare at the problem. Sometimes the
answer comes from someone with a rod, pointing the way.
Sometimes the answer comes from someone with a tamborine,
leading in song. In all cases, the answer comes from within, in
a desire to be part of the solution.

Tefilat HaLev - Shabbat/Festivals — שבת/חג - תפלת הלב

מִי כָמְכָה בָּאֵלִים יהוה? מִי כָּמְכָה נֶאְדָּר בַּקֹּדֶשׁ,
נוֹרָא תְהִלֹּת, עֹשֵׂה פֶלֶא?
מַלְכוּתְךָ רָאוּ בָנֶיךָ, בּוֹקֵעַ יָם
לִפְנֵי מֹשֶׁה, זֶה אֵלִי עָנוּ וְאָמְרוּ:
יהוה יִמְלֹךְ לְעוֹלָם וָעֶד.
וְנֶאֱמַר: כִּי פָדָה יהוה אֶת יַעֲקֹב, וּגְאָלוֹ מִיַּד חָזָק
מִמֶּנּוּ. בָּרוּךְ אַתָּה יהוה, גָּאַל יִשְׂרָאֵל עַמֶּךָ:

Mi cha**mo**cha ba-ei**lim**, Ado**nai**?
Mi ka**mo**cha, ne**dar** ba**ko**desh, **no**ra tehi**lot**, o**sei** fe**leh**?
Malechute**cha** ra-**u** va**ne**cha, bo**kei**-a yam lif**nei**
Mo**sheh**; Zeh Ei**li** a**nu** ve-ame**ru**. "Ado**nai** yim**loch**
le'**o**lam va'**ed**." Vene-e**mar**: Ki fa**da** Ado**nai** et Ya'a**kov**,
Uge-a**lo** mi**yad** cha**zak** mi**me**nu.
Baruch **A**ta Ado**nai**, ga-**al** Yisra-**eil** ame**cha**.

Who is like You, Eternal One, among the gods that are worshipped? Who is like You, majestic in holiness, awesome in splendor, doing wonders?
In their escape from the sea, Your children saw Your sovereign might displayed.
"This is my God!" they cried.
"The Eternal One will reign through all time and space."
And it has been said: "The Eternal One delivered Jacob, and redeemed us from the hand of one stronger than ourselves."
A Source of Blessing are You, Eternal One, Redeemer of Israel.

We are a people in whom the past endures, in whom the present is inconceivable without moments gone by. The Exodus lasted a moment, a moment enduring forever. What happened once upon a time happens all the time.

Abraham J Heschel

Mitzrayim means tight or narrow place. Our Sages have taught that we are to remember being delivered out of our own tight places, our own *Mitzrayim* as we sing *Mi Chamocha*. Yearly, on *Pesach* (Passover), we are enjoined to experience the exodus personally.

Tefilat HaLev - Shabbat/Festivals — שבת/חג

הַשְׁכִּיבֵנוּ יהוה אֱלֹהֵינוּ לְשָׁלוֹם, וְהַעֲמִידֵנוּ מַלְכֵּנוּ לְחַיִּים וּפְרוֹשׂ עָלֵינוּ סֻכַּת שְׁלוֹמֶךָ, וְתַקְּנֵנוּ בְּעֵצָה טוֹבָה מִלְּפָנֶיךָ, וְהוֹשִׁיעֵנוּ לְמַעַן שְׁמֶךָ. וְהָגֵן בַּעֲדֵנוּ, וְהָסֵר מֵעָלֵינוּ אוֹיֵב, דֶּבֶר, וְחֶרֶב, וְרָעָב וְיָגוֹן, וְהָסֵר שָׂטָן מִלְּפָנֵינוּ וּמֵאַחֲרֵינוּ, וּבְצֵל כְּנָפֶיךָ תַּסְתִּירֵנוּ. כִּי אֵל שׁוֹמְרֵנוּ וּמַצִּילֵנוּ אָתָּה, כִּי אֵל מֶלֶךְ חַנּוּן וְרַחוּם אָתָּה, וּשְׁמֹר צֵאתֵנוּ וּבוֹאֵנוּ, לְחַיִּים וּלְשָׁלוֹם, מֵעַתָּה וְעַד עוֹלָם. וּפְרֹשׂ עָלֵינוּ סֻכַּת שְׁלוֹמֶךָ. בָּרוּךְ אַתָּה יהוה, הַפּוֹרֵשׂ סֻכַּת שָׁלוֹם עָלֵינוּ וְעַל כָּל עַמּוֹ יִשְׂרָאֵל וְעַל יְרוּשָׁלָיִם.

Hashkive**inu**, Ado**nai** Elo**heinu**, lesha**lom**, veha'ami**deinu** mal**keinu** lechay**yiym**, uf**ros** a**leinu** su**kat** shlo**mecha**, vetak**neinu** be'ei**tzah** to**vah** milfa**necha**, vehoshi'**einu** lema'an she**mecha**. Vehagein ba-a**deinu**, veha**seir** mei-a**leinu** o**yeiv**, **dever**, veche**rev**, vera'**av**, veya**gon**, veha**seir** sa**tan** milfa**neinu** umei-acha**reinu**, uve**tzeil** kena**fecha** tasti**reinu**, ki El shom**reinu** umatzi**leinu** Ata, ki El **Melech** cha**nun** vera**chum** Ata, Ush**mor** tzei**teinu** uvo-**einu** lechay**yiym** ulesha**lom**, mei-**atah** ve'ad **olam**. Uf**ros** a**leinu** su**kat** shlo**mecha**. **Baruch A**ta, Ado**nai**, hapo**reis** su**kat** sha**lom** a**leinu** ve'**al** kol **amo** Yisra-**eil** ve'**al** Yerusha**layim**.

May we lie down tonight in peace, and rise up to life renewed. May night spread over us a shelter of peace, of quiet and calm, the blessing of rest.

There will come a time when morning will bring no word of war or famine or anguish; there will come a day of happiness, of contentment and peace. Praised be the source of joy within us, for the night and its rest, for the promise of peace.

Tefilat HaLev - Shabbat/Festivals   שבת/חג - תפלת הלב

וּפְרוֹשׂ עָלֵינוּ סֻכַּת שָׁלוֹם,

Ufros aleinu sukat shalom,
Spread over us wings of peace,
Draw water in joy from the living well,
Mayim chayim, waters of Life, Shalom.
© Rabbi Aryeh Hirschfield

There are times when life throws us a curve,
when we feel turbulent inside, conflicted, ill at ease.
Those are times that it helps to remember to call out to You.
In the darkest night, the roughest seas, You are still there.

Night can be scary, when I am left in the darkness.
Sometimes I feel all alone. Sometimes I am scared.
Those are the times it is helpful to remember I am not alone.
Those are the times I need to remember You are there.

I have been one acquainted with the night.
I have walked out in rain—and back in rain.
I have outwalked the furthest city light.
   I have looked down the saddest city lane.
   I have passed by the watchman on his beat
   And dropped my eyes, unwilling to explain.
I have stood still and stopped the sound of feet
When far away an interrupted cry
Came over houses from another street,
   But not to call me back or say good-bye;
   And further still at an unearthly height,
   One luminary clock against the sky
Proclaimed the time was neither wrong nor right.
I have been one acquainted with the night.   © Robert Frost

44

Tefilat HaLev - Shabbat/Festivals   שבת/חג - תפלת הלב

The Covenant of Shabbat, Veshamru   ושמרו

✡ For us, Shabbat is about doing, not ceasing to do. All week long we struggle to create a brief time where we can just BE.

And to BE requires work - soul work.
It requires the work of stepping back
from the everyday rushing
long enough to really be present in the moment
and to appreciate Shabbat and community.

Thus, by "Do"ing Shabbat, we ensure that the Exodus which defines us will continue, for us and for our future generations.

❃ What does it mean to *La'asot et haShabbat*, to "do" Shabbat? The Sages take its placement in Torah, right after the details of the *Mishkan*, as indicating the types of activities to be forbidden on Shabbat. But the Hebrew says 'DO Shabbat' -- because on the seventh day, Adonai did Shabbat and *yinafash*. That is also a verb meaning to give life, soul. So for six days we worry about the furniture, the details, who does what -- and then we DO Shabbat. In the Holy One's image, we give ourselves *nefesh* -- life, soul. This is a covenant forever.

✿ The mystics teach that the relationship between Israel and God is that of a marriage, and a marriage requires the giving of something valuable from the Groom (the *Kadosh Baruch Hu*, the Holy One, Blessed Be) to the Bride (Israel). Shabbat is the gift from God to us and the text from Exodus, the *Veshamru*, is the verification of this gift because it says that Shabbat is *Ot hi le'olam*, a "sign forever" between us and God. In that sense, this passage becomes a love song:

Tefilat HaLev - Shabbat/Festivals   שבת/חג - תפלת הלב

🌴 Ahad Ha-Am said,
"More than the Jewish people has kept Shabbat,
Shabbat has kept the Jewish people."

Shabbat is a special time for us to celebrate life.
The ancients taught us to imitate God
By stepping back from the everyday to remember
And to do Shabbat.
> *Shabbat is special time with family and friends,*
> *Singing, praying, and feeling connected*
> *To each other, to God, to the universe, and to ourselves.*

🔔 The allegory of Shabbat as a wedding between God, in the sense of Tiferet (an attribute of God) and Israel, in the sense of Shechinah, is rooted in Talmud (Shab. 119a). As such, that allegory is expressed throughout the observance of Shabbat, making it a day of rest and of celebration.

וְשָׁמְרוּ בְנֵי יִשְׂרָאֵל אֶת הַשַּׁבָּת, לַעֲשׂוֹת אֶת הַשַּׁבָּת לְדֹרֹתָם בְּרִית עוֹלָם:
בֵּינִי וּבֵין בְּנֵי יִשְׂרָאֵל אוֹת הִיא לְעוֹלָם, כִּי שֵׁשֶׁת יָמִים עָשָׂה יהוה אֶת הַשָּׁמַיִם וְאֶת הָאָרֶץ,
וּבַיּוֹם הַשְּׁבִיעִי שָׁבַת וַיִּנָּפַשׁ.

Veshamru ve**nei** Yisra-**eil**, et haSha**bat**, La-a**sot** et haSha**bat** ledoro**tam**, brit o**lam**.
Beini u**vein** be**nei** Yisra-**eil**, ot hi, le-o**lam**.
Ki **shei**shet yami**ym** a**sa** Adonai, et hashama**yim** ve-**et** ha-**aretz**. Uva**yom** hashvi'**i** sha**vat** vayi**nafash**.

And the children of Israel protect the Shabbat, doing Shabbat for their generations, a covenant forever. Between Me and the children of Israel, it is a sign forever, for in six days, Adonai made the heavens and the earth and on the seventh day God rested and gave the world Soul.

Tefilat HaLev - Shabbat/Festivals — שבת/חג

יִשְׂמְחוּ בְמַלְכוּתְךָ שׁוֹמְרֵי שַׁבָּת וְקוֹרְאֵי עֹנֶג, עַם מְקַדְּשֵׁי שְׁבִיעִי, כֻּלָּם יִשְׂבְּעוּ וְיִתְעַנְּגוּ מִטּוּבֶךָ, וּבַשְּׁבִיעִי רָצִיתָ בּוֹ וְקִדַּשְׁתּוֹ, חֶמְדַּת יָמִים אוֹתוֹ קָרָאתָ, זֵכֶר לְמַעֲשֵׂה בְרֵאשִׁית.

Yismechu vemalechutecha shomrei Shabat vekorei oneg. Am mekadeshei shevi-i kulam yisbe-u veyitangu mituvecha. Uvashvi-i ratzita bo vekidashto, chemdat yamim oto karata, zeicher lema-asei vereishiyt.

We delight in Divine sovereignty by guarding our Shabbat time to make it a delight. We are a people who teach the sanctity of the seventh day as a source of fulfillment, filled with Your goodness. This day is Israel's festival of the spirit, sanctified and blessed by You, the most precious of days, a symbol of the joy of creation.

Amidah — תפילה

✡ As we come to the heart of our worship, which is sometimes called the "Silent Meditation," we ask God to "open our lips." At first this sounds contradictory; why do we ask God to open our lips for silence?

And then we look more deeply into the Hebrew in the prayer and we see that Adonai itself, not the YHVH, is used as the Name of God and Adonai means "connector." When we really connect with God, then the contradictions of life become gates of connectivity and it is those gates that we ask help in opening.

🔔 We come now to the heart of our worship. Some call it the *Shmoneh Esrei*, the "Eighteen Benedictions," but on the Shabbat there are only seven! Some say, the *Amidah*, the time for standing. But it is also known, in its simplicity, as *HaTefilah*, "The Prayer."

Tefilat HaLev - Shabbat/Festivals שבת/חג – תפלת הלב

The great rationalist Rabbi Mordecai M. Kaplan said, "To say 'I believe in praying' sounds to me as absurd as to say 'I believe in thinking.' The question whether prayer is effective is only a special form of the question whether thought is effective. And just as we make use of the best thoughts of others in order to channel our own thinking into the surest and most beneficial effectiveness, so should we make use of the most noble and sincere prayers of others to channel our own prayers into a life of the greatest nobility and sincerity."

Prayer invites God
to let the divine presence suffuse our spirits,
to let the divine will prevail in our lives.
Prayer cannot bring water to parched fields,
nor mend a broken bridge nor rebuild a ruined city;
but prayer can water an arid soul, mend a broken heart, and rebuild a weakened will.
Abraham J Heschel, adapted

To pray is to take notice of wonder, to regain a sense of the mystery that animates all beings, the divine margin in all attainments. Prayer is our humble answer to the inconceivable surprise of living.
Abraham J Heschel

Sometimes I do not know the words to the prayers I want to or need to say.
Sometimes, I wonder if God can hear my prayers.
That is the place of silent prayer, the prayer of our hearts.
Even when we do not know the words to the prayers,
Our hearts and souls always do.
So when words will not come to the mind,
the heart and soul pray.
All they need from us to be able to pray, is silence.

Tefilat HaLev - Shabbat/Festivals שבת/חג - תפלת הלב

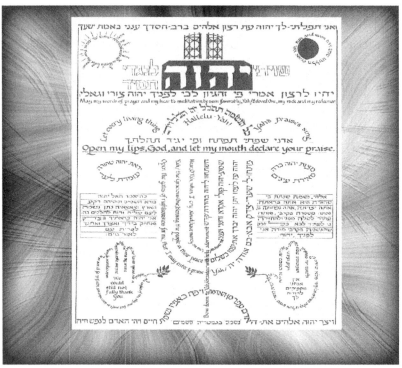

(If you are comfortable doing so, please rise as the ark is opened)

אֲדֹנָי שְׂפָתַי תִּפְתָּח וּפִי יַגִּיד תְּהִלָּתֶךָ:

Adonai sefatai tiftach ufi yagiyd tehilatecha.
Oh, God open up my lips, as I begin to pray.
Eternal God, open up my lips,
that my mouth may declare Your glory
(Psalm 51:17)

[Amidah in Guided imagery is on pages 73-76.]
[Intermediate Amidah Prayers for a weekday start on page 181]

Why is the instruction to "do Shabbat" placed in Torah after the *Mishkan*, the portable dwelling place? The *Mishkan* was very important, but we always end on a key point and that key is Shabbat. So as important as the *Mishkan* is/was, Shabbat is the key to remember. We still have Shabbat (if we choose to DO it), even though we no longer have the physical *Mishkan*. Of course, by DOing Shabbat, by giving ourselves *nefesh*, life, soul (DOing Soul work), we create the inner *Mishkan*.

The art on this page is called a *shviti*. It is a focusing or meditative device based on the phrase from Psalms 16:8 "*Shviti Adonai negdi tamid*, I have set Adonai before me always."

Tefilat HaLev - Shabbat/Festivals שבת/חג - תפלת הלב

✡ Let us remember our spiritual and physical mothers and fathers, who made us, the fathers and the mothers who made them and the fathers and the mothers who made them.
*We are the product of all of our ancestors
as we stand here in their light before You who made us all.*
Each of them understood You differently
and they are the voices behind us.

🕊 We invoke the memories of our fathers and our mothers and their fathers and mothers.
Each of them sought You
and found You in their lives in different ways.
No two of them experienced You the same way.
*May we learn from them
to value and honor the differences among us
in how we seek You. May we learn from them
that no matter how we seek You,
it is the same You we are seeking.*

 After these things the word of Adonai came to Abraham in a vision, saying, "Fear not, Abram; I am a shield for you and your reward will be great. ... Look now toward heaven, and count the stars, if you are able to count them, so your seed will be." And he trusted in Adonai; Who counted it for his merit.
*The merit of our ancestors was so great
that there is still reserve left for us
and for our future generations.*

 God, I sometimes think of you as my father, and at other times, as my mother.
*A parent loves a child, even when that child misbehaves.
Thank You, God, for loving me,
especially when I have not earned it.*

Tefilat HaLev - Shabbat/Festivals - שבת/חג – תפלת הלב

🌴 We are shaped by those who came before us just as the seedling grown from the plant was formed by it, nourished by it and released by it. And yet, that seedling grows into its own unique plant, experiencing its own life. How it will grow and thrive is caused by the interaction between what it receives genetically and what it experiences in the course of its own life.

Avot / God of All Generations — אבות

בָּרוּךְ אַתָּה יהוה אֱלֹהֵינוּ וֵאלֹהֵי אֲבוֹתֵינוּ וְאִמּוֹתֵינוּ, אֱלֹהֵי אַבְרָהָם, אֱלֹהֵי יִצְחָק, וֵאלֹהֵי יַעֲקֹב, אֱלֹהֵי שָׂרָה, אֱלֹהֵי רִבְקָה, אֱלֹהֵי לֵאָה, וֵאלֹהֵי רָחֵל. הָאֵל הַגָּדוֹל הַגִּבּוֹר וְהַנּוֹרָא, אֵל עֶלְיוֹן, גּוֹמֵל חֲסָדִים טוֹבִים, וְקוֹנֵה הַכֹּל, וְזוֹכֵר חַסְדֵי אָבוֹת וְאִמָּהוֹת, וּמֵבִיא גְאֻלָּה לִבְנֵי בְנֵיהֶם לְמַעַן שְׁמוֹ בְּאַהֲבָה:

Baruch Ata Adonai, Ehloheinu, veilohei avoteinu ve-imoteinu: Elohei Avraham, Elohei Yitzchak, vEilohei Ya-akov. Elohei Sarah, Elohei Rivkah, Elohei Lei-ah, vEilohei Racheil. Ha-eil hagadol hagibor vehanora, eil elyon, gomeil chasadim tovim vekonei hakol, vezocheir chasdei avot ve-imahot, Umeivi geula livnei veneihem, lema-an shemo, ba-ahava:

A Source of Blessing are you, Adonai our God and God of our Fathers and our Mothers. God of Abraham, God of Isaac, and God of Jacob, God of Sarah, God of Rebecca, God of Rachel and God of Leah. Great God, powerful and awesome, God of the Highest, who bestows kindness and goodness, master of all, who remembers the good deeds of our fathers and mothers and brings redemption to the children of their children for God's sake with love.

Tefilat HaLev - Shabbat/Festivals   שבת/חג – תפלת הלב

Our Ancestors Support us in our Journey.
We thank You, Infinite Source, for the power within us,
The power that gave our ancestors their strength:
Power of Abraham, Power of Isaac, Power of Jacob,
Power of Sarah, Power of Rebekah, Power of Rachel, Power of
Leah, each in their own way,
and according to their needs.
You hear truth in every age,
generation after generation,
Boundless, vibrant, awesome, sublime,
Surrounding and filling all space and time.
Gradually embracing all things into One.
We seek the blessing of the Infinite Source,
alive within us.
Rabbis Marcia Prager, Mordechai and Devora Bartnoff z"l, adapted

On Shabbat Shuvah, add:

זָכְרֵנוּ לְחַיִּים, מֶלֶךְ חָפֵץ בַּחַיִּים, וְכָתְבֵנוּ בְּסֵפֶר הַחַיִּים, לְמַעַנְךָ אֱלֹהִים חַיִּים.

Zoch**rei**nu lecha**yim**, **Me**lech cha**feitz** bacha**yim**, vechot**vei**nu be**sei**fer hacha**yim**, lema'an**cha** Elo**hiym** cha**yim**.
Remember us for life, Sovereign who wants us to live,
and write us in the Book of Life, for Your sake, Living God.

מֶלֶךְ עוֹזֵר וּמוֹשִׁיעַ וּמָגֵן: בָּרוּךְ אַתָּה יהוה,
מָגֵן אַבְרָהָם וְעֶזְרַת (וּפוֹקֵד) שָׂרָה:

Melech o**zeir** umo**shi**'a uma**gein**: Ba**ruch** Ata Ado**nai**,
ma**gein** Avra**ham** ve'e**zrat** (ufo**keid**) Sa**rah**.
Sovereign, who is our Help, our redemption and our protector. A Blessing are You, Adonai, Shield of Abraham and Helper of (One who remembers) Sarah.

In keeping with modern Reform practices, the Avot prayer includes the option of *ezrat Sarah* (helped Sarah) and *pokeid Sarah* (remembered or accounted for Sarah, Gen 21:1; *magein Avraham*, the Shield of Abraham, comes from Gen 15:1): Traditional choreography is that one bends the knee and bows at *Baruch* (beginning and end) and stands erect at *Adonai*.

Tefilat HaLev - Shabbat/Festivals — שבת/חג - תפלת הלב

✡ Your might, Adonai, is everlasting;
Help us use our strength for good and not for evil.
You are the Source of life and blessing;
Help us choose life for ourselves and our children.
You are the support of the falling;
Help us lift up the fallen.
You are the Author of freedom;
Help us set free the captive.
You are our hope in death as in life;
Help us keep faith with those who sleep in the dust.
Your might, Adonai, is everlasting;
Help us use our strength for good.

Adonai, there was a time for each of us when we felt almost paralyzed with the burdens of life, when everything was overpowering. We wanted to lie still without moving, feeling almost deadened inside.
Slowly, something started to change;
a little glow started deep inside,
almost imperceptibly at first.
We became like a young plant
reaching to the heavens,
feeling the radiated Warmth and Energy
on us and through us.
Help us to know that it is from You
that the radiance comes,
that we might rejoice in life itself.

You sustain life through love,
reviving the deadened, giving life to all.
Just as the rabbis did in ancient times,
let us recognize the things in our lives
that need reviving: old friendships,
a passion for justice and loving kindness,
and ourselves after sleep.

Tefilat HaLev - Shabbat/Festivals — שבת/חג - תפלת הלב

❁ We pray that we might know
before Whom we stand: the Power whose gift is Life,
even for those who have forgotten how to live.
We pray for winds that disperse the choking air of sadness,
and for the rains that refresh withered or shriveled hope,
that we might rise up.
We pray for the love that blossoms
into persons and into community,
giving us power over our own lives with dignity.
We pray that we might be
the healers and the helpers of all who are in need.
We pray for opened eyes,
we, who are blind to our own inner Self.
Praised is Adonai, whose gift is life,
whose cleansing rains cause parched men and women
to flower in a sunlit world.

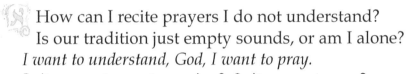

❦ How can I recite prayers I do not understand?
Is our tradition just empty sounds, or am I alone?
I want to understand, God, I want to pray.
Is it wrong to want meaning? Is it wrong to care?
No, for meaning is found in the seeking,
and seeking and learning takes effort and caring.

Gevurot / Power — גבורות

אַתָּה גִבּוֹר לְעוֹלָם אֲדֹנָי מְחַיֵּה הַכֹּל (מֵתִים) אַתָּה רַב לְהוֹשִׁיעַ:

**Ata gibor leolam Adonai, mechayei hakol (maytiym)
Ata, rav lehoshiy'a.**

Winter	Summer
מַשִּׁיב הָרוּחַ וּמוֹרִיד הַגָּשֶׁם:	מוֹרִיד הַטָּל:
Mashiyv haru-ach umoriyd hagashem.	Moriyd hatal.
Who causes the wind to blow and rain to fall.	Who brings the dew.

54

Tefilat HaLev - Shabbat/Festivals — שבת/חג - תפלת הלב

מְכַלְכֵּל חַיִּים בְּחֶסֶד, מְחַיֵּה הַכֹּל
(מֵתִים) בְּרַחֲמִים רַבִּים, סוֹמֵךְ
נוֹפְלִים, וְרוֹפֵא חוֹלִים, וּמַתִּיר
אֲסוּרִים, וּמְקַיֵּם אֱמוּנָתוֹ לִישֵׁנֵי
עָפָר, מִי כָמוֹךָ בַּעַל גְּבוּרוֹת וּמִי
דוֹמֶה לָךְ, מֶלֶךְ מֵמִית וּמְחַיֶּה וּמַצְמִיחַ יְשׁוּעָה:

Mechal**keil** chay**im** beche**sed**, mecha**yei** ha**kol**
(may**tiym**) beracha**miym** ra**biym**, so**meich** nof**liym**
vero**fei** cho**liym** uma**tiyr** asu**riym**, umka**yeim** emuna**to**
liyshei**nei** a**far**, mi chamo**cha ba**-al gevu**rot** umiy
domeh lach, **me**lech meimi**yt** umcha**yeh** umatz**miy**ach
yeshu-**a**.

🍃 Divine Essence and Power.
Who is like You! Source of all strength,
Source of all compassion, Source of all healing.
You are also a source of inspiration in times of despair,
Please keep alive in us our ideals, hopes and dreams,
that the dead may live again through us.
Rabbis Marcia Prager, Mordechai and Devora Bartnoff z"l, adapted

On Shabbat Shuvah, add:

מִי כָמוֹךָ אַב הָרַחֲמִים, זוֹכֵר יְצוּרָיו לְחַיִּים בְּרַחֲמִים:

Mi chamo**cha** Av haRacha**miym**, zo**cheir** yetzu**rav** lecha**yim** beracha**miym**.
Who can compare to You, a nurturing parent, who remembers and nurtures all creatures for life.

וְנֶאֱמָן אַתָּה לְהַחֲיוֹת הַכֹּל (הַמֵּתִים).
בָּרוּךְ אַתָּה יהוה, מְחַיֵּה הַכֹּל (הַמֵּתִים):

Vene-e**man A**ta lehacha**yot** ha**kol** (ha**may**tiym).
Baruch **A**ta Adonai, mecha**yei** ha**kol** (ha**may**tiym).

Tefilat HaLev - Shabbat/Festivals   שבת/חג – תפלת הלב

You are strength forever, Adonai. Giving life to all (the deadened), You are great to save us. You bring the dew. You support life with mercy, You give life to all (the deadened) with great compassion. You support the fallen and heal the sick, You release the captives and establish faith for those who sleep in the dust. Who is like You, master of strength, and who can compare to You, Sovereign of life and death, who causes salvation to blossom. Who is like You, compassionate parent, who remembers Your creatures for life with compassion. And You are faithful in giving life to all (the deadened).
A blessing are You, Adonai, who gives life to all (the deadened).

Kadosh / Holy   קדשה

🔔 We say Kadosh three times
to signify three levels of spiritual awareness.
First is the sensation
that there is something beyond us
and that we are not
the center of the universe.
The second level is the recognition
that the something beyond us
is so immense and beyond definition,
that it is beyond knowing.
The third level is the sense of wholeness
that comes from the realization
that the One is right here,
in our hearts,
and has always been there.

🌴 A time may come to us when our hearts are filled with awe, when suddenly the noise of life is stilled for a moment. Our eyes open to a world just beyond the border of our minds. All at once there is a glory in our souls, and we proclaim, "O Holy God, majestic Presence!"

By reciting the prayers for rain and dew, we are connecting ourselves with the land of Israel. We are praying for a healthy environment (where the rains and dew come in the appropriate time and quantity) for them, and through them, for us and the entire world as well.

Tefilat HaLev - Shabbat/Festivals   שבת/חג - תפלת הלב

✡ Days pass and even the years vanish. We walk
through life blind to Your miracles all around us. God,
open our eyes that we might see, open our hearts that
we might feel. Grant knowing to our minds. May there
be moments when Your Presence, like lightning,
illuminates the darkness in which we walk.
*Help us to take the time and to see, wherever we gaze,
that the bush burns unconsumed.*
And we, mere clay touched by God,
will reach out for holiness, and exclaim in wonder:
*How filled we are with You in this place,
and we did not know it!
Blessed is the Eternal One, the holy God!*

✡ Holiness feels different from the ordinary,
the unrealized potential.
Holiness is being fulfilled, and not hollow.
Holiness is the feeling that grows from inside,
when one soul connects to another
with love and dignity.
*And so we separate the holy from the hollow,
the elevated from the ordinary, the wheat from the chaff.*
Sometimes, we can feel the holiness
of the One we call Holy.
It is through that holiness that we can find
the connection between our souls.
*And we can be and feel holy when we acknowledge
the holiness of all human beings and all life.
And then the illusion of separateness
disappears into the holiness of connecting.*

✡ Holy means special, sacred, intense.
God said, "Be holy because I am holy."
God left it up to us to seek the best in all people, being holy.

Tefilat HaLev - Shabbat/Festivals שבת/חג – תפלת הלב

❀ How does one praise holiness?
What does it mean for God to be Holy?
These are questions our ancestors asked
of themselves and of God.
They did not find holiness by finding God,
they found holiness in the seeking.
> To call God Holy is to seek God.
> To see the holiness in God's Essence is to find
> the holiness in our selves and in our being.

From that place, God is Holy, every day.

🍃 We Name the Holy. You are Holy.
We who seek to be holy, praise You every day, for all eternity!
Holy is all life in the world.
Holy are all who struggle for freedom,
Who seek and reveal the sacred in each living being.

<small>Rabbis Marcia Prager, Mordechai and Devora Bartnoff z"l, adapted</small>

אַתָּה קָדוֹשׁ וְשִׁמְךָ קָדוֹשׁ וּקְדוֹשִׁים בְּכָל יוֹם
יְהַלְלוּךָ, סֶלָה. בָּרוּךְ אַתָּה יהוה, הָאֵל הַקָּדוֹשׁ.

Ata kadosh veshim**cha** ka**dosh** ukdo**shim** be**chol** yom
yehale**lucha, Se**la.
Baruch **Ata**, Ado**nai** ha-Eil haka**dosh**.

You are Holy, and Your Name is Holy; We acknowledge Your holiness every day, Selah. A Source of Blessing are You, Adonai, You are Divine Holiness.

(All are seated - - Ark is closed)

> How does a person
> achieve holy fulfillment?
> When power and goodness are combined
> to promote justice, harmony and peace.
> That is the path to sanctifying God
> and making God's Name holy.
> R. Sholom Silver

Kadosh   קָדוֹשׁ

Kadosh   קָדוֹשׁ

Kadosh   קָדוֹשׁ

Tefilat HaLev - Shabbat/Festivals   שבת/חג – תפלת הלב

✡ O God, Your gift to us is the Shabbat
and we answer You by guarding it and by doing it.
By remembering to Do Shabbat,
we honor You and Your wisdom.
> *We might think that it is okay to skip Shabbat*
> *and continue our daily routine,*
> *never stepping back*
> *and achieving the rest and perspective*
> *that we may not even recognize we need.*

Thank You, Adonai,
for the gift of this day of stepping back and reflecting.
Shabbat is Your gift for life.

🕊 What a Gift You have given us in Shabbat.
It is a time of healing and nurturing and purifying.
It is a glimpse of what Life can be.
> *By giving us Shabbat, You give us ourselves.*
> *By giving us Shabbat, You give us community.*
> *By giving us Shabbat, You give us time and hope.*

May we take from Shabbat the drive to serve You
by making the world a better place.
> *May we take from Shabbat*
> *the insight and perspective that guides our effort.*

Then, together, we make Shabbat Holy.

❀ On Shabbat, we turn from the world of creating
to the creating of the world.
> *On Shabbat, we seek to Be, not to manipulate.*

May we help the hurt to find comfort and healing.
> *May we help those who hunger to find nourishment.*

May we help those who struggle to find rest.
> *May we help those who despair to find hope.*

On Shabbat, we seek to live, not merely to survive.
> *By bringing Shabbat into our lives,*
> *may we be brought to action, not to slumber.*

Tefilat HaLev - Shabbat/Festivals שבת/חג – תפלת הלב

🌴 In Your gracious love, Adonai,
let Your holy Shabbat remain our heritage,
that all Israel may find rest and peace.
*A Source of Blessing are You, Adonai,
for the Shabbat and for its holiness.*

🍃 Let us open ourselves to Sacredness in Shabbat.
May my heart see the world that can be,
A world of fulfillment, justice, and peace.
As we rest and celebrate on Shabbat, Your sacred day,
Lifting out voices together as one,
May we delight in our love for each other,
A foretaste of the way things can and will be!
Rabbis Marcia Prager, Mordechai and Devora Bartnoff z"l, adapted

[Intermediate Amidah Prayers for a weekday start on page 181]

אֱלֹהֵינוּ וֵאלֹהֵי אֲבוֹתֵינוּ
וְאִמּוֹתֵינוּ, רְצֵה בִמְנוּחָתֵנוּ,
קַדְּשֵׁנוּ בְּמִצְוֹתֶיךָ וְתֵן חֶלְקֵנוּ
בְּתוֹרָתֶךָ, שַׂבְּעֵנוּ מִטּוּבֶךָ
וְשַׂמְּחֵנוּ בִּישׁוּעָתֶךָ, וְטַהֵר לִבֵּנוּ לְעָבְדְּךָ בֶּאֱמֶת,
וְהַנְחִילֵנוּ יהוה אֱלֹהֵינוּ בְּאַהֲבָה וּבְרָצוֹן שַׁבַּת
קָדְשֶׁךָ, וְיָנוּחוּ בוֹ יִשְׂרָאֵל מְקַדְּשֵׁי שְׁמֶךָ.
בָּרוּךְ אַתָּה יהוה, מְקַדֵּשׁ הַשַּׁבָּת:

Eloheinu velo**hei** avo**tei**nu veimo**tei**nu, ret**zei**
vimnucha**tei**nu, kad**shei**nu bemitzvo**te**cha ve**tein**
chel**kei**nu betora**te**cha, sab'**ei**nu mituve**cha**
vesam**chei**nu biyshu'a**te**cha, Veta**heir** li**bei**nu
le'av**de**cha be-**emet**. Vehanchi**lei**nu Adonai Elo**hei**nu
be-a**ha**va uvra**tzon** Sha**bat** kod**she**cha, veya**nu**chu vo
Yisra-**eil** mekad**shei** she**me**cha.
Baruch Ata Adonai, meka**deish** haSha**bat**.

Tefilat HaLev - Shabbat/Festivals שבת/חג - תפלת הלב

Our God and the God of our fathers and mothers, may our rest be pleasing, may we be sanctified through Your mitzvot and find our portion in Your Torah; may we find satisfaction in Your goodness and joy in Your deliverance. Purify our hearts to serve You with Truth, guide us, Adonai, our God with love and desire to the holiness of Shabbat. May Israel rest thereon for the sake of Your holy Name. A Source of blessing are You, Adonai, Who makes Shabbat holy.

קָדוֹשׁ Holy means special, sacred, intense.
God said, "Be holy because I am holy."
God left it us to learn how to be holy.
Is it holy when we make mistakes in our learning?
It can be holy,
but only when we learn from our mistakes.
Torah teaches us to aplogize
and to repair more than we hurt.
When we do that we can be holy.
And we can see and feel the holiness in everyone.

✡ Adonai, show Your love to us, Your people Israel.
Help us to know that You are there
and that You receive our prayers with love.
Fill us with the knowledge that You are near to us
whenever we seek You truthfully.
Let us feel Your Presence in our midst   קָדוֹשׁ
and in the midst of all peoples in Tzion.
Adonai, You are the Source of Blessing,
whose Presence gives life to Tzion,   קָדוֹשׁ
all Israel and all of the world.

The prayer says that Israel rests on Shabbat as a way to make God's Essence (Name) holy. Holiness is fulfillment, the opposite of hollow, empty. Holiness is achieving one's potential. We are invited to recognize that the realization of achieving potential is only possible when one sits back long enough to see that the potential has indeed been reached. The act of recognition is part of the completion. The completion of a painting is stepping back and saying, the creating is complete, the painting has achieved its potential.

Tefilat HaLev - Shabbat/Festivals   שבת/חג – תפלת הלב

✿ Be gracious, Eternal God, to Your people Israel;
receive our prayers with love.
May our worship always be acceptable to You.
Since You are a God near to all who call upon You,
be gracious unto Your servants.
Pour Your spirit upon us.
May we one day see Your merciful return to Tzion.
Blessed are You, Eternal One,
who restores Shechinah to Tzion.

✡ Adonai, show Your love to us, Your people Israel.
Help us to know that You are there and that You
receive our prayers with love.
Fill us with the knowledge that You are near to us
whenever we seek You truthfully.
Let us feel Your Presence in our midst
and in the midst of all peoples in Tzion.
Adonai, You are the Source of Blessing,
whose Presence gives life to Tzion,
all Israel and all of the world.

🕊 When we experience our love for God
and God's love for us,
we experience a flame that burns within us.
Our hearts yearn to be of service to the Divine.
There is a longing and a passion to our seeking.
  God, You said to build a Mishkan, a holy place for You,
  so You could dwell within us.
  Please help us feel Your Divine Presence within us.
  Then we can serve You truthfully
  by helping to rebuild Tzion and the world.
You are the Source of Blessing, Adonai.
Shechinah gives life to Tzion,
all Israel and all of the world.

Tefilat HaLev - Shabbat/Festivals שבת/חג - תפלת הלב

 May the spirit of the Universe
   Bring sunshine into your heart
 Today,
   Tomorrow,
       and forever.

Pawnee Blessing

🍃 We Open Ourselves to Sacred Service.
We bless the One who enables us to feel deeply,
To know our needs, and the needs of our world.
May our actions flow with Your goodness, grace, love and care.
May our prayer arise and find acceptance with love.
May our lives turn always towards You,
So Your Shechinah will dwell within us always.

Rabbis Marcia Prager, Mordechai and Devora Bartnoff z"l, adapted

Retzei / Receive Our Prayers   רצה

רְצֵה, יהוה אֱלֹהֵינוּ, בְּעַמְּךָ יִשְׂרָאֵל,
וּתְפִלָּתָם בְּאַהֲבָה תְקַבֵּל, וּתְהִי
לְרָצוֹן תָּמִיד עֲבוֹדַת יִשְׂרָאֵל עַמֶּךָ.
אֵל קָרוֹב לְכָל קֹרְאָיו, פְּנֵה אֶל
עֲבָדֶיךָ וְחָנֵּנוּ, שְׁפוֹךְ רוּחֲךָ עָלֵינוּ.

Retzei Ado**nai** elo**hei**nu, be-am**cha** Yisra-**eil**,
Utefila**tam** ba-a**ha**va teka**beil**. U**te**hi lerat**zon** ta**mid**
avo**dat** Yisra-**eil** a**me**cha. Eil ka**rov** le**chol** kor'**av**, pe**nei**
el ava**de**cha vecha**nei**nu. She**foch** rucha**cha** a**lei**nu.

Tefilat HaLev - Shabbat/Festivals — שבת/חג – תפלת הלב

For Festivals:

אֱלֹהֵינוּ וֵאלֹהֵי אֲבוֹתֵינוּ, יַעֲלֶה וְיָבֹא, וְיִזָּכֵר זִכְרוֹנֵנוּ, וְזִכְרוֹן כָּל עַמְּךָ בֵּית יִשְׂרָאֵל לְפָנֶיךָ, לְטוֹבָה, לְחֵן וּלְחֶסֶד וּלְרַחֲמִים, לְחַיִּים וּלְשָׁלוֹם, בְּיוֹם

Elo**hei**nu velo**hei** avo**tei**nu, ya-**aleh** veya**vo**, veyiza**cheir** zichro**nei**nu, vezich**ron** kol am**cha** beit Yisra-**eil** lefa**ne**cha, leto**va** le**chein**, ule**che**sed ulerach**a**miym, lecha**yim** uleshal**om**, be**yom**

Our God and God of all ages, be mindful of Your people Israel on this

first day of the new month,

Rosh ha**cho**desh ha**zeh**   רֹאשׁ הַחֹדֶשׁ הַזֶּה

day of Pesach,

chag haMa**tzot** ha**zeh**   חַג הַמַּצּוֹת הַזֶּה

day of Shavuot,

chag haShavu-**ot** ha**zeh**   חַג הַשָּׁבֻעוֹת הַזֶּה

day of Sukkot,

chag haSu**kot** ha**zeh**   חַג הַסֻּכּוֹת הַזֶּה

day of Shmini Atzeret,

haShmini, Chag haAtzeret ha**zeh**   הַשְּׁמִינִי, חַג הָעֲצֶרֶת הַזֶּה

and renew in us love and compassion, goodness, life and peace.

זָכְרֵנוּ, יהוה אֱלֹהֵינוּ, בּוֹ לְטוֹבָה. אָמֵן.
Zochreinu, Ado**nai** Elo**hei**nu, bo leto**va**. A**mein**.
This day remember us for well-being. Amen

וּפָקְדֵנוּ בּוֹ לִבְרָכָה. אָמֵן.
Ufok**dei**nu vo livra**cha**. A**mein**.
This day bless us with Your nearness. Amen.

וְהוֹשִׁיעֵנוּ בּוֹ לְחַיִּים. אָמֵן.
Vehoshi**yei**nu vo lecha**yim**. A**mein**.
This day help us to a fuller life. Amen.

Tefilat HaLev - Shabbat/Festivals שבת/חג - תפלת הלב

וְתֶחֱזֶינָה עֵינֵינוּ בְּשׁוּבְךָ לְצִיּוֹן בְּרַחֲמִים.
בָּרוּךְ אַתָּה יהוה, הַמַּחֲזִיר שְׁכִינָתוֹ לְצִיּוֹן.

**Vetechezena eyneinu beshuvecha
letziyon berachamiym.
Baruch Ata Adonai,
hamachazir shechinato letziyon.**

Find favor, Adonai our God, in Your people Israel and accept their prayer with love. May You always be pleased with Your people Israel's service. You are a God near to all who call to You. Turn toward us and be gracious to us, pour Your Spirit upon us. Allow our eyes to see Your return to Tzion with compassion. A Source of Blessing are You, Adonai, who returns Shechina to Tzion.

God, we are taught that you answer prayers.
How can I know that you hear and answer mine?
*Sometimes, when I hurt badly,
my prayers are said in tears.
Sometimes, when I am afraid, my prayers are said in fear.*
It is especially important to know,
that God indeed hears the prayers of tears
and the prayers we say when we are afraid.
*Help me hear Your answer.
Please help me know my prayers were heard.*

> Meditation
> God did not create a completed world.
> Rather, God gave us
> a purpose in life
> and challenges to make ourselves
> and the world whole.
> Rabbi Sholom Silver
> (1921-1974)

Tefilat HaLev - Shabbat/Festivals שבת/חג – תפלת הלב

✡ We gratefully acknowledge that You are Adonai our God, the God of all generations. You are the Rock of our life and the Power that shields us in every age.
We thank You and sing praises to You:
for our lives, which are in Your hand;
for our souls, which are in Your keeping;
for the signs of Your presence we encounter each day;
and for Your wondrous gifts at all times, morning, noon,
and night.
You are Goodness, endlessly merciful, compassionate. Your love never fails. You have always been our hope.

🕊 The bird soars in the sky,
   making flight look effortless.
The large whale glides through the water.
And after a ferocious storm, the birds sing again.
Adonai, help us to see the wonders before us every hour,
every minute, every second.
In looking out at the world You and we hold dear,
let us remember to say Thank You for the gift of life
and the gift of wonder.
Thank You, Adonai,
for signs of Your handiwork in our lives.
When we see those signs, we say Thank You.
Thank You for life and for hope
and for meaning in our lives.

🌴 A time of pausing and looking around allows us to see the many things for which we need to say "Thank You" to God. Our gratitude allows us to recognize God as the anchor that grounds us, protects us from our own panics and fears. This is the God that saves us now and has been our deliverance in generations past.

Tefilat HaLev - Shabbat/Festivals — שבת/חג - תפלת הלב

❁ How does a person say "Thank You"
to the Source of all Life, to the Fountain of all Blessing?
How can we acknowledge the Rock of our Lives,
that which remains steadfast and open to us,
even in the depth of our own despair?

*It may not always be easy to say "Thank You,"
unless we take the time to look and see the wonder of life.
When we do that, we are brought to the "Thank You"
that connects You to us and us to You.
Thank You, Adonai, our connectivity to the fullness of life.*

אּ Life is Your gift to us,
  and our lives are filled with Your gifts.
*Thank You, God, for the gift of life, for loving family,
for Shabbat, and for special times.*

Hoda-ah / For All These Gifts — הודאה

מוֹדִים אֲנַחְנוּ לָךְ, שָׁאַתָּה הוּא, יהוה אֱלֹהֵינוּ
וֵאלֹהֵי אֲבוֹתֵינוּ (אִמּוֹתֵינוּ), לְעוֹלָם וָעֶד, צוּר
חַיֵּינוּ מָגֵן יִשְׁעֵנוּ אַתָּה הוּא לְדוֹר וָדוֹר.

Modiym anach**nu** lach, sha-**A**ta Hu, Adonai Elo**hei**nu
vei**lo**hei avo**tei**nu, (imo**tei**nu) le-**o**lam va-**ed**, tzur
cha**yei**nu, ma**gein** yish'**ei**nu, **A**ta Hu le**dor** va**dor**.

On Shabbat Shuvah insert:

וּכְתוֹב לְחַיִּים טוֹבִים כָּל בְּנֵי בְרִיתֶךָ.

Uch**tov** lechay**yiym** to**viym** kol be**nei** vri**techa**.
Let abundant life be the heritage of all Your children.

Tefilat HaLev - Shabbat/Festivals שבת/חג - תפלת הלב

ON CHANUKAH AND PURIM:
We give thanks for the redeeming wonders
and the mighty deeds by which at this season
our people was saved in days of old.
Through the power of Your spirit, the weak defeated the strong,
the few prevailed over the many,
and the righteous were triumphant.

עַל הַנִּסִּים, וְעַל הַפֻּרְקָן, וְעַל הַגְּבוּרוֹת, וְעַל הַתְּשׁוּעוֹת,
וְעַל הַמִּלְחָמוֹת, שֶׁעָשִׂיתָ לַאֲבוֹתֵינוּ בַּיָּמִים הָהֵם בַּזְּמַן הַזֶּה.

Al hani**siym** ve'**al** hapur**kan** ve'**al** hagvu**rot**, ve'**al** hatshu-**ot**,
ve'**al** hamilcha**mot**, she'a**si**ta la-avo**tei**nu baya**miym** ha**heim**
baz**man** ha**zeh**.

CHANUKAH

וְקָבְעוּ שְׁמוֹנַת יְמֵי חֲנֻכָּה אֵלּוּ,
לְהוֹדוֹת וּלְהַלֵּל לְשִׁמְךָ הַגָּדוֹל.

Vekav'**u** shmo**nat** ye**mei** chanu**ka** ei**lu**
leho**dot** ulha**leil** leshim**cha** haga**dol**.
Then Your children returned to Your house, to purify the
sanctuary and kindle its lights. And they dedicated these days to
give thanks and praise to Your great name. We honor their
struggle and take our turn at maintaining the light.

🍃 We Open to Gratitude.
We are thankful for all the generations that came before us,
For our parents, who brought us into this world,
For the miracles that greet us every day,
For morning, noon, and night,
For the joy of continual discovery,
For the beauty that surrounds us, and is us.
For all these things may Your Name be praised forever.
Rabbis Marcia Prager, Mordechai and Devora Bartnoff z"l, adapted

Tefilat HaLev - Shabbat/Festivals — שבת/חג — תפלת הלב

בָּרוּךְ אַתָּה יהוה, הַטּוֹב שִׁמְךָ וּלְךָ נָאֶה לְהוֹדוֹת.

Baruch **Ata** A**do**nai,
ha**tov** shim**cha** ule**cha** na-**eh** leho**dot**.

A Source of blessing are You, Adonai,
Your Essence is goodness and it is fitting to be grateful to You.

Shalom / Peace — שלום

✡ May we find peace with those we love.
  May we grow together over time,
  finding new delights in each other.
May we find peace with ourselves.
  May we find satisfaction in our labors
  and purpose in our days.
May we facilitate peace
in our world.
  May we do so with gentleness
  and kindness and compassion.
May we be at peace with the Source.
  May we find wisdom and understanding
  and a true sense of Being.

❁ Our tradition teaches: If others are in turmoil
and disharmony rules their lives,
there can be no peace for us.
When the violence in our lives
drowns out the music for which we yearn,
others likewise can find no peace.
A prayer for peace for one requires peace for the other.
We do not have to make peace with our friends.
Peace for all Israel. Peace for all humankind.

We are invited to start each day with a thank you as we awaken and to include a thank you in our evening prayers. By bracketing our days in thank you's, we give ourselves a sense of well-being that provides perspective on our days and helps us through the periodic rough times. The Holy One of Blessing does not need our "thank you"s, we do.   R. Sholom Silver

Tefilat HaLev - Shabbat/Festivals — שבת/חג - תפלת הלב

What is peace? Is it simply the absence of war?
Our tradition teaches that Shalom, peace,
is a sense of wholeness, completeness,
a sense of healthy well-being.

*It comes at a price, though,
a price that is not always easy to pay.*
Perhaps that is why the Hebrew also means to pay.
What is the price we must pay?
The price of the ego, the price of pride and willfulness.
The price of letting go,
the ceasing to control and manipulate.
*That is the work of Shabbat, a taste of resting,
a taste of letting go.*
Shabbat is a time for Shalom.
May this Shabbat be the start of a week of peace.

As long as there is someone in the world who is not free, there can be no peace for us.
Peace for all Israel. Peace for all humankind.

Making peace is more than not fighting.
Making peace is partnering with God
to make the world a better place.
*Making peace means treating everyone with respect.
Making peace means not doing mean things to others,
even when they are mean.*

עוֹד יָבוֹא שָׁלוֹם עָלֵינוּ וְעַל כֻּלָּם,
שַׁלְאַאם עָלֵינוּ וְעַל כָּל הָעוֹלָם.

Od yavo sha**lom** aleinu Ve'al ku**lam**
Sa**laam** Aleinu ve'al kol ha'**o**lam, Sa**laam**.

There is still the chance of peace for us and for everyone. Peace! For us and for the entire world.   © Sheva, an Israeli band

שלום שלום **שלום** שלום **שלום** שלום   שלום   שלום שלום

Tefilat HaLev - Shabbat/Festivals — שבת/חג — תפלת הלב

🔔 Let Israel, Your people, and all peoples, know peace.
Peace destroys your enemies
by making them allies and partners.
Let the great shofar of freedom
be sounded for us and all peoples.
Let peace and freedom reign in all the world.
Let every wanderer come home
from the bitterness of exile.
And may our eyes see Your return to Tzion in mercy.
Then will Jerusalem, the city of David,
be the city of peace, the joy of all the world.
The land of Israel and its people
and its neighbors will see freedom and peace.

🍃 **We Open to Wholeness, Completeness, Fulfillment, Peace.**
Source of Shalom: Fulfillment and Peace
May we drink deeply from the fountain of peace,
May we know peace in ourselves,
Live in peace with our neighbors, create peace in the world.
We bless the Holy One,
Creator of Wholeness, Source of Peace.
Rabbis Marcia Prager, Mordechai and Devora Bartnoff z"l, adapted

Shalom Rav / With Abundant Love — שלום רב

שָׁלוֹם רָב עַל יִשְׂרָאֵל עַמְּךָ תָּשִׂים לְעוֹלָם,
כִּי אַתָּה הוּא מֶלֶךְ אָדוֹן לְכָל הַשָּׁלוֹם.
וְטוֹב בְּעֵינֶיךָ לְבָרֵךְ אֶת עַמְּךָ יִשְׂרָאֵל
בְּכָל עֵת וּבְכָל שָׁעָה בִּשְׁלוֹמֶךָ.

Shalom rav al Yisra-**eil** am**cha** tasim le-olam ki Ata Hu **Melech adon lechol** hashalom. Vetov be-einecha levareich et amcha Yisra-eil. Bechol eit uvechol sha'ah bishlomecha.

The dove artwork is the Arabic words *Houb* (Love) and *Salaam* (Peace), styled in Arabic Diwani calligraphy by Mamoun Sakkal.

Tefilat HaLev - Shabbat/Festivals　שבת/חג – תפלת הלב

Grant a lasting and abundant peace upon Israel and the world, for You are the Sovereign who connects all to peace. And it is good in Your eyes to bless Your people Israel with peace in every moment and in every hour.

On Shabbat Shuvah

בְּסֵפֶר חַיִּים, וּבְרָכָה נִכָּתֵב לְחַיִּים טוֹבִים וּלְשָׁלוֹם.

Be**seif**er cha**yim** ubra**cha** nika**teiv** lecha**yim** tovi**ym** ulesha**lom**.
Teach us then to find our happiness in the search for righteousness and peace.

בָּרוּךְ אַתָּה יהוה, עוֹשֶׂה הַשָּׁלוֹם.

Ba**ruch** Ata Ado**nai**, **o**seh hasha**lom**.
A Source of Blessing are You, Adonai, Who makes peace.

🔔 The bomb measured 20 inches, the bomb's destruction: 7 yards. Four were killed and eleven wounded. Two hospitals and one cemetery absorbed the wounded and the dead. One of the women killed was buried within 30 miles of where she was born. The man who mourns her lives an ocean away.

There are others who mourn those who were killed. And there are those who love the wounded and the mourners. We have circled the world.　　　　Let us work for peace.

It is the time for our hearts and souls
to have their voice as we pray silently.

Tefilat HaLev - Shabbat/Festivals שבת/חג - תפלת הלב

The Amidah in Guided Imagery

Adapted from "Amidah in Movement" by Talia de Lone in P'nai Or Religious Fellowship Siddur Or Chadash 1989

1. **Avot**: We Call upon our Ancestors for Support in our Journey.

The image
Visualize Avraham and Sarah standing before you. They can be seen as two radiant light sources. Extend from them two rays of interwoven light. The light forms a chain that comes down through the generations into you. Receive the light from your feet. Connect it to the ground. Allow the light to grow up around you, following your spine until it comes to rest on the crown of your head. Spiral it down until you are enclosed in this light. The light is your protection.

Once you have established the image, chant its blessing:

מֶלֶךְ עוֹזֵר וּמוֹשִׁיעַ וּמָגֵן: בָּרוּךְ אַתָּה יהוה, מָגֵן אַבְרָהָם וְעֶזְרַת (וּפוֹקֵד) שָׂרָה:

Melech **o**zeir umoshi'a umagein: **B**aruch Ata A**do**nai, ma**gein** Avra**ham** ve'ez**rat** (ufo**keid**) **S**arah.

Sovereign, who is our Help, our redemption and our protector. A Blessing are You, Adonai, Shield of Abraham and Helper of (One who remembers) Sarah.

2. **Chesed and Gevurah**: We Open to Divine Expansiveness and Power.

The Image
See yourself in a time of your life in which you felt lost., confused, despairing. See a light come into your heart. Allow it to grow until you shine with your own Source. Imagine yourself lying down at first, and gradually, as the light fills you, you come to standing.

Once you have established the image, chant its blessing:

Tefilat HaLev - Shabbat/Festivals — שבת/חג

וְנֶאֱמָן אַתָּה לְהַחֲיוֹת הַכֹּל (הַמֵּתִים).
בָּרוּךְ אַתָּה יהוה, מְחַיֵּה הַכֹּל (הַמֵּתִים):

Vene-e**man** A**ta** lehacha**yot** ha**kol** (hamay**tiym**).
B**aruch** Ata Ado**nai**, mecha**yei** ha**kol** (hamay**tiym**).
And You are faithful in giving life to all (the deadened).
A blessing are You, Adonai, who gives life to all (the deadened).

3. Kedushat Ha-Shem: We Name the Holy.

The Image
Breathe in and out, seeing the purity of your breath come into your body. Breathe out slowly, allowing all impurities to leave you. Experience the wholeness and completeness of each breath. Feel its circularity, its roundness, its holiness, God's Name is in each breath.

Once you have established the image, chant its blessing:

אַתָּה קָדוֹשׁ וְשִׁמְךָ קָדוֹשׁ וּקְדוֹשִׁים בְּכָל יוֹם יְהַלְלוּךָ,
סֶלָה. בָּרוּךְ אַתָּה יהוה, הָאֵל הַקָּדוֹשׁ.

A**ta** ka**dosh** veshim**cha** ka**dosh** ukdo**shim** be**chol** yom yehale**lucha**, **Sela**. B**aruch** ata, Ado**nai** ha-Eil haka**dosh**.
You are Holy, and Your Name is Holy; We acknowledge Your holiness every day, Selah. A Source of Blessing are You, Adonai, You are Divine Holiness.

4. Kedushat Ha-Yom: We Open Ourselves to the Sacred in Shabbat.

The Image
Rabbi Abraham Joshua Heschel taught: "The meaning of Shabbat is to turn from the results of creation to the mystery of creation; from the world of creation to the creation of the world."

Look around the space you are in. Allow your eyes to see each object, each person fresh and new, as if you were seeing them for the first time. Appreciate with delight

Tefilat HaLev - Shabbat/Festivals — שבת/חג - תפלת הלב

the creation process that brought all this into being. Can you feel how, by your very looking, you are creating the world you see? Rest in your delight in this way of seeing.

Once you have established the image, chant its blessing:

בָּרוּךְ אַתָּה יהוה, מְקַדֵּשׁ הַשַּׁבָּת:

Baruch Ata Adonai, mekadeish haShabat.
A Source of blessing are You, Adonai, Who makes Shabbat holy.

🍃 🍃 🍃 🍃 🍃 🍃 🍃 🍃 🍃 🍃 🍃

5. **Avodah**: We Open Ourselves to Sacred Service.

The Image
See yourself as a flame, offering yourself to God. Feel the flame burning inside you. Feel your longing, your desire to know God, to serve God. Experience the great yearning that rests in that flame.

Once you have established the image, chant its blessing:

וְתֶחֱזֶינָה עֵינֵינוּ בְּשׁוּבְךָ לְצִיּוֹן בְּרַחֲמִים.
בָּרוּךְ אַתָּה יהוה, הַמַּחֲזִיר שְׁכִינָתוֹ לְצִיּוֹן.

**Vetechezena eyneinu beshuvecha letziyon berachamiym.
Baruch Ata Adonai, hamachazir shechinato letziyon.**
Allow our eyes to see Your return to Tzion with compassion. A Source of Blessing are You, Adonai, who returns Shechina to Tzion.

🍃 🍃 🍃 🍃 🍃 🍃 🍃 🍃 🍃 🍃 🍃

6. **Modim**: We Open Ourselves to Gratitude.

Think about something in your life about which you are grateful. Recognize that miracles happen every day in your life. Think of one of these miracles now. Feel the appreciation of these miracles rise within you. Recognize that you are the vessel for Divine action and that the One acts through you and with you. Be a conduit for Warmth and Energy from the heavens to the earth and back again.

Tefilat HaLev - Shabbat/Festivals   שבת/חג – תפלת הלב

Once you have established the image, chant its blessing:

בָּרוּךְ אַתָּה יהוה, הַטּוֹב שִׁמְךָ וּלְךָ נָאֶה לְהוֹדוֹת.

Baruch **A**ta Ado**nai**, ha**tov** shim**cha** ule**cha** na-**eh** leho**dot**.
A Source of blessing are You, Adonai, Your Essence is goodness and it is fitting to be grateful to You.

🍃 🍃 🍃 🍃 🍃 🍃 🍃 🍃 🍃 🍃 🍃 🍃 🍃

7. **Shalom:** We Open Ourselves to Wholeness, Completeness, Fulfillment and Peace.

See a glow of light approaching you. It surrounds you and envelops you. You are bathed in this light. This light is contentment and it comes to you from those around you and you send it back out to those arround you and to your family and the ones you love. Watch as the light spreads from person to person until it surrounds and envelops the world.

Once you have established the image, chant its blessing:

בָּרוּךְ אַתָּה יהוה, עוֹשֶׂה הַשָּׁלוֹם.

Baruch **A**ta Ado**nai**, **o**seh hasha**lom**.
A Source of Blessing are You, Adonai, Who makes peace.

It is the time for our hearts and souls
to have their voice as we pray silently.

76

Tefilat HaLev - Shabbat/Festivals — שבת/חג — תפלת הלב

אֱלֹהַי, נְצוֹר לְשׁוֹנִי מֵרָע. וּשְׂפָתַי מִדַּבֵּר מִרְמָה:
וְלִמְקַלְלַי נַפְשִׁי תִדֹּם,
וְנַפְשִׁי כֶּעָפָר לַכֹּל תִּהְיֶה.
פְּתַח לִבִּי בְּתוֹרָתֶךָ,
וּבְמִצְוֹתֶיךָ תִּרְדּוֹף נַפְשִׁי.

Elohai netzor leshoni meira. Usfatai midabeir mirma:
Velimkalelai nafshi tidom, venafshi ke-afar lakol tihye.
Petach libiy betoratecha, uvemitzvotecha tirdof nafshi.
My God, Guard my tongue from all evil
and my lips from spouting lies.
May I think before I begin to speak,
may my words be gentle and wise.
Help me ignore those who wish me ill,
help me be humble before all.
Open my heart to Your Torah
that I may know how to answer Your call. Juliet Spitzer

יִהְיוּ לְרָצוֹן אִמְרֵי פִי וְהֶגְיוֹן לִבִּי לְפָנֶיךָ,
יהוה צוּרִי וְגֹאֲלִי.

Yiheyu leratzon imrei fi vehegyon libi lefanecha,
Adonai tzuri vego-ali.
May the words of my mouth and the meditations of my heart be acceptable before You, Adonai, my rock and my redeemer.

Tefilat HaLev - Shabbat/Festivals — שבת/חג - תפלת הלב

עֹשֶׂה שָׁלוֹם בִּמְרוֹמָיו הוּא יַעֲשֶׂה שָׁלוֹם עָלֵינוּ
וְעַל כָּל יִשְׂרָאֵל, (וְעַל כָּל יוֹשְׁבֵי תֵבֵל,)
וְאִמְרוּ אָמֵן:

O**seh** sha**lom** bimro**mav**, hu ya-a**seh** sha**lom** a**lei**nu,
ve'**al** kol Yisra-**eil**, (ve'al kol yosh**vei** tei**veil**,)
ve-im**ru**: a**mein**.
May the One who makes peace in the high places, make peace for us, for Israel, and all the world, and let us say, Amen.

Kaddish Shalem (Full) - page 144

Torah Service - page 146

Gomeil Blessing - page 151

Prayers for Healing - page 152

Aleinu - page 169

Kiddush - page 180 (eve), page 181 (morn)

Motzie - page 191

Weekday Amidah - page 183

Hallel - page 189

Yizkor - page 201

Tefilat HaLev - Shabbat/Festivals — שבת/חג - תפלת הלב

Shabbat Morning Service
SHABBAT SHALOM!

Nishmati ahuvah
lehitchareit haklipah
letshu-vah uslichah
letodah uvrachah
HalelluhYahh,
HalelluhYahh

נִשְׁמָתִי אֲהוּבָה
לְהִתְחָרֵט הַקְלִיפָּה
לִתְשׁוּבָה וּסְלִיחָה
לְתוֹדָה וּבְרָכָה
הַלְלוּיָהּ הַלְלוּיָהּ

O my Soul, I Love You,
Pain and Sorrow from my life
Repenting and Releasing
Thanks to You, Blessings come HalelluhYahh
HalelluhYahh

מוֹדָה אֲנִי לְפָנֶיךָ, רוּחַ חַי וְקַיָּם,
שֶׁהֶחֱזַרְתָּ בִּי נִשְׁמָתִי בְּחֶמְלָה רַבָּה אֱמוּנָתֶךָ.

Modah/deh ani lifanecha, ru-ach chai vekayam,
shechazarta biy nishmati bechemla
rabah emunatecha.

I gratefully acknowledge the face of God; Spirit lives and endures; You return my soul to me with compassion; How great is your faith in me. © R. Shefa Gold

וַאֲנַחְנוּ נְבָרֵךְ יָהּ, מֵעַתָּה וְעַד עוֹלָם, הַלְלוּיָהּ:

Va-anachnu nevarech Yahh, Me'ata ve'ad olam,
Halelu-Yahh:

Praise Adonai (Yahh): And we will bless Adonai (Yahh)
from now and until eternity, Praise Adonai (Yahh):

Tefilat HaLev - Shabbat/Festivals — שבת/חג - תפלת הלב

When I sing the Name of God my spirit rises
From the depths she soars in the light

שַׁדַּי, שְׁכִינָה, יהוה צְבָאוֹת, הֲוָיָה, מְקוֹר חַיִּים, צוּר, מָקוֹם, אֵל עֶלְיוֹן, יָהּ, רוּחַ, אֱלוֹהִים.

Shaddai, Shechina, Adonai Tzeva-ot, Havaya, Mekor Chayim, Tzur, Makom, Eil Elyon, Yahh, Ruach, Elohiym. © R. Hanna Tiferet Siegel

בָּרוּךְ שֶׁאָמַר, בְּרוּכָה שֶׁאָמְרָה, וְהָיָה הָעוֹלָם.

Baruch she-amar, Bruchah she-amrah vehayah ha-olam.

Blessed is He, Blessed is She, Blessed are We,
who speak and are heard. © R. Hanna Tiferet Siegel

Bar'chu, Dear One, Shechinah, Holy Name,
When I call on the Light of my Soul, I come home.
 © Lev Friedman

Ma Tovu / Oh How Good — מה טבו

מַה טֹּבוּ אֹהָלֶיךָ יַעֲקֹב, מִשְׁכְּנֹתֶיךָ יִשְׂרָאֵל.

Mah tovu ohalecha Ya-akov, Mishkenotecha Yisra-eil.
O how good are your tents, Jacob, your dwelling-places, Israel.
Blessings flow into the world from the Source of Life.
Be a vessel for the love-song of God © R. Hanna Tiferet Siegel

הִנֵּה מַה טּוֹב וּמַה נָּעִים שֶׁבֶת אַחִים גַּם יָחַד.

Hinei ma tov umah na-iym shevet achiym gam yachad.
Behold how good and how pleasant it is when brethren dwell together.

80

Tefilat HaLev - Shabbat/Festivals — שבת/חג - תפלת הלב

"Our deepest Fear is not that we are inadequate. Our deepest fear is that we are powerful beyond measure. It is our light, not our darkness that most frightens us. We ask ourselves, "Who am I to be brilliant, gorgeous, talented, fabulous?" Actually, who are you not to be? You are a child of God. Your playing small does not serve the world. There is nothing enlightened about shrinking so that other people won't feel insecure around you. We are all meant to shine, as children do. We were born to make manifest the glory of God that is within us. It's not just in some of us; it's in everyone. And as we let our own light shine, we unconsciously give other people permission to do the same. As we are liberated from our own fear, our presence automatically liberates others."

© Marianne Williamson, *A Return to Love*.

וַאֲנִי תְפִלָּתִי לְךָ יהוה, עֵת רָצוֹן, אֱלֹהִים בְּרָב חַסְדֶּךָ, עֲנֵנִי בֶּאֱמֶת יִשְׁעֶךָ.

Va-ani tefilati lecha Adonai eit ratzon Elohiym berov hasdecha aneini be-emet yish'echa.

I am hope and my prayer to You, through You Adonai, blending in with Your desire and Your great mercy. Answer me with Your truth, O great One.

Psalm 69:14 Rev Maya Kashtelyan and Rabbi Shafir Lobb

Tefilat HaLev - Shabbat/Festivals שבת/חג – תפלת הלב

Barchi nafshi et Adonai. בָּרְכִי נַפְשִׁי אֶת יהוה.
My Soul, acknowledge Adonai.

The wearing of a tallit may be considered "time-bound" because it is worn in daylight in order to "see" the fringes, and the blue strand, if it is present.

Are not all humans bound by time in our modern world? By choosing to wear a tallit, we choose to set aside a time to pray, a time to connect; the tallit serves to wrap us in the past and it invites us to wrestle with our present and look to the future.

"What is your kavanah, your intention, when you pray," the tallit asks us. Physically or virtually, we put the tallit on in two steps, first saying the bracha or blessing to remind ourselves that it is a mitzvah, a way to feel connected to the Source of Life. Then we pause for a moment with the tallit over our heads, a second or two of deep privacy, allowing us to focus and feel that connection.

We are reminded, that like all spiritual practices, "It's about the seeking, the striving."

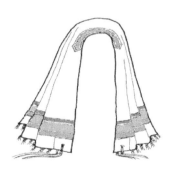

בָּרוּךְ אַתָּה יהוה אֱלֹהֵינוּ מֶלֶךְ הָעוֹלָם, אֲשֶׁר קִדְּשָׁנוּ בְּמִצְוֹתָיו, וְצִוָּנוּ לְהִתְעַטֵּף בַּצִּיצִת.

Baruch ata Adonai Eloheinu melech ha-olam, asher kidshanu bemitzvotav, vetzivanu, lehitateif batzitzit.
The Source of Blessing are You, Eternal Sovereign. You make us special with Mitzvot and instruct us to enwrap ourself with tzitzit (tallit).

Tefilat HaLev - Shabbat/Festivals שבת/חג - תפלת הלב

✡ Traditional morning prayers include reminders that our bodies are amazing in many ways. We have veins, arteries, synapses, opening and closings. We are reminded that we are here this morning only because more of our bodies are working as they should than are not. We are here because we choose to be and because our bodies allow us to function enough to so do. How amazing is that body. And even more amazing is the Soul, the Life-force within that body. Our Tradition teaches us that the Soul is pure. Every time we wake, we are invited to remind ourselves that the Divine Spark within us is that bit of the Divine within each of us. How will you treat and use your Soul today?

🕊 According to Talmud (Brachot 60b), 1600 years ago, Abaye would say the *asher yatzar* blessing upon exiting the privy. It is easy to ridicule the concept of attaching holy words of prayer to such basic functions, until our bodies stop working as well as they should. A young student, who would become a doctor one day, scoffed at the signs in his day school that reminded him and his friends to say this blessing after every visit. He thought the idea humorous.

Later, upon becoming a doctor, he thought of patients whose lives revolved around dialysis machines and others with colostomies and urinary catheters, and he realized how wise the rabbi had been. He asked if Abaye could have foreseen that "blockage" of the "cavity," or lumen, of the coronary artery would lead to "the commonest cause of death in industrialized countries some 16 centuries later?" For all of us, this is a prayer we will say in one form or another when the time is right. And so, it is part of our morning prayers.

The doctor is Dr. Kenneth Prager, M.D.

Tefilat HaLev - Shabbat/Festivals — שבת/חג - תפלת הלב

בָּרוּךְ אַתָּה יהוה אֱלֹהֵינוּ מֶלֶךְ הָעוֹלָם, אֲשֶׁר יָצַר אֶת הָאָדָם בְּחָכְמָה, וּבָרָא בוֹ נְקָבִים נְקָבִים, חֲלוּלִים חֲלוּלִים, גָּלוּי וְיָדוּעַ לִפְנֵי כִסֵּא כְבוֹדֶךָ שֶׁאִם יִפָּתֵחַ אֶחָד מֵהֶם, אוֹ יִסָּתֵם אֶחָד מֵהֶם, אִי אֶפְשַׁר לְהִתְקַיֵּם וְלַעֲמוֹד לְפָנֶיךָ: **בָּרוּךְ אַתָּה יהוה, רוֹפֵא כָל בָּשָׂר, וּמַפְלִיא לַעֲשׂוֹת:**

Baruch ata Adonai Eloheinu melech ha-olam, asher et ha-adam bechochma uvara vo nekeiviym nekeiviym, chaluliym chaluliym, galuy veyadu'a lifnei chisei kevodecha she-im yipatei-ach echad meihem o yisateim echad meihem iy efshar lehitkayeim vela'amod lefanecha.
Baruch Ata Adonai, rofei chol basar umafli la-asot.

A Source of blessings are You, Adonai, our God, Sovereign of the universe, Who fashioned humans with wisdom and created many openings and cavities within. It is obvious and known before Your Throne of Glory that if but one of them were to be ruptured or but one of them were to be blocked it would be impossible to survive and to stand before You. A Source of blessings are You, Adonai, who heals all flesh and acts wonderously.

בָּרוּךְ אַתָּה יהוה אֱלֹהֵינוּ מֶלֶךְ הָעוֹלָם, אֲשֶׁר קִדְּשָׁנוּ בְּמִצְוֹתָיו, וְצִוָּנוּ לַעֲסוֹק בְּדִבְרֵי תוֹרָה:

Baruch Ata Adonai Eloheinu melech ha-olam, asher kidshanu bemitzvotav, vetzivanu la'asok bedivrei Torah.
The Source of Blessing are You, Eternal Sovereign. You make us special with Mitzvot and instruct us to engage with words of Torah.

אֵלּוּ דְבָרִים שֶׁאֵין לָהֶם שִׁעוּר: שֶׁאָדָם אוֹכֵל פֵּרוֹתֵיהֶם בָּעוֹלָם הַזֶּה וְהַקֶּרֶן קַיֶּמֶת לוֹ לָעוֹלָם הַבָּא, וְאֵלּוּ הֵן:

Eilu devariym she-ein lahem shiur: she-adam ochail peirotaihem ba'olam hazeh vehakeren kayemet lo le'olam haba, ve-eilu hein:
These are the things that that have no limit: A person enjoys their fruit in this world, and lives upon their principal in the world to come:

תפלת הלב – שבת/חג — Tefilat HaLev - Shabbat/Festivals

כִּבּוּד אָב וָאֵם, kibud av ve-aim,
honoring father and mother;

וּגְמִילוּת חֲסָדִים, ugmilut chasadiym,
performing acts of love and kindness;

וְהַשְׁכָּמַת בֵּית הַמִּדְרָשׁ שַׁחֲרִית וְעַרְבִית, vehashkamat beit hamidrash shachariyt ve'arviyt,
participate at the house of study at least twice daily;

וְהַכְנָסַת אוֹרְחִים, vehachnassat orchim,
welcome strangers;

וּבִקּוּר חוֹלִים, uvikur choliym,
visit the sick;

וְהַכְנָסַת כַּלָּה, vehachnasat kalah,
contribute to newlyweds;

וּלְוָיַת הַמֵּת, ulvayat hameit,
helping to bury the dead;

וְעִיּוּן תְּפִלָּה, ve'iyun tefila,
praying with devotion;

וַהֲבָאַת שָׁלוֹם בֵּין אָדָם לַחֲבֵרוֹ, vehava-at shalom bein adam lechaveiro,
bringing peace between individuals;

וְתַלְמוּד תּוֹרָה כְּנֶגֶד כֻּלָּם. vetalmud Torah keneged kulam
And studying Torah leads to them all.

Tefilat HaLev - Shabbat/Festivals — שבת/חג

אֱלֹהַי נְשָׁמָה שֶׁנָּתַתָּ בִּי טְהוֹרָה הִיא.
Elohai neshamah shenatata bi tehorah hi.
My God, the life and soul which You placed within me are pure.

When we say that the soul is pure, what do we mean? We are reminding ourselves that each day is a fresh start, for ourselves and for others. We are reminded to see the best in ourselves and in others. The soul with each and every one of us is pure. Live today in a way worthy of your soul.

בָּרוּךְ אַתָּה יהוה אֱלֹהֵינוּ מֶלֶךְ הָעוֹלָם, ...
Baruch Ata Adonai Eloheinu Melech ha'olam, ...
A Source of Blessing are You, Adonai, Sovereign of the Universe...

...אֲשֶׁר נָתַן לַשֶּׂכְוִי בִינָה, לְהַבְחִין בֵּין יוֹם וּבֵין לָיְלָה:
... asher natan lasechvi vina, lehavchiyn bein yom uvein laila.
...who has given the mind the capacity to distinguish between day and night.

... she'asani betzalmo. ...שֶׁעָשַׂנִי בְּצַלְמוֹ:
... who made me in the divine image.

... she'asani Yisra-eil. ...שֶׁעָשַׂנִי יִשְׂרָאֵל:
... who made me of the people Israel.

...שֶׁעָשַׂנִי בֶּן/בַּת חוֹרִין:
... she'asani ben/bat choriyn.
... who made me free.

Tefilat HaLev - Shabbat/Festivals - שבת/חג - תפלת הלב

... pokei-ach 'ivriym. ‎…פּוֹקֵחַ עִוְרִים:
... who gives sight to the blind.

... malbiysh 'arumiym. ‎…מַלְבִּישׁ עֲרֻמִּים:
... who clothes the naked.

... matiyr asuriym. ‎…מַתִּיר אֲסוּרִים:
... who frees the captive.

... zokeif kefufiym. ‎…זוֹקֵף כְּפוּפִים:
... who straightens the bent.

‎…רוֹקַע הָאָרֶץ עַל הַמָּיִם:
... roka ha-aretz al hamayim.
... who stretches out the earth upon the waters.

... she'asah li kol tzorki. ‎…שֶׁעָשָׂה לִי כָּל צָרְכִּי:
... who provides me with all I need.

‎…הַמֵּכִין מִצְעֲדֵי גָבֶר:
... hameichiyn mitz'adei gaver.
... who makes firm a person's steps.

... ozeir Yisra-eil bigvurah. ‎…אוֹזֵר יִשְׂרָאֵל בִּגְבוּרָה:
... who girds Israel with strength.

‎…עוֹטֵר יִשְׂרָאֵל בְּתִפְאָרָה:
... 'oteir Yisra-eil betif-arah.
... who crowns Israel with splendor.

... hanotein laya'eif ko-ach. ‎…הַנּוֹתֵן לַיָּעֵף כֹּחַ:
... who gives strength to the weary.

‎…הַמַּעֲבִיר שֵׁנָה מֵעֵינַי וּתְנוּמָה מֵעַפְעַפָּי:
... hama'aviyr sheinah mei'einai utnumah mei-afapai.
... who removes sleep from my eyes and slumber from my eyelids.

(translations: Rabbi Marcia Prager, ©1998, *the Path of Blessing*)

Tefilat HaLev - Shabbat/Festivals — שבת/חג – תפלת הלב

אַנְעִים זְמִירוֹת וְשִׁירִים אֶאֱרוֹג,
כִּי אֵלֶיךָ נַפְשִׁי תַעֲרוֹג.
נַפְשִׁי חָמְדָה בְּצֵל יָדֶךָ, לָדַעַת כָּל רָז סוֹדֶךָ.

An'im zemi**rot** veshi**riym** e-e**rog**. Ki ei**le**cha naf**shi** ta'a**rog**. Naf**shi** chem**da** bet**zeil** yade**cha**, lada'at kol raz so**de**cha.

The joy in my heart is weaving a song.
For You my soul is longing.
We touch, we embrace, in the shelter of love.
In Your light, I know who I am.
© R. Hanna Tiferet Siegel

There are only two ways to live your life. One is as though nothing is a miracle. The other is as though everything is a miracle.   Albert Einstein

טוֹב לְהֹדוֹת לַיהוה וּלְזַמֵּר
לְשִׁמְךָ עֶלְיוֹן: לְהַגִּיד בַּבֹּקֶר
חַסְדֶּךָ וֶאֱמוּנָתְךָ בַּלֵּילוֹת:

Tov leho**dot** la'Ado**nai**.
Uleza**meir** leshim**cha** El**yon**,
Leha**gid** babo**ker** chas**de**cha ve-emuna**te**cha balei**lot**.

It is good to give thanks to Adonai and to sing of God's great Name, to tell of God's compassion in the morning and faithfulness in the evening.

Brachot or blessings say thank You by acknowledging God's role in our lives as that force that connects us with all that is and gives our lives purpose and meaning. We are reminded that we are not alone, not now, not ever.

Tefilat HaLev - Shabbat/Festivals שבת/חג - תפלת הלב

צַדִּיק כַּתָּמָר יִפְרָח
כְּאֶרֶז בַּלְּבָנוֹן יִשְׂגֶּה:
שְׁתוּלִים בְּבֵית יהוה
בְּחַצְרוֹת אֱלֹהֵינוּ יַפְרִיחוּ:
עוֹד יְנוּבוּן בְּשֵׂיבָה
דְּשֵׁנִים וְרַעֲנַנִּים יִהְיוּ:
לְהַגִּיד כִּי יָשָׁר יהוה
צוּרִי וְלֹא עַוְלָתָה בּוֹ.

Tzadik katamar yifrach ke-erez balvanon yisgeh,
Shetuliym beveit Adonai bechatzrot Eloheinu yafrichu.
Od yenuvun beseivah
desheiniym vera'ananiym yihyu,
Lehagiyd ki yashar Adonai, Tzuri, velo avlatah bo.

❀ The righteous ones will flourish like the palm tree, thrive and grow tall, like a cedar in Lebanon.
They are rooted in the house of Adonai,
In God's own courtyards.
Even as they age, they will be fruitful, fresh and evergreen,
Proclaiming that Adonai is just, my Rock,
there is no hardship [coming from God].

🕊 Psalms are traditionally attributed to David, although less than half of them specifically mention David. Others are unattributed, or attributed to Solomon, the sons of Korach, the rebellious one, or Asaph, who is traditionally understood as a Temple musician, or guild of musicians, during the times of David and Solomon.

Tefilat HaLev - Shabbat/Festivals שבת/חג - תפלת הלב

🔔 The earliest public prayers were Psalms, and we still use many of them in congregational and private worship today. Psalms express joy, lamentations, fear, and confidence. The Psalms remind us of our connection to God and to universe. Later prayers are often poems written to aid us in the process of introspection, healing, and community building. There is never just one proper way to pray, and different prayers help different people at different times. That diversity is a true reflection of God's abundance and love for us and for all of creation.

בָּרוּךְ שֶׁאָמַר וְהָיָה הָעוֹלָם, בָּרוּךְ הוּא,
Baruch she-amar vehayah ha-olam, Baruch Hu!

בָּרוּךְ עֹשֶׂה בְרֵאשִׁית, בָּרוּךְ שְׁמוֹ.
Baruch oseh vereishiyt, Baruch Shemo!

בָּרוּךְ אוֹמֵר וְעֹשֶׂה, בָּרוּךְ הוּא,
Baruch omeir v'oseh, Baruch Hu!

בָּרוּךְ גּוֹזֵר וּמְקַיֵּם, בָּרוּךְ שְׁמוֹ.
Baruch gozeir umkayeim, Baruch Shemo!

בָּרוּךְ מְרַחֵם עַל הָאָרֶץ, בָּרוּךְ הוּא,
Baruch meracheim al ha-aretz, Baruch Hu!

בָּרוּךְ מְרַחֵם עַל הַבְּרִיּוֹת, בָּרוּךְ שְׁמוֹ.
Baruch meracheim al habriyot, Baruch Shemo!

בָּרוּךְ מְשַׁלֵּם שָׂכָר טוֹב לִירֵאָיו, בָּרוּךְ הוּא,
Baruch meshaleim sachar tov liyrei-av, Baruch Hu!

בָּרוּךְ חַי לָעַד וְקַיָּם לָנֶצַח, בָּרוּךְ שְׁמוֹ.
Baruch chai la-ad vekayam lanetzach, Baruch Shemo!

בָּרוּךְ פּוֹדֶה וּמַצִּיל, בָּרוּךְ הוּא, בָּרוּךְ שְׁמוֹ.
Baruch podeh umatziyl, Baruch Hu!
Baruch Shemo! (Baruch Hu! Baruch Shemo!)

Tefilat HaLev - Shabbat/Festivals — שבת/חג - תפלת הלב

Blessings from the one, who spoke and all things came to be! Blessed are You!
Blessings from the one, who created all in the beginning! Blessed is Your Name!
Blessings from the one, who speaks and acts! Blessed are You!
Blessings from the one, who determines and fulfills! Blessed is Your Name!
Blessings from the one, who deals kindly with the world! Blessed are You!
Blessings from the one, who acts kindly toward all creatures!   Blessed is Your Name!
Blessings from the one, who responds with good to those in awe! Blessed are You!
Blessings from the one, who removes the dark and brings the light!   Blessed is Your Name!
Blessings from the one, who lives eternally! Blessed are You!
Blessings from the one, who lasts forever! Blessed is Your Name!
Blessings from the one, who delivers and redeems! Blessed are You!
Blessings are You and Your name! Blessed is Your Name!

בָּרוּךְ אַתָּה יהוה, מֶלֶךְ מְהֻלָּל בַּתִּשְׁבָּחוֹת׃

Baruch Ata Adonai Eloheinu Melech mehulal batishbachot.

A Source of Blessing are You, Adonai, Sovereign, worthy of psalms of praise.

רוֹמְמוּ יהוה אֱלֹהֵינוּ וְהִשְׁתַּחֲווּ לְהַר קָדְשׁוֹ
כִּי־קָדוֹשׁ יהוה אֱלֹהֵינוּ׃

**Romemu Adonai Eloheinu vehishtachavu lehar kodsho.
Ki Kadosh Adonai Eloheinu.**

Exalt Adonai, our God and worship at God's holy mountain,
for Adonai, our God is holy.

Tefilat HaLev - Shabbat/Festivals — שבת/חג - תפלת הלב

הוֹדוּ לַיהוה כִּי טוֹב, כִּי לְעוֹלָם חַסְדּוֹ:
Hodu laAdonai ki-tov -- ki le-olam chasdo
Give thanks to Adonai, for God is good, God's compassion endures through all time and space;

הוֹדוּ לֵאלֹהֵי הָאֱלֹהִים, כִּי לְעוֹלָם חַסְדּוֹ:
Hodu leilohei ha-Elohiym -- ki le-olam chasdo
Give thanks to the God above all gods, God's compassion endures through all time and space;

הוֹדוּ לַאֲדֹנֵי הָאֲדֹנִים, כִּי לְעוֹלָם חַסְדּוֹ:
Hodu la-adonei ha-adoniym -- ki le-olam chasdo
Give thanks to the Connector of connectiveness, God's compassion endures through all time and space;

(2x)

לְעֹשֵׂה נִפְלָאוֹת גְּדֹלוֹת לְבַדּוֹ, כִּי לְעוֹלָם חַסְדּוֹ:
Le-osei nifla-ot gedolot levado -- ki le-olam chasdo
To the One who alone does great wonders, God's compassion endures through all time and space;

לְעֹשֵׂה הַשָּׁמַיִם בִּתְבוּנָה, כִּי לְעוֹלָם חַסְדּוֹ:
Le-osei hashamayim bitvuna -- ki le-olam chasdo
To the One who made the heavens with purpose, God's compassion endures through all time and space;

לְרוֹקַע הָאָרֶץ עַל הַמָּיִם, כִּי לְעוֹלָם חַסְדּוֹ:
Leroka ha-aretz al-hamayim -- ki le-olam chasdo
To the One who stretched the earth over the waters, God's compassion endures through all time and space;

(2x)

Tefilat HaLev - Shabbat/Festivals — שבת/חג

לְעוֹשֵׂה אוֹרִים גְּדוֹלִים, כִּי לְעוֹלָם חַסְדּוֹ:

Le-osei oriym gedoliym -- ki le-olam chasdo
To the One who made the great lights, God's compassion endures through all time and space;

אֶת הַשֶּׁמֶשׁ לְמֶמְשֶׁלֶת בַּיּוֹם, כִּי לְעוֹלָם חַסְדּוֹ:

Et hashemesh lememshelet **bayom -- ki le-olam chasdo**
The sun to reign by day, God's compassion endures through all time and space;

אֶת הַיָּרֵחַ וְכוֹכָבִים // לְמֶמְשְׁלוֹת בַּלַּיְלָה, כִּי לְעוֹלָם חַסְדּוֹ:

Et hayarei-ach vechochaviym // lememshelot balaila -- ki le-olam chasdo
The moon and the stars to reign by night, God's compassion endures through all time and space;

שֶׁבְּשִׁפְלֵנוּ זָכַר לָנוּ, כִּי לְעוֹלָם חַסְדּוֹ:

Shebeshifleinu zachar lanu -- ki le-olam chasdo
Who remembered us when we were low, God's compassion endures through all time and space;

וַיִּפְרְקֵנוּ מִצָּרֵינוּ, כִּי לְעוֹלָם חַסְדּוֹ:

Vayifrekeinu mitzareinu -- ki le-olam chasdo
And released us from our foes, God's compassion endures through all time and space;

נוֹתֵן לֶחֶם לְכָל בָּשָׂר, כִּי לְעוֹלָם חַסְדּוֹ:

Notein lechem lechol-basar -- ki le-olam chasdo
Who gives food to all creatures, God's compassion endures through all time and space;

הוֹדוּ לְאֵל הַשָּׁמַיִם, כִּי לְעוֹלָם חַסְדּוֹ:

Hodu le-Eil hashamayim -- ki le-olam chasdo
Give thanks to God of all heaven, God's compassion endures through all time and space;

Tefilat HaLev - Shabbat/Festivals   שבת/חג – תפלת הלב

Source of Life, You are the still small voice within us. May we slow down and be quiet enough to hear You. May the voice be loud enough to hear, yet also soft enough to hear; may we learn to listen.

In pondering our day and the coming week we may face indecision. We may not be able to determine which course to take. Here we ask You for inspiration, an intuitive thought or guidance. May we relax and "do" Shabbat. When we pause to let go and cease our struggle to manipulate and control, the answers we seek often come.

שִׁירוּ לַיהוה שִׁיר חָדָשׁ שִׁירוּ לַיהוה כָּל הָאָרֶץ:
שִׁירוּ לַיהוה בָּרְכוּ שְׁמוֹ
בַּשְּׂרוּ מִיּוֹם לְיוֹם יְשׁוּעָתוֹ:

Shiru laAdo**nai** shir cha**dash**,
Shiru laAdo**nai** kol ha-**a**retz
Shiru laAdo**nai** bar**chu** she**mo**
bas**ru** mi**yom** le**yom** yeshua**to**.
Sing to Adonai a new song,
Sing to Adonai all the earth!
Sing to Adonai, acknowledge God's Essence,
noble every day, source of salvation.

MEDITATION
The word *Shabbat* is related to *lashevet* - to sit or to dwell. It is related to the *yeshiva* (sitting) mode of praying. The very act of sitting and taking the time to make Shabbat is a sign of freedom. The gift of Shabbat is being able to take the time to view things from the perspective of sitting back, relaxing and considering the larger picture. When we can really do that, then we achieve Shabbat.　　　R. Sholom Silver

יִשְׂמְחוּ הַשָּׁמַיִם וְתָגֵל הָאָרֶץ יִרְעַם הַיָּם וּמְלֹאוֹ:

Yisme**chu** hasha**ma**yim veta**geil** ha-**a**retz. Yir'**am** ha**yam** umelo-**o**.
Rejoice O Heavens and unfurl O Earth; Roar O Seas, may all be fulfilled.

Tefilat HaLev - Shabbat/Festivals – שבת/חג

הַלְלוּיָהּ, הַלְלוּ אֵל בְּקָדְשׁוֹ, הַלְלוּהוּ בִּרְקִיעַ עֻזּוֹ:
הַלְלוּהוּ בִגְבוּרֹתָיו, הַלְלוּהוּ כְּרֹב גֻּדְלוֹ:
הַלְלוּהוּ בְּתֵקַע שׁוֹפָר, הַלְלוּהוּ בְּנֵבֶל וְכִנּוֹר:
הַלְלוּהוּ בְּתֹף וּמָחוֹל, הַלְלוּהוּ בְּמִנִּים וְעֻגָב:
הַלְלוּהוּ בְצִלְצְלֵי שָׁמַע, הַלְלוּהוּ בְּצִלְצְלֵי תְרוּעָה:
כֹּל הַנְּשָׁמָה תְּהַלֵּל יָהּ הַלְלוּיָהּ.

HaleluYahh, Halelu Eil bekodsho.
Haleluhu birkiy'a uzo.
Haleluhu bigvurotav. Haleluhu kerov gudlo.
Haleluhu beteika shofar. Haleluhu beneivel vechinor.
Haleluhu betof umachol. Haleluhu beminim ve'ugav.
Haleluhu betziltzelei shama. Haleluhu betziltzelei tru'ah. Kol hanshamah tehaleil Yahh, HaleluYahh.

Praise the Source in the holy space! Praise the Source in the heights above! Praise the Source through mightiness! Praise the Source in its infinite expanse! Praise the Source with Shofar blast! Praise the Source with lyre and string! Praise the Source with drum, tambourines and dance! Praise the Source with passion and enthusiasm!
Praise the Source with crashing cymbals! Praise the Source with resounding voice!
Let all who breathe now praise their Source! Hallelujah (Praise Yahh)!
(Psalm 150)

Tefilat HaLev - Shabbat/Festivals שבת/חג - תפלת הלב

HALLELUJAH!

Now I've heard there was a secret chord,
That David played, and it pleased the Lord,
But you don't really care for music, do you?
It goes like this: The fourth, the fifth, The minor fall,
the major lift,
The baffled king composing Hallelujah,
Hallelujah, Hallelujah, Hallelujah, Hallelujah
> Your faith was strong but you needed proof,
> You saw her bathing on the roof,
> Her beauty and the moonlight overthrew you.
> She tied you to a kitchen chair,
> She broke your throne, and she cut your hair,
> And from your lips she drew the Hallelujah.

Baby I have been here before, I know this room,
I've walked this floor,
I used to live alone before I knew you.
I've seen your flag on the marble arch,
Love is not a victory march,
It's a cold and it's a broken Hallelujah.
Hallelujah, Hallelujah, Hallelujah, Hallelujah.

> You say I took the name in vain,
> I don't even know the name,
> But if I did, well really, what's it to you?
> There's a blaze of light in every word,
> It doesn't matter which you heard,
> The holy or the broken Hallelujah
> Hallelujah, Hallelujah, Hallelujah, Hallelujah.

I did my best, it wasn't much, I couldn't feel,
so I tried to touch,
I've told the truth, I didn't come to fool you.
And even though it all went wrong
I'll stand before the Lord of Song
With nothing on my tongue but Hallelujah.
Hallelujah, Hallelujah, Hallelujah, Hallelujah.
© Leonard Cohen

Tefilat HaLev - Shabbat/Festivals — שבת/חג - תפלת הלב

 Our breath connects us with all life and with
the Source of All.
How can my breath honor that connection?
When I choose to live this day and this
moment fully,
Then my breath becomes so deep that, it, too, becomes
both praise and blessing.

נִשְׁמַת כָּל חַי, תְּבָרֵךְ אֶת שִׁמְךָ יהוה אֱלֹהֵינוּ.
Nishmat kol chai, teva**reich** et shim**cha** (Yahh or
Ado**nai**) Elo**hei**nu.
The breath of all life, Praises You, (Yahh or Adonai)
our God.

If the world was meant to be "all the same,"
there would be one kind of tree,
one kind of flower, and one kind of person.
Instead, we live in an amazing world and universe
with countless shades of green, many flowers,
abundant diversity, you, me, and everyone else.

There are many ways to approach the Divine.
Some reach out with song, some with meditation.
Some seek God through movement, as the great Akiva did.
How shall I seek You? Where can I find You?
God is not a thing or person, locked in time and space.
God is to be experienced, not believed or conceived.
God is when we are present to each other.
God is when we feel life fully,
a connection through time and space,
yesterday, today, and also tomorrow.

Tefilat HaLev - Shabbat/Festivals – שבת/חג – תפלת הלב

Shochein Ad - You Dwell For All Time
שׁוֹכֵן עַד

Shochein, shochein ad
Marom vekadosh Shemo
vechatuv, kadosh Shemo...
Shochein...

שׁוֹכֵן שׁוֹכֵן עַד,
מָרוֹם וְקָדוֹשׁ שְׁמוֹ:
וְכָתוּב, קָדוֹשׁ שְׁמוֹ...
שׁוֹכֵן...

Ranenu tzadikiym ba'Adonai,
layeshariym navah tehilah
vechatuv, kadosh Shemo...
Shochein...

רַנְּנוּ צַדִּיקִים בַּיהוה,
לַיְשָׁרִים נָאוָה תְהִלָּה.
וְכָתוּב, קָדוֹשׁ שְׁמוֹ... שׁוֹכֵן...

Befi yeshariym titromam
uvdivrei tzadikiym titbarach
vechatuv, kadosh Shemo... Shochein...

בְּפִי יְשָׁרִים תִּתְרוֹמָם.
וּבְדִבְרֵי צַדִּיקִים תִּתְבָּרַךְ.
וְכָתוּב, קָדוֹשׁ שְׁמוֹ...... שׁוֹכֵן...

Uvilshon chasiydiym titkadash
uvekerev kedoshiym tit'halal
vechatuv, kadosh Shemo... Shochein...

וּבִלְשׁוֹן חֲסִידִים תִּתְקַדָּשׁ.
וּבְקֶרֶב קְדוֹשִׁים תִּתְהַלָּל:
וְכָתוּב, קָדוֹשׁ שְׁמוֹ...... שׁוֹכֵן...

You dwell within, for all time
Exalted, sacred are You
It is written, Sacred are You...
Shochein...

The righteous rejoice in You
The upright seek Your glory
It is written, Sacred are You... Shochein...

The words of the upright praises You
The righteous draw blessing from You
It is written, Sacred are You... Shochein...

The talk of the faithful exalts You
In the holy You are made holy
It is written, Sacred are You... Shochein...

Tefilat HaLev - Shabbat/Festivals — שבת/חג

וּבְמַקְהֲלוֹת רִבְבוֹת עַמְּךָ בֵּית יִשְׂרָאֵל,
בְּרִנָּה יִתְפָּאַר שִׁמְךָ מַלְכֵּנוּ, בְּכָל דּוֹר וָדוֹר.

**Uvmakehalot rivevot amcha beit Yisra-eil,
berina yitpa-ar shimcha malkeinu, bechol dor vador.**

With the great chorus of Your people, Israel,
with joy we exalt Your sovereign name, in and to every generation.

When I sing the Name of God my spirit rises
From the depths she soars in the light

שַׁדַּי, שְׁכִינָה, יהוה צְבָאוֹת, הֲוָיָה, מְקוֹר חַיִּים,
צוּר, מָקוֹם, אֵל עֶלְיוֹן, יָהּ, רוּחַ, אֱלוֹהִים.

Shaddai, Shechina, Adonai Tzeva-ot, Havaya, Mekor Chayim, Tzur, Makom, Eil Elyon, Yahh, Ruach, Elohiym.

© R. Hanna Tiferet Siegel

Hebrew has many names for God,
and many words for joy.
  There are one hundred and fifty psalms
  that Praise the Source of Life, God, our redeemer.
Praising God helps us through any rough times.
Praising God helps us live life fully.

Tefilat HaLev - Shabbat/Festivals — שבת/חג - תפלת הלב

יִשְׁתַּבַּח שִׁמְךָ לָעַד מַלְכֵּנוּ,
הָאֵל הַמֶּלֶךְ הַגָּדוֹל וְהַקָּדוֹשׁ בַּשָּׁמַיִם וּבָאָרֶץ.
כִּי לְךָ נָאֶה, יהוה אֱלֹהֵינוּ וֵאלֹהֵי אֲבוֹתֵינוּ:
שִׁיר וּשְׁבָחָה, הַלֵּל וְזִמְרָה, עֹז וּמֶמְשָׁלָה, נֶצַח, גְּדֻלָּה
וּגְבוּרָה, תְּהִלָּה וְתִפְאֶרֶת, קְדֻשָּׁה וּמַלְכוּת.
בְּרָכוֹת וְהוֹדָאוֹת מֵעַתָּה וְעַד עוֹלָם.

Yishta**bach** shim**cha** la'**ad** mal**kei**nu, ha-**eil** ha**Me**lech
haga**dol** vehaka**dosh** basha**may**im uva-**a**retz. Ki le**cha**
na-**eh** Ado**nai** Elo**hei**nu veilo**hei** avo**tei**nu: Shir ushva**cha**,
ha**leil** vezim**ra**, oz umemsha**la**, **ne**tzach, gedu**la** ugvu**ra**,
tehi**la** vetif-**eret**, kedu**sha** umal**chut**.
Be**ra**chot vehoda-**ot** mei'**a**ta ve-**ad** o**lam**.

Your holy name is always to be praised, Mighty One, holy and great sovereign
of heaven and earth. Such praises befit You, Adonai, our God and God of our
ancestors. Songs and praise, psalms of adoration and glory, exalting and
acknowledging, telling of Your Eternal Essence, greatness, and might, revealing
Your spendor, sanctity, grandeur, and sovereignty. You are a source of blessings
and make us forever grateful, through all time and space.

בָּרוּךְ אַתָּה יהוה, אֵל מֶלֶךְ גָּדוֹל בַּתִּשְׁבָּחוֹת,
אֵל הַהוֹדָאוֹת, אֲדוֹן הַנִּפְלָאוֹת,
הַבּוֹחֵר בְּשִׁירֵי זִמְרָה, מֶלֶךְ, אֵל, חֵי הָעוֹלָמִים.

Ba**ruch** Ata Ado**nai**, eil **Me**lech ga**dol** batishba**chot**,
eil hahoda-**ot**, **adon** hanifla-**ot**, habo**cheir** beshi**rei**
zim**ra**, **Me**lech, eil, chei ha'ola**miym**.

✡ A source of blessings are You, Adonai, Sovereign
God, worthy of all praise, worthy of all gratitude,

wellspring of wonders,
who delights in song and
prayer, eternal and
majestic, the living God
in all realms.

100

Tefilat HaLev - Shabbat/Festivals — שבת/חג

God does not need our songs of praise, we do.
Remember, we feel better when we Praise the One!

Chatzie Kaddish - Short Kaddish — חצי קדיש

יִתְגַּדַּל וְיִתְקַדַּשׁ שְׁמֵהּ רַבָּא. בְּעָלְמָא דִּי בְרָא
כִרְעוּתֵיהּ, וְיַמְלִיךְ מַלְכוּתֵיהּ בְּחַיֵּיכוֹן וּבְיוֹמֵיכוֹן
וּבְחַיֵּי דְכָל בֵּית יִשְׂרָאֵל. בַּעֲגָלָא וּבִזְמַן קָרִיב
וְאִמְרוּ אָמֵן:

> On Shabbat Shuvah, drop the italicized words and say the bracketed gray.

Yitga**dal** veyitka**dash** shimei raba be'alma di vra chiru**tei**,
veyam**lich** malchu**tei** bechayei**chon** uveyomei**chon**
uvcha**yei** dechol beit Yisra-**eil**, ba-aga**la**, uviz**man** ka**riv**,
ve-i**mru**: A**mein**.

יְהֵא שְׁמֵהּ רַבָּא מְבָרַךְ לְעָלַם וּלְעָלְמֵי עָלְמַיָּא:

Ye**hei** shmei raba mevarach le'alam ul'almei almaya.

יִתְבָּרַךְ וְיִשְׁתַּבַּח וְיִתְפָּאַר וְיִתְרוֹמַם וְיִתְנַשֵּׂא
וְיִתְהַדָּר וְיִתְעַלֶּה וְיִתְהַלָּל שְׁמֵהּ דְּקֻדְשָׁא בְּרִיךְ
הוּא לְעֵלָּא מִן כָּל [לְעֵלָּא מִכָּל] בִּרְכָתָא וְשִׁירָתָא
תֻּשְׁבְּחָתָא וְנֶחֱמָתָא, דַּאֲמִירָן בְּעָלְמָא, וְאִמְרוּ
אָמֵן:

Yitba**rach**, veyishta**bach**, veyitpa-**ar**, veyitro**mam**,
veyitna**sei**, veyit-ha**dar**, veyit-a**leh**, veyit-ha**lal** she**mei**
dekud**sha**, brich hu. Le'**eila** *min kol* [le'**eila** mi**kol**]
bircha**ta** veshira**ta**, tushbecha**ta** venechema**ta**
da-ami**ran** be'alma, ve-i**mru**: A**mein**.

God's gloriousness is to be extolled, God's great Name to be hallowed in the world whose creation God willed. And may God's reign be in our day, during our life, and the life of all Israel, let us say: Amen. Let God's great Name be praised forever and ever. Let the Name of the Holy One, the Blessing One, be glorified, exalted, and honored, though God is beyond all the praises, songs, and adorations that we can utter, and let us say: Amen.

Tefilat HaLev - Shabbat/Festivals שבת/חג – תפלת הלב

✡ When we contemplate the Divine,
there is something about us that expands and connects
to All That Is; what amazing acts that Entity does,
and what amazing thoughts that Entity must have.

מַה גָּדְלוּ מַעֲשֶׂיךָ יהוה מְאֹד
עָמְקוּ מַחְשְׁבֹתֶיךָ. הַלְלוּיָהּ.

Ma godlu ma'a**se**cha Yahh me-**od**
amku machshevo**te**cha. (Hallelu**Yahh**)

How great are Your actions, Adonai; Your thoughts are very deep.
(HalleluYahh - Praise God)

❀ When we rise together, we come together
as a *"Kehilah Kedoshah,"* a holy congregation.
Once we come together as community,
we are ready to start the main body of our service.
 If we were not participants prior to this point,
 we become so now, active and engaged.
 Some of us participate with singing, some with speaking
 and some with hearing.
 Together we achieve Kadosh, holy and fulfilled.

🌴 Coming together is the beginning;
 staying together is making progress;
working and achieving together is success.

🕊 It's when we start working together that the real
 healing takes place... it's when we start spilling
our sweat, and not our blood.   David Hume

Tefilat HaLev - Shabbat/Festivals שבת/חג - תפלת הלב

As we bless the Source of Life
So we are blessed.
And our blessings give us strength,
and make our visions clear,
and our blessings give us peace,
and the courage to dare,
As we bless the Source of Life,
So we are blessed.
© Faith Rogow

**If you are comfortable doing so,
please rise and let us sing the 'BARCHU'**

בָּרְכוּ אֶת יהוה הַמְבֹרָךְ:

Barchu et Adonai hamevorach.
Let us acknowledge Adonai, the Source of Blessing, Who blesses.

בָּרוּךְ יהוה הַמְבֹרָךְ לְעוֹלָם וָעֶד:

Baruch Adonai hamevorach le'olam va'ed.
A Source of Blessing are you, Adonai, through all time and space.

Praise the One to whom all praise is due.
Praised be the One to whom all praise is due,
Now and forever.
Praise the One to whom all praise is due.
Praised be the One to whom all praise is due
Now and forever, now and forever, now and forever,
praise the One.

If you are more comfortable sitting, please do so at this time or at any time.

Tefilat HaLev - Shabbat/Festivals   שבת/חג – תפלת הלב

🕊 Sometimes,
   as the morning light breaks over the horizon,
It is still possible to see the brighter stars
and a planet or two.
Sometimes, the moon is still visible in the morning sky.
  Even as the morning light fills the sky and our lives,
  We are still aware of the immensity of the universe.
  We see Your light shining across time and space
  And coming into our lives in so many ways.
Your vessels pour light upon the universe
Flooding the cracks in our own darkness
With the beams of Your compassion.

We seek to find Your light
on our path
Illuminating our lives,
Filling the dark spaces
We seek to hide
from ourselves.
How much of life reveals
Your presence!
How much Torah unfolds
from each new flower,
From each new wave that breaks upon the sand.
  You are Praised, Who forms from the clay of our lives,
  The delicate vessels which are our light.
In Your light, we see light.

❀ Bereishiyt records: "And God said,
"Let there be light" and there was light.
God saw that the light was good;
and God separated the light from the darkness.
God called the light day, and the darkness night.
And there was evening and there was morning,
day one."   Gen 1:3-5

If you are more comfortable sitting, please do so at this time or at any time.

Tefilat HaLev - Shabbat/Festivals   שבת/חג - תפלת הלב

✡ You are the One who created at the very beginning,
forming light and creating darkness,
ordaining peace and fashioning all things.

*With compassion You give light to the earth and to all life,
renewing creation every day.*

*How extensive are Your mysteries and deeds, Adonai,
a wisdom beyond depth.*

Everything is Yours, everything is Your creation.

Let us acknowledge You,
feeling Your expansive and awesome handiwork,
the light from distant stars, our moon and sun.
Your creation is fitting to Your Glory
through all time and space.
A source of blessings are You, Adonai,
fashioner of Lights.

🌴 The Isaiah reference behind this prayer says God made peace and created *ra*. The Hebrew word *ra*, occurs over 600 times in Scriptures. Mostly, *ra* is translated as "evil." Other times *ra* is translated as "wicked," "bad," "hurt," "harm," "ill," "sorrow," "mischief," "displeased," "adversity," "affliction," "trouble," "calamity," "grievous," and "misery." While the word does not require a translation as "evil," there is cleary a sense of strife, which the rabbis did not want in prayer. And so they changed the prayer to: God made peace and created all.

🔔 What does it mean in our lives that God creates both good and bad? What lessons can be learned from any experience in our lives? Do we learn better from one side of the balance or from the other. It is said that when we do not learn the lesson, it is repeated. In all cases, we can choose to learn.

If you are more comfortable sitting, please do so at this time or at any time.

Tefilat HaLev - Shabbat/Festivals — שבת/חג — תפלת הלב

Baruch Ata, Adonai Eloheinu **me**lech ha-O**lam**, **yo**tzeir or, uvo**rei cho**shech, **O**seh sha**lom** uvo**rei** et ha**kol**. Hamei-**iyr** la-**a**retz velada**riym a**le-ah beracha**miym**. Uvtu**vo** mecha**deish** be**chol** yom ta**mid** ma'a**sei** verei**shiyt**. Mah ra**bu** ma-a**se**cha Ado**nai**. Ku**lam** be**choch**ma a**si**ta mal-**a** ha-**a**retz kinya**ne**cha: Titba**rach** Adonai Elo**hei**nu, al **she**vach ma'a**sei** ya**de**cha, ve'al me-o**rei** or she'a**si**ta: yefa-a**ru**cha. **Se**lah. Ba**ruch** Ata Adonai, **yo**tzeir hame-o**rot**.	בָּרוּךְ אַתָּה יהוה, אֱלֹהֵינוּ מֶלֶךְ הָעוֹלָם, יוֹצֵר אוֹר, וּבוֹרֵא חֹשֶׁךְ, עֹשֶׂה שָׁלוֹם וּבוֹרֵא אֶת הַכֹּל. הַמֵּאִיר לָאָרֶץ וְלַדָּרִים עָלֶיהָ בְּרַחֲמִים. וּבְטוּבוֹ מְחַדֵּשׁ בְּכָל יוֹם תָּמִיד מַעֲשֵׂה בְרֵאשִׁית. מָה רַבּוּ מַעֲשֶׂיךָ יהוה. כֻּלָּם בְּחָכְמָה עָשִׂיתָ, מָלְאָה הָאָרֶץ קִנְיָנֶךָ: תִּתְבָּרַךְ יהוה אֱלֹהֵינוּ, עַל שֶׁבַח מַעֲשֵׂה יָדֶיךָ, וְעַל מְאוֹרֵי אוֹר שֶׁעָשִׂיתָ: יְפָאֲרוּךָ. סֶלָה. בָּרוּךְ אַתָּה יהוה, יוֹצֵר הַמְּאוֹרוֹת:

A Source of Blessing are You, Adonai, our God, Sovereign of the universe, who forms light and creates darkness, makes peace and creates everything. With compassion, You are the illumination to the earth and to those who live on it. With Your goodness, you continually renew everything every day as part of the mystery of creation. How great is the mystery of You, Adonai. Your wisdom permeates Your deeds, the earth is Yours and filled with Your Presence. Your splendor shines through in the lights that cause to shine, Selah! A Source of Blessing are You, Adonai, our God, who forms the lights.

If you are more comfortable sitting, please do so at this time or at any time.

Tefilat HaLev - Shabbat/Festivals שבת/חג - תפלת הלב

❀ We seek to feel Your love, God,
And we sometimes fail to notice
that it is surrounding us at all times.
When we choose to feel Your Love,
Then we can move into the light of that Love
and feel it throughout.
Help us know that we are loved by an unending love.
Your Love encourages us to form community,
And to support our community
with actions and with effort.
And when we support our community,
Then we receive back that love in soothing waves.
Torah is the guide to the Service we are instructed to give
To our community and to each other.
When we are also generous with acts of loving kindness,
We partner with You to establish our world.
You are the Source of Blessings, Beloved One,
who loves Your people Israel.

✌ Shabbat is about Your Love and our connections
To You, to our past, to our future and each other.
Shabbat enters with candles,
Flames that purify, soften, and renew.
Shabbat leaves with flame whose wicks entertwine.
Between the flames is Your Presence,
reminding us of the beauty that touches our hearts.
May we take from Shabbat the Love and the Courage
to work for the Great Shabbat of Peace.

🌴 The prayers between the Barchu and the Shema
talk about lights and love, preparing us to move from
coming together as community to connecting with the
One who is the Source of All Life.

If you are more comfortable sitting, please do so at this time or at any time.

Tefilat HaLev - Shabbat/Festivals — שבת/חג - תפלת הלב

אַהֲבָה רַבָּה אֲהַבְתָּנוּ, יהוה אֱלֹהֵינוּ, חֶמְלָה גְדוֹלָה
וִיתֵרָה חָמַלְתָּ עָלֵינוּ. אָבִינוּ מַלְכֵּנוּ, בַּעֲבוּר אֲבוֹתֵינוּ
וְאִמּוֹתֵינוּ שֶׁבָּטְחוּ בְךָ, וַתְּלַמְּדֵם חֻקֵּי חַיִּים, כֵּן תְּחָנֵּנוּ
וּתְלַמְּדֵנוּ. אָבִינוּ, הָאָב הָרַחֲמָן, הַמְרַחֵם, רַחֵם עָלֵינוּ, וְתֵן
בְּלִבֵּנוּ לְהָבִין וּלְהַשְׂכִּיל, לִשְׁמֹעַ, לִלְמֹד וּלְלַמֵּד, לִשְׁמֹר
וְלַעֲשׂוֹת וּלְקַיֵּם אֶת כָּל דִּבְרֵי תַלְמוּד תּוֹרָתֶךָ בְּאַהֲבָה.

Ahava raba ahavtanu Adonai Eloheinu, chemla gedola viyteira chamalta aleinu. Avinu Malkeinu, ba-**avur** avoteinu veimo**teinu** shebat**chu** ve**cha**, vatlam**deim** chu**kei** chayim, kein techa**neinu** utlam**deinu**. Avinu ha-**av** haracha**man** hamra**cheim**, ra**cheim** aleinu, ve**tein** beli**beinu** leha**viyn** ulhaskil, lishmo-a lil**mod** ulela**meid**, lish**mor** vela-a**sot** ulkayeim et kol divrei talmud toratecha be-ahavah.

✽ With abundant love have You loved us, Adonai, our God. With the greatest compassion have You been compassionate to us. *Avinu Malkeinu*, for the sake of our ancestors who trusted in You and whom You taught the mysteries of life, may You be so gracious to us and teach us. Our Parent, merciful Parent, Who is compassionate, be compassionate with us, instill in our hearts understanding and wisdom, to listen, learn, teach, safeguard, perform, and fulfill all the words of Your Torah's teaching with love.

🔔 *Ahava raba* is recited here to incur the obligation to recite verses from the Torah. Since the Shema is composed of verses from the Torah, its recital fulfills that obligation. *Ahava raba* also fulfills the mitzvah of saying a blessing before Torah study.

If you are more comfortable sitting, please do so at this time or at any time.

Tefilat HaLev - Shabbat/Festivals — שבת/חג - תפלת הלב

וְהָאֵר עֵינֵינוּ בְּתוֹרָתֶךָ, וְדַבֵּק לִבֵּנוּ בְּמִצְוֹתֶיךָ, וְיַחֵד לְבָבֵנוּ לְאַהֲבָה וּלְיִרְאָה אֶת שְׁמֶךָ, שֶׁלֹּא נֵבוֹשׁ וְלֹא נִכָּלֵם וְלֹא נִכָּשֵׁל לְעוֹלָם וָעֶד: כִּי בְשֵׁם קָדְשְׁךָ הַגָּדוֹל וְהַנּוֹרָא בָּטָחְנוּ, נָגִילָה וְנִשְׂמְחָה בִּישׁוּעָתֶךָ.

Veha-eir eineinu betoratecha, vedabeik libeinu bemitzvotecha, veyacheid levaveinu le-ahava uleyir-a et shemecha, shelo nevosh velo nikaleim velo nikasheil le-olam va-ed. Ki vesheim kodshecha hagadol vehanora batachnu, nagila venismecha biyshu'atecha.

Enlighten our eyes through Your Torah, attach our hearts to Your mitzvot, and unify our hearts to love and honor Your Essence. May we not feel shame nor disgrace and may we not stumble for all eternity. Because we have trusted in Your great and awesome holy Name, we exult and rejoice in Your salvation.

Looking at a flower,
it is easy to see the intricate relationship
between the various parts of the flower.
The stem, the petals, the pistil and the stamen
are all positioned just so,
each with their unique function.

All of life is that delicate, all of life requires balance.
Your love gives us the balance we need to live
Our very complicated lives.
Help us feel Your love today and every day.

Love is a primary theme in Torah. Traditional Judaism teaches that all of Torah is a demonstration of God's love for us, even the more challenging accounts. How can we understand that love today and in our own lives?

If you are more comfortable sitting, please do so at this time or at any time.

Tefilat HaLev - Shabbat/Festivals — שבת/חג — **תפלת הלב**

❀ If a person is wearing a tallit, there is a traditional practice of gathering the tzitzit during this prayer in preparation for the recitation of the Shema. The four sets of fringes are gathered up into one hand and held together as a unity, often placed over the heart. We gather together all of our parts, much as we pray for God to gather in all of our people from the four corners of the earth. The concept of exile and redemption, of *galut* and *ge-ulah*, is ritualized in this pose of healing and wholeness. May this be the beginning of a true healing for our own fractures, those within the Jewish community, and the world.

🌴 The act of gathering the tzitzit and placing them over our hearts is a prayer for healing. May that healing be powerful within you and overflow from you to those around you and to those you love.

וַהֲבִיאֵנוּ לְשָׁלוֹם מֵאַרְבַּע כַּנְפוֹת הָאָרֶץ,
וְתוֹלִיכֵנוּ קוֹמְמִיּוּת לְאַרְצֵנוּ. וְקָרַבְתָּנוּ לְשִׁמְךָ
הַגָּדוֹל סֶלָה בֶּאֱמֶת לְהוֹדוֹת לְךָ וּלְיַחֶדְךָ בְּאַהֲבָה.
בָּרוּךְ אַתָּה יהוה, אוֹהֵב עַמּוֹ יִשְׂרָאֵל.

Vahavi-**ei**nu lesha**lom** mei-ar**ba** kan**fot** ha-**a**retz,
vetoli**chei**nu komemi**yut** le-ar**tzei**nu. Vekeravta**nu**
leshim**cha** haga**dol se**lah be-**e**met, leho**dot** le**cha**
ulyached**cha** be-a**ha**va.
Baruch Ata Ado**nai**, **o**heiv amo Yisra-**eil**.

Bring us in to peacefulness from the four corners
of the earth and grant us independence in our land. And bring
us close to You with truth to thank You and proclaim Your
Oneness with love.
A Source of Blessing are You, who loves Your people Israel.

If you are more comfortable sitting, please do so at this time or at any time.

Tefilat HaLev - Shabbat/Festivals – שבת/חג – תפלת הלב

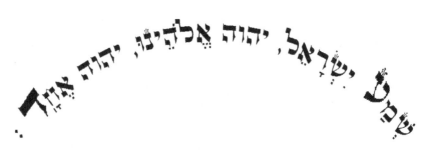

שְׁמַע יִשְׂרָאֵל, יהוה אֱלֹהֵינוּ, יהוה אֶחָד:

Shema Yisra-eil: Adonai Eloheinu, Adonai Echad!
Listen up, O Israel: Adonai is our God, Adonai is One!

(softly)

בָּרוּךְ שֵׁם כְּבוֹד מַלְכוּתוֹ לְעוֹלָם וָעֶד.

Baruch sheim kevod malechuto le-olam va-ed!
Blessings from God's glorious majesty extend through all time and space.

We are seated

וְאָהַבְתָּ אֵת יהוה אֱלֹהֶיךָ בְּכָל־לְבָבְךָ וּבְכָל־נַפְשְׁךָ וּבְכָל־מְאֹדֶךָ: וְהָיוּ הַדְּבָרִים הָאֵלֶּה אֲשֶׁר אָנֹכִי מְצַוְּךָ הַיּוֹם עַל־לְבָבֶךָ: וְשִׁנַּנְתָּם לְבָנֶיךָ וְדִבַּרְתָּ בָּם בְּשִׁבְתְּךָ בְּבֵיתֶךָ וּבְלֶכְתְּךָ בַדֶּרֶךְ וּבְשָׁכְבְּךָ וּבְקוּמֶךָ: וּקְשַׁרְתָּם לְאוֹת עַל־יָדֶךָ וְהָיוּ לְטֹטָפֹת בֵּין עֵינֶיךָ: וּכְתַבְתָּם עַל־מְזֻזוֹת בֵּיתֶךָ וּבִשְׁעָרֶיךָ:

Ve-ahavta eit Adonai Elohecha; bechol levavcha uvechol nafshecha uvechol me-odecha. Vehayu hadvariym ha-eileh asher Anochi metzavcha hayom al levavecha. Veshinantam levanecha vedibarta bam; beshivtecha beveitecha uvlechtecha vaderech uvshochbecha uvkumecha. Ukshartam le-ot 'al yadecha; vehayu letotafot bein 'einecha. Uchtavtam 'al-mezuzot beitecha uvish'arecha. (Deut 6:4-9)

Tefilat HaLev - Shabbat/Festivals　שבת/חג – תפלת הלב

✡ And you must love Adonai your God, with all your passions, with every breath, with every fiber of your being. Take these words, by which I join Myself to you today, into your heart. Pattern your days on them so that your children will discover Torah within you. Make your life into a voice of God, both in your stillness and in your movement. Renew these words each evening and morning with devotion. Bind them as t'fillen on your forehead and arm as symbols of thoughts and acts sacred to Me. Write them in Mezuzot at the entrances to your homes as a sign that all people may discover Me as they enter your home and your life.

✡ And thou shalt love the Lord, thy God, with all of thy heart, with all thy soul, and with all of thy might. And all these words which I command ye on this day shall be in thy heart. And thou shalt teach them diligently unto thy children. And thou shalt speak of them when thou sittest in thy house, when thou walkest by the way, and when you risest up and when thou liest down. And thou shalt bind them for a sign upon thy hand. And they shall be for frontlets between thine eyes. And thou shalt bind them on the door posts of thy house, and upon thy gates. That ye may remember and do all of my commandments and be holy unto thy God.

✎ The middle paragraph of the shema is often recited silently. For many years, some prayer books did not even include it as part of the service because it was seen as indicating a punishing God. In today's understanding of the climate and the changing world, this part of the shema is now seen as an instruction to care for the world and its inhabitants.

Tefilat HaLev - Shabbat/Festivals — שבת/חג — תפלת הלב

וְהָיָ֗ה אִם־שָׁמֹ֤עַ תִּשְׁמְעוּ֙ אֶל־מִצְוֺתַ֔י אֲשֶׁ֧ר אָנֹכִ֛י מְצַוֶּ֥ה אֶתְכֶ֖ם הַיּ֑וֹם לְאַהֲבָ֞ה אֶת־יְהוָ֤ה אֱלֹֽהֵיכֶם֙ וּלְעָבְד֔וֹ בְּכָל־לְבַבְכֶ֖ם וּבְכָל־נַפְשְׁכֶֽם: וְנָתַתִּ֧י מְטַֽר־אַרְצְכֶ֛ם בְּעִתּ֖וֹ יוֹרֶ֣ה וּמַלְק֑וֹשׁ וְאָסַפְתָּ֣ דְגָנֶ֔ךָ וְתִֽירֹשְׁךָ֖ וְיִצְהָרֶֽךָ: טו וְנָתַתִּ֛י עֵ֥שֶׂב בְּשָׂדְךָ֖ לִבְהֶמְתֶּ֑ךָ וְאָכַלְתָּ֖ וְשָׂבָֽעְתָּ: הִשָּֽׁמְר֣וּ לָכֶ֔ם פֶּן־יִפְתֶּ֖ה לְבַבְכֶ֑ם וְסַרְתֶּ֗ם וַעֲבַדְתֶּם֙ אֱלֹהִ֣ים אֲחֵרִ֔ים וְהִשְׁתַּחֲוִיתֶ֖ם לָהֶֽם: וְחָרָ֨ה אַף־יְהוָ֜ה בָּכֶ֗ם וְעָצַ֤ר אֶת־הַשָּׁמַ֙יִם֙ וְלֹֽא־יִהְיֶ֣ה מָטָ֔ר וְהָ֣אֲדָמָ֔ה לֹ֥א תִתֵּ֖ן אֶת־יְבוּלָ֑הּ וַאֲבַדְתֶּ֣ם מְהֵרָ֗ה מֵעַל֙ הָאָ֣רֶץ הַטֹּבָ֔ה אֲשֶׁ֥ר יְהוָ֖ה נֹתֵ֣ן לָכֶֽם: וְשַׂמְתֶּם֙ אֶת־דְּבָרַ֣י אֵ֔לֶּה עַל־לְבַבְכֶ֖ם וְעַֽל־נַפְשְׁכֶ֑ם וּקְשַׁרְתֶּ֨ם אֹתָ֤ם לְאוֹת֙ עַל־יֶדְכֶ֔ם וְהָי֥וּ לְטוֹטָפֹ֖ת בֵּ֥ין עֵינֵיכֶֽם: וְלִמַּדְתֶּ֥ם אֹתָ֛ם אֶת־בְּנֵיכֶ֖ם לְדַבֵּ֣ר בָּ֑ם בְּשִׁבְתְּךָ֤ בְּבֵיתֶ֙ךָ֙ וּבְלֶכְתְּךָ֣ בַדֶּ֔רֶךְ וּֽבְשָׁכְבְּךָ֖ וּבְקוּמֶֽךָ: וּכְתַבְתָּ֛ם עַל־מְזוּז֥וֹת בֵּיתֶ֖ךָ וּבִשְׁעָרֶֽיךָ: לְמַ֨עַן יִרְבּ֤וּ יְמֵיכֶם֙ וִימֵ֣י בְנֵיכֶ֔ם עַ֚ל הָֽאֲדָמָ֔ה אֲשֶׁ֨ר נִשְׁבַּ֧ע יְהוָ֛ה לַאֲבֹתֵיכֶ֖ם לָתֵ֣ת לָהֶ֑ם כִּימֵ֥י הַשָּׁמַ֖יִם עַל־הָאָֽרֶץ:

And it will be, if you really listen and hear My *mitzvot* which I instruct you today, to love Adonai your God and to serve with all your heart and with all your being, I [have designed the world so that there] will be rain for your land at the proper time, the early rain and the late rain, and you will gather in your grain, your wine and your oil. And I will see that there is grass in your fields for your cattle, and you will eat and be sated. Take care lest your heart be seduced by your cravings, and you turn astray and worship other things as gods and serve them. For then the fury of Adonai will

flare up inside you, and the heavens will close so that there will be no rain and the earth will not yield its produce, and you will swiftly perish from the good land which Adonai gives you. Therefore, place these words of mine upon your heart and upon your being, and bind them for a sign on your hand, and they shall be *totafot* between your eyes. You shall teach them to your children, to speak of them when you sit in your home and when you go on your way, when you lie down and when you rise. And inscribe them on the doorposts of your house and on your gates - so that your days and the days of your children may be long and full on the land which Adonai swore to your fathers to give to them for heavenly days on the earth.

וַיֹּאמֶר יְהוָה אֶל־מֹשֶׁה לֵּאמֹר: דַּבֵּר אֶל־בְּנֵי יִשְׂרָאֵל וְאָמַרְתָּ אֲלֵהֶם וְעָשׂוּ לָהֶם צִיצִת עַל־כַּנְפֵי בִגְדֵיהֶם לְדֹרֹתָם וְנָתְנוּ עַל־צִיצִת הַכָּנָף פְּתִיל תְּכֵלֶת: וְהָיָה לָכֶם לְצִיצִת וּרְאִיתֶם אֹתוֹ וּזְכַרְתֶּם אֶת־כָּל־מִצְוֹת יְהוָה וַעֲשִׂיתֶם אֹתָם וְלֹא תָתֻרוּ אַחֲרֵי לְבַבְכֶם וְאַחֲרֵי עֵינֵיכֶם אֲשֶׁר־אַתֶּם זֹנִים אַחֲרֵיהֶם: לְמַעַן תִּזְכְּרוּ וַעֲשִׂיתֶם אֶת־כָּל־מִצְוֹתָי וִהְיִיתֶם קְדֹשִׁים לֵאלֹהֵיכֶם: אֲנִי יְהוָה אֱלֹהֵיכֶם אֲשֶׁר הוֹצֵאתִי אֶתְכֶם מֵאֶרֶץ מִצְרַיִם לִהְיוֹת לָכֶם לֵאלֹהִים אֲנִי יְהוָה אֱלֹהֵיכֶם:

Transliteration and translation next page.

Tefilat HaLev - Shabbat/Festivals שבת/חג – תפלת הלב

Vayomer Adonai el Moshe leimor: Dabeir el benei Yisra-eil ve-amarta aleihem v'asu lahem tzitzit al kanfei bigdeihem ledorotam venatnu al tzitzit hakanaf petiyl techeilet. Vehaya lachem letzitzit ur'iytem oto uzchartem et kol mitzvot Adonai va-asitem otam velo taturu acharei levavchem ve-acharei eineichem asher atem zoniym achareihem. Lema-an tizkeru, va'asitem et kol mitzvotai viheyitem kedoshiym l'Eiloheichem. Ani Adonai Eloheichem, asher hotzeiti etchem mei-eretz Mitzrayim, lihiyot lachem l'Eilohiym. Ani Adonai Eloheichem. (Numb 15:40-41) **(Emet)**

Adonai spoke to Moshe, saying: "Speak to the children of Israel and tell them to make for themselves reminder fringes on the corners of their garments for the sake of their generations, and to put a thread of *techelet* blue on the reminder fringe of each corner. They are to be to you as tzizit, reminder fringes, and when you look at them, remember all the mitzvot of Adonai and do them, and you will not wander after your heart and after your eyes, lest you hunger after cravings; So that you may remember and do all of My *mizvot* and be holy to your God. I am Adonai, your God, who brought you out of the land of Egypt to be your God; I, Adonai, am your God." [It is True.]

Meditation

Our innermost thoughts are reflected in our body language and action,
even when we think that they are not.
Therefore, speak to yourself only those thoughts that you want others to see.

אמת אָמֶת אָמֶת אמת אמת אמת אָמֶת אמת אָמֶת אמת

Tefilat HaLev - Shabbat/Festivals שבת/חג - תפלת הלב

Shema Yisrael

Listen! you Yisrael person
יהוה who is, is our God.
יהוה who is, is One,
unique, all there is.

Through Time and Space
Your Glory Shines
Majestic One!

Love, that יהוה
who is your God,
in what your heart is in,
in what you aspire to,
in what you have made
your own.

May these values
which I connect
with your life
be implanted
in your feelings.

May they become
the norm for your children,
addressing them
in the privacy
of your home,
on the errands you run.

May they help you relax,
and activate you
to be productive.

Display them visibly
on your arm.
Let them focus
your attention.
See them in all transitions,
at home and in your
environment.

How good it will be
when you really listen
and hear My directions
which I give you today,
for loving יהוה
who is your God,
and acting Godly
with feeling and
inspiration.

Your earthly needs
will be met
at the right time,
appropriate to the season.
You will reap
what you have planted
for your delight and health.

And your animals
will have ample feed.
All of you will eat
and be content.

Be careful -- watch out!
Don't let your cravings
delude you.
Don't become alienated.
Don't let your cravings
become your gods.
Don't debase yourself
to them,
because the God-sense
within you
will become distorted.
Heaven will be shut to you.
Grace will not descend.
Earth will not produce.
Your rushing
will destroy you

116

Tefilat HaLev - Shabbat/Festivals — שבת/חג — תפלת הלב

and Earth will not be able
to recover her good balance
in which
God's gifts manifest.

May these values of Mine
reside in your aspirations
marking what you produce,
guiding what you perceive.

Teach them
to your children,
so that they
be addressed by them
in making their homes,
how they deal with traffic;
when you are depressed
when you are elated.

Mark your entrances
and exits
with them
so you are more aware.

Then you and your children
will live out on earth
that divine promise
given to your ancestors
to live heavenly days
right here on this earth.

יהוה, who is, said to Moshe
"Speak, telling
the Israel folks
to make tzitzit
on the corners

of their garments
so they will have
generations to follow them.
On each tzitzit-tassel
let them set a blue thread.
Glance at it,
and in your seeing,
remember
all the other directives
of יהוה who is,
and act on them.

This way
you will not be led astray,
craving to see and want,
and then prostitute yourself
for your cravings.

This way
you will be mindful
to actualize My directions
for becoming
dedicated to your God,
to be aware that
I AM
יהוה who is your God --
the One who freed you
from the oppression
in order to God you.
I am יהוה your God."
That is the truth.

Interpretive translation by
Rabbi Zalman Schachter-Shalomi

Adonai **Elo**heichem. **Emet**.. ..אֱמֶת׃ אֱלֹהֵיכֶם יהוה

Tradition takes the *emet*, "true" from the prayer which follows (True and established) and appends it onto the Shema as an immediate affirmation of the Shema's truth for us.

Tefilat HaLev - Shabbat/Festivals — שבת/חג — תפלת הלב

אֱמֶת אֱמֶת אֱמֶת אֱמֶת אֱמֶת אֱמֶת אֱמֶת אֱמֶת

אֱמֶת וְיַצִּיב וְנָכוֹן וְקַיָּם וְיָשָׁר וְנֶאֱמָן וְאָהוּב
וְחָבִיב וְנֶחְמָד וְנָעִים וְנוֹרָא וְאַדִּיר וּמְתֻקָּן
וּמְקֻבָּל וְטוֹב וְיָפֶה הַדָּבָר הַזֶּה עָלֵינוּ לְעוֹלָם וָעֶד.

Emet ve-ya**tziv** vena**chon** veka**yam** veya**shar**
vene-**eman** ve-a**huv** vecha**viyv** venech**mad** vena-**iym**
veno**ra** ve-a**dir** umtu**kan** umku**bal** ve**tov** veya**feh**
hada**var** ha**zeh** a**lei**nu le-o**lam** va-**ed**. (2x)

True and established, and correct, and upright, and faithful, and beloved,
and adored, and desired, and pleasant, and awesome, and mighty, and
powerful, and receiving, and good, and beautiful, is this principal for us
through all time and space.

Long ago,
   Moshe and Miriam had a choice
They could stay in Egypt, the tight place
Where they knew the routine
and what was expected of them
Or they could make a change
in their lives and the world.

   Our ancestors had to choose between the sure destruction
   of the advancing Egyptian army they were facing
   And the impassable wall of water behind them.
   They asked the question of where should they turn
   and saw no answer.

Moshe turned to God and God said,
"Why are you crying to me?
Speak to the Children of Israel
and they will move forward."
God explained that Moshe
already had the power he needed;
it was in his hand in the form of a rod.

118

Tefilat HaLev - Shabbat/Festivals שבת/חג – תפלת הלב

And so Moshe turned us around
that we might see the miracle,
The parting of the sea, the path to freedom and birth,
the path to our own self-determination
To the freedom of being responsible for our own actions.

And so we journeyed forward
into the freedom of responsibility
and the responsibility of freedom.
And we did so on dry ground, safely,
even though danger was on both sides,
close enough to touch.

May we turn around now and see the miracles around us,
May we find the path to freedom and responsibility
May we see the danger around us and not succumb
May we join with Moshe and Miriam in their song to God.

❁ We are invited every day
to remember that our exodus
from Mitzrayim, the narrow or tight place,
is truly one of our defining moments,
both as individuals and as a people.

May we remember that You are there for us,
in the hugs and smiles from others
as we reach the distant shore.
May we realize that the sea was always meant to split
at just the right time and place,
presenting us with a dry, safe path, reaching the far shore.

Whether we are in a tight place right now,
whether we are just starting our own escape,
or whether we have just reached the far shore,
let us remember that there are no other Gods like You.

Thank You, God, for helping us reach the shore,
safely, walking on the dry ground.

Tefilat HaLev - Shabbat/Festivals — שבת/חג — תפלת הלב

Mi chamocha ba-eilim, Adonai?	מִי כָמֹכָה בָּאֵלִים יהוה?
Mi kamocha, nedar bakodesh, nora tehilot, osei feleh?	מִי כָּמֹכָה נֶאְדָּר בַּקֹּדֶשׁ, נוֹרָא תְהִלֹּת, עֹשֵׂה פֶלֶא?
Shira chadasha shibchu ge-uliym leshimcha al sfat hayam, yachad kulam hodu vehimliychu ve-amru:	שִׁירָה חֲדָשָׁה שִׁבְּחוּ גְאוּלִים לְשִׁמְךָ עַל שְׂפַת הַיָּם, יַחַד כֻּלָּם הוֹדוּ וְהִמְלִיכוּ וְאָמְרוּ:
"Adonai yimloch le'olam va'ed"	יהוה יִמְלֹךְ לְעוֹלָם וָעֶד:
Tzur Yisra-eil, kuma b'ezrat Yisra-eil ufdei chinumecha Yehuda veYisra-eil. Go-aleinu Adonai Tzeva-ot Shemo, Kedosh Yisra-eil. Baruch Ata Adonai, ga-al Yisra-eil.	צוּר יִשְׂרָאֵל, קוּמָה בְּעֶזְרַת יִשְׂרָאֵל, וּפְדֵה כִנְאֻמֶךָ יְהוּדָה וְיִשְׂרָאֵל. גֹּאֲלֵנוּ יהוה צְבָאוֹת שְׁמוֹ, קְדוֹשׁ יִשְׂרָאֵל. בָּרוּךְ אַתָּה יהוה, גָּאַל יִשְׂרָאֵל:

Who is like You, Eternal One, among the gods that are worshipped? Who is like You, majestic in holiness, awesome in splendor, doing wonders? The redeemed sang a new song of praise to You on the shores of the sea. Together everyone gave thanks and enthroned You saying: "Adonai will reign forever and ever." Rock of Israel, rise up and help Israel, redeem us as You promised Judah and Israel. The One whose Name is Adonai Tzeva-ot, saves us, O Holy One of Israel. A Source of Blessing are You, Adonai, redeemer of Israel.

You helped us through the Sea of Reeds
for our sake and for Yours,
So that we could work together
to make this world a better place
For all of Your creatures, everywhere.
Adonai, help us do that work this coming week.

Tefilat HaLev - Shabbat/Festivals — שבת/חג - תפלת הלב

[The ARK is OPENED]
If you are comfortable doing so,
please rise as we open the ark for the Tefilah (the Prayer),
the Amidah (the time for standing), the central part of our prayers.

אֲדֹנָי שְׂפָתַי תִּפְתָּח וּפִי יַגִּיד תְּהִלָּתֶךָ:

Adonai sefatai tif**tach** ufi yagiyd tehilatecha.
Oh, God open up my lips, as I begin to pray.
Eternal God, open up my lips,
that my mouth may declare Your glory.
(Psalm 51:17)

The art on this page is called a *shviti*. It is a focusing or meditative device based on the phrase from Psalms 16:8 "*Shviti Adonai negdi tamid,* I have set Adonai before me always."

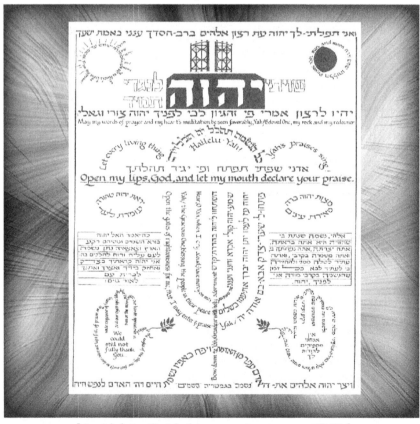

[Amidah in Guided imagery is on pages 73-76.]
[Intermediate Amidah Prayers for a weekday start on page 181]

Tefilat HaLev - Shabbat/Festivals   שבת/חג – תפלת הלב

❁ We invoke the memories
of our spiritual and physical mothers and fathers
who made us,
the fathers and the mothers who made them,
all the way back to Abraham and Sarah.
*We are the product of all of our ancestors
as we stand here in their light before You who made us all.*
Each of them sought You
and found You in their lives in different ways.
No two of them experienced You the same way
and they honored those differences.
*May we learn from them to value and honor
the differences among us in how we seek You.
May we learn from them that no matter how we seek You,
it is the same You we are seeking.*

✡ We remind ourselves that our ancestors
established a relationship with God.
Each of them did so, and each in their own way.
The prayer reflects this by saying:
**Elohei Avraham, Elohei Yitzchak, vEilohei Ya-akov.
Elohei Sarah, Elohei Rivkah, Elohei Lei-ah,
vEilohei Racheil.** *The God of Abraham, the God of Isaac, the
God of Jacob, the God of Sarah, the God of Rebecca,
the God of Leah, and the God of Rachel.*
The prayer does not say, **Elohei Avraham, Yitzchak,
Ya-akov, Sarah, Rivkah, Lei-ah, vRacheil.**
The God of Abraham, Isaac, Jacob, Sarah, Rebecca,
Leah, and Rachel.
By repeating "the God of," we are reminded
that while it is the same God, they each had
their own unique experience of that same God.

If you are more comfortable sitting, please do so at this time or at any time.

Tefilat HaLev - Shabbat/Festivals — שבת/חג – תפלת הלב

🍃 Our Ancestors Support us in our Journey.
We thank You, Infinite Source, for the power within us,
The power that gave our ancestors their strength:
Power of Abraham, Power of Isaac, Power of Jacob,
Power of Sarah, Power of Rebekah, Power of Rachel, Power of Leah, each in their own way,
and according to their needs.
You hear truth in every age,
generation after generation,
Boundless, vibrant, awesome, sublime,
Surrounding and filling all space and time.
Gradually embracing all things into One.
We seek the blessing of the Infinite Source, alive within us.

Rabbis Marcia Prager, Mordechai and Devora Bartnoff z"l, adapted

Avot - God of All Generations — אבות

בָּרוּךְ אַתָּה יהוה אֱלֹהֵינוּ וֵאלֹהֵי אֲבוֹתֵינוּ וְאִמּוֹתֵינוּ, אֱלֹהֵי אַבְרָהָם, אֱלֹהֵי יִצְחָק, וֵאלֹהֵי יַעֲקֹב, אֱלֹהֵי שָׂרָה, אֱלֹהֵי רִבְקָה, אֱלֹהֵי לֵאָה, וֵאלֹהֵי רָחֵל. הָאֵל הַגָּדוֹל הַגִּבּוֹר וְהַנּוֹרָא, אֵל עֶלְיוֹן, גּוֹמֵל חֲסָדִים טוֹבִים, וְקוֹנֵה הַכֹּל, וְזוֹכֵר חַסְדֵי אָבוֹת וְאִמָּהוֹת, וּמֵבִיא גְאֻלָּה לִבְנֵי בְנֵיהֶם לְמַעַן שְׁמוֹ בְּאַהֲבָה:

Baruch Ata Adonai, Eloheinu, veilohei avoteinu
ve-imoteinu: Elohei Avraham, Elohei Yitzchak,
vEilohei Ya-akov. Elohei Sarah, Elohei Rivkah, Elohei
Lei-ah, vEilohei Racheil. Ha-eil hagadol hagibor
vehanora, eil elyon, gomeil chasadim tovim vekonei
hakol, Vezocheir chasdei avot ve-imahot, Umeivi
ge-ula livnei Veneihem, lema-an shemo, be-ahava:

Tefilat HaLev - Shabbat/Festivals שבת/חג – תפלת הלב

A Source of Blessing are you, Adonai our God and God of our Fathers and our Mothers. God of Abraham, God of Isaac, and God of Jacob, God of Sarah, God of Rebecca, God of Rachel and God of Leah. Great God, powerful and awesome, God of the Highest, who bestows kindness and goodness, master of all, who remembers the good deeds of our fathers and mothers and brings redemption to the children of their children for God's sake with love.

On Shabbat Shuvah, please add:

זָכְרֵנוּ לְחַיִּים, מֶלֶךְ חָפֵץ בַּחַיִּים, וְכָתְבֵנוּ בְּסֵפֶר הַחַיִּים, לְמַעַנְךָ אֱלֹהִים חַיִּים.

Zochreinu lechayiym, **Me**lech cha**fetz** bachayiym, vechot**vei**nu be**sei**fer hachayiym, lema-an**cha** Elo**hiym** chayiym.

מֶלֶךְ עוֹזֵר וּמוֹשִׁיעַ וּמָגֵן: בָּרוּךְ אַתָּה יהוה, מָגֵן אַבְרָהָם וְעֶזְרַת (וּפוֹקֵד) שָׂרָה:

Melech o**zeir** umo**shi**-a uma**gein**: B**aruch** Ata Ado**nai**, ma**gein** Avra**ham** ve'e**zrat** (ufo**keid**) **Sarah**.

Remember us for life, O Sovereign who favors life, and write us into the Book of Life, for Your sake, O God of Life, Sovereign who is our Help, our redemption and our protector. A Blessing are You, Adonai, Shield of Abraham and Helper of (One who remembers) Sarah.

❀ Adonai, help us remember that You are there for us,
even when we feel deadened.
When we seek You, then we we might just feel You,
awakening us from inside.
Let us feel Your Presence within us
and know that You are there.
A Source of Blessing are You,
who helps us feel alive this day and every day.

124

Tefilat HaLev - Shabbat/Festivals — שבת/חג - תפלת הלב

✡ When we move from thoughts of our ancestors
to thoughts of life, we can recognize that life is a gift.
And although there are hard and even tragic times,
times beyond belief,
we can still choose to feel Your Presence.

Although there are times when it is hard for us,
You are always there for us, patiently waiting,
wanting us to connect even more than we seek You.

Thank You God, for upholding those who fall,
healing the sick, setting free the captives,
and keeping faith with those who sleep in the dust.

Thank You God, for the hope of life.
Thank You God, for renewing us day by day.

You delight in life and teach us to live.
You bring meaning to our days,
and hope in our dispair.

May we become free from our entanglements,
May we learn to face the challenges of life
with joy and strength renewed.

May we find inspiration in our hope.
May we find connection with You and all life.

Divine Essence and Power.
Who is like You! Source of all strength,
Source of all compassion, Source of all healing.
You are also a source of inspiration in times of despair,
Please keep alive in us our ideals, hopes and dreams,
that the dead may live again through us.

Rabbis Marcia Prager, Mordechai and Devora Bartnoff z"l, adapted

The prayer says that You keep faith with those
who sleep in the dust. Does that include those
who sleep in the dusty streets of life? And what does
this prayer mean for me?

If you are more comfortable sitting, please do so at this time or at any time.

Tefilat HaLev - Shabbat/Festivals — שבת/חג - תפלת הלב

Gevurot - Power   גבורות

אַתָּה גִבּוֹר לְעוֹלָם אֲדֹנָי מְחַיֵּה
הַכֹּל (מֵתִים) אַתָּה רַב לְהוֹשִׁיעַ:

Ata gibor le'olam Adonai,
mechayei hakol (meitiym) Ata, rav lehoshiy'a.

summer: **Moriyd** hatal.   מוֹרִיד הַטָּל: summer

summer: Who brings the dew.

מַשִּׁיב הָרוּחַ וּמוֹרִיד הַגֶּשֶׁם: winter

winter: **Mashiyv** haru-ach umoriyd hagashem.
winter: Who causes the wind to blow and rain to fall.

מְכַלְכֵּל חַיִּים בְּחֶסֶד, מְחַיֵּה הַכֹּל (מֵתִים)
בְּרַחֲמִים רַבִּים, סוֹמֵךְ נוֹפְלִים, וְרוֹפֵא חוֹלִים,
וּמַתִּיר אֲסוּרִים, וּמְקַיֵּם אֱמוּנָתוֹ לִישֵׁנֵי עָפָר, מִי
כָמוֹךָ בַּעַל גְּבוּרוֹת וּמִי דּוֹמֶה לָּךְ, מֶלֶךְ מֵמִית
וּמְחַיֶּה וּמַצְמִיחַ יְשׁוּעָה:

Mechal**keil** cha**yim** be**che**sed, mecha**yei** ha**kol**
(mei**tiym**) beracha**miym** ra**biym**, so**meich** nof**liym**
vero**fei** cho**liym** uma**tiyr** asu**riym**, umka**yeim** emuna**to**
liyshei**nei** a**far**, mi cha**mo**cha **ba**-al gevu**rot** u**miy**
domeh lach, **me**lech mei**miyt** umcha**yeh** umatzmi**yach**
yeshu-**a**.

On Shabbat Shuvah, please add:

מִי כָמוֹךָ אַב הָרַחֲמִים, זוֹכֵר יְצוּרָיו לְחַיִּים בְּרַחֲמִים:

Mi cha**mo**cha Av haracha**miym**, zo**cheir** yetzu**rav** lecha**yiym**
beracha**miym**.

If you are more comfortable sitting, please do so at this time or at any time.

126

Tefilat HaLev - Shabbat/Festivals — שבת/חג — תפלת הלב

וְנֶאֱמָן אַתָּה לְהַחֲיוֹת הַכֹּל (מֵתִים).
בָּרוּךְ אַתָּה יהוה, מְחַיֵּה הַכֹּל (מֵתִים):

Vene-eman Ata lehachayot hakol (meitiym).
Baruch Ata Adonai, mechayei hakol (meitiym).

You are strength forever, Adonai. Giving life to all (the deadened), You are great to save us. You bring the dew. You support life with mercy, You give life to all (the deadened) with great compassion. You support the fallen and heal the sick, You release the captives and establish faith for those who sleep in the dust. Who is like You, Master of strength and who can compare to You, Sovereign of life and death, who causes salvation to blossom. Who is like You, compassionate parent, who remembers Your creatures for life with compassion. And You are faithful in giving life to all (the deadened).
A Blessing are You, Adonai, who gives life to all (the deadened).

🍃 **We Name the Holy. You are Holy.**
We who seek to be holy, praise You every day,
for all eternity!
Holy is all life in the world.
Holy are all who struggle for freedom,
Who seek and reveal the sacred in each living being.
Rabbis Marcia Prager, Mordechai and Devora Bartnoff z"l, adapted

✡ Holiness is a complex idea.
What do we mean when we say God is holy?
  What do we mean when we say God's Name is holy?
  What do we do to make ourselves holy?
How do we live up to being holy today and every day?

Kedushah/Holiness — קדושה

אַתָּה קָדוֹשׁ וְשִׁמְךָ קָדוֹשׁ וּקְדוֹשִׁים בְּכָל יוֹם
יְהַלְלוּךָ, סֶּלָה. בָּרוּךְ אַתָּה יהוה, הָאֵל הַקָּדוֹשׁ.

Ata kadosh veShimcha kadosh ukdoshim bechol yom yehalelucha, Sela.
Baruch Ata, Adonai ha-Eil hakadosh.

You are Holy, and Your Name is Holy; We acknowledge Your holiness every day, Selah. A Source of Blessing are You, Adonai, You are Divine Holiness.

[Intermediate Amidah Prayers for a weekday start on page 181]
If you are more comfortable sitting, please do so at this time or at any time.

Tefilat HaLev - Shabbat/Festivals — שבת/חג - תפלת הלב

Nekadesh/Kedushah/Holiness — נקדש\קדושה

נְקַדֵּשׁ אֶת שִׁמְךָ בָּעוֹלָם, כְּשֵׁם שֶׁמַּקְדִּישִׁים אוֹתוֹ בִּשְׁמֵי מָרוֹם, כַּכָּתוּב עַל יַד נְבִיאֶךָ, וְקָרָא זֶה אֶל זֶה וְאָמַר:

Nekadeish et shim**cha** ba-**o**lam ke**s**heim shemakdiy**shiym** oto bish**mei** ma**rom**, kaka**tuv** al yad nevi-**e**cha ve**ka**ra zeh el zeh ve-a**mar**:

We sanctify Your name for all time and space, just as Your Holy Name was sanctified in the highest places, as it was written by the hand of Your prophets, and they [the angels] called out to each other:

Alternate Kedushah — קדושה שונה

נַעֲרִיצְךָ וְנַקְדִּישְׁךָ, כְּסוֹד שִׂיחַ שַׂרְפֵי קֹדֶשׁ. הַמַּקְדִּישִׁים שִׁמְךָ בַּקֹּדֶשׁ, כַּכָּתוּב עַל יַד נְבִיאֶךָ, וְקָרָא זֶה אֶל זֶה וְאָמַר:

Na'ariytzecha venakdiy**she**cha, ke**sod siy**-ach sar**fei ko**desh. Hamakdiy**shiym** shim**cha** ba**ko**desh, kaka**tuv** al yad neviy**e**cha, ve**ka**ra zeh el zeh ve-a**mar**:

We appreciate and sanctify You, like the hidden chanting of the holy serphim. They sanctify Your Name with holiness, as it is written by Your prophet, "They called out one another saying:"

קָדוֹשׁ קָדוֹשׁ קָדוֹשׁ יהוה צְבָאוֹת, מְלֹא כָל הָאָרֶץ כְּבוֹדוֹ.

Kadosh ka**dosh** ka**dosh** Ado**nai** Tzeva-**ot**, me**lo** chol ha-**a**retz kevo**do**.

Holy, Holy, Holy are You, Adonai Tzeva-ot, all the earth is filled with Your glory.

If you are more comfortable sitting, please do so at this time or at any time.

Tefilat HaLev - Shabbat/Festivals - שבת/חג

אַדִּיר אַדִּירֵנוּ, יהוה אֲדֹנֵינוּ, מָה אַדִּיר שִׁמְךָ בְּכָל הָאָרֶץ.

Adiyr adi**yrei**nu, Ado**nai** Ado**nei**nu, mah **adiyr** shim**cha** be**chol** ha-aretz.

Strength of our strength, connectivity of our connectivity, how mighty is Your Name in all the earth.

כְּבוֹדוֹ מָלֵא עוֹלָם, מְשָׁרְתָיו שׁוֹאֲלִים זֶה לָזֶה, אַיֵּה מְקוֹם כְּבוֹדוֹ, לְעֻמָּתָם בָּרוּךְ יֹאמֵרוּ:

Kevo**do** malei olam, meshartav sho-a**liym** zeh lazeh, a**yei** mekom kevodo, le'umatam baruch yo**mei**ru:

Your Glory fills the universe. When Your ministering beings ask one another "Where is the One's Glory?", they answer with this blessing saying:

 בָּרוּךְ כְּבוֹד יהוה, מִמְּקוֹמוֹ.

Baruch ke**vod** Ado**nai** mimkomo.
A Source of Blessing is Adonai's glory, radiating [everywhere] from the Source.

אֶחָד הוּא אֱלֹהֵינוּ, הוּא אָבִינוּ, הוּא מַלְכֵּנוּ, הוּא מוֹשִׁיעֵנוּ, וְהוּא יַשְׁמִיעֵנוּ בְּרַחֲמָיו שֵׁנִית לְעֵינֵי כָּל חָי:

Hu Elo**hei**nu, Hu Avinu, Hu Mal**kei**nu, Hu Moshi-**ei**nu, veHu Yashmi-**ei**nu bera**cha**mav shei**niyt** le'einei kol chai.

One is our God, God is our parent, God is our Sovereign, God is our salvation. And God will declare again with compassion for the eyes of all that live:

If you are more comfortable sitting, please do so at this time or at any time.

Tefilat HaLev - Shabbat/Festivals – שבת/חג – תפלת הלב

מִמְּקוֹמוֹ הוּא יִפֶן בְּרַחֲמִים, וְיָחוֹן עַם הַמְיַחֲדִים שְׁמוֹ עֶרֶב וָבֹקֶר בְּכָל יוֹם תָּמִיד, פַּעֲמַיִם בְּאַהֲבָה שְׁמַע אוֹמְרִים:

Mimko**mo** hu **yi**fen beracha**miym**, veya**chon** am hamyacha**diym** she**mo** **e**rev vavo**ker** be**chol** yom ta**mid**, pa-a**ma**yim be-aha**va** she**ma** om**riym**:

From the Divine dwelling place comes nurturing, gracious to all those who join themselves to the Name, evening and morning, every day, twice, by lovingly reciting the Shema:

שְׁמַע יִשְׂרָאֵל, יהוה אֱלֹהֵינוּ, יהוה אֶחָד:

Shema Yisra-**eil** Ado**nai** Elo**hei**nu, Ado**nai** e**chad**.

Listen Yisra-eil, Adonai is our God, Adonai is One.

הוּא אֱלֹהֵינוּ הוּא אָבִינוּ, הוּא מַלְכֵּנוּ, הוּא מוֹשִׁיעֵנוּ, וְהוּא יַשְׁמִיעֵנוּ בְּרַחֲמָיו שֵׁנִית לְעֵינֵי כָּל חָי, לִהְיוֹת לָכֶם לֵאלֹהִים:

Hu Elo**hei**nu Hu A**vi**nu, Hu Mal**kei**nu, Hu Moshi**yei**nu, veHu yashmi**yei**nu beracha**mav** shei**niyt** le'ei**nei** kol chai, lih**yot** la**chem** l'Elo**hiym**:

Our God! Our Parent! Our Sovereign! Our Rescuer! We will be redeemed by Divine nurturing as You once again declare before all who live that You are the One:

אֲנִי יהוה אֱלֹהֵיכֶם:

Ani Ado**nai** Elohei**chem**.

I am Adonai your God.

וּבְדִבְרֵי קָדְשְׁךָ כָּתוּב לֵאמֹר:

Uvdiv**rei** kod**she**cha ka**tuv** lei**mor**:

As it is written in the holy writings:

If you are more comfortable sitting, please do so at this time or at any time.

Tefilat HaLev - Shabbat/Festivals — שבת/חג

יִמְלֹךְ יהוה לְעוֹלָם, אֱלֹהַיִךְ צִיּוֹן לְדֹר וָדֹר, הַלְלוּיָהּ.

Yimloch Adonai le'olam, elohayich tziyon ledor vador. Hallelu-Yahh.

Adonai will reign forever, Your God, Tzion, from generation to generation. Praise Yahh (Adonai).

לְדוֹר וָדוֹר נַגִּיד גָּדְלֶךָ וּלְנֵצַח נְצָחִים קְדֻשָּׁתְךָ נַקְדִּישׁ, וְשִׁבְחֲךָ אֱלֹהֵינוּ מִפִּינוּ לֹא יָמוּשׁ לְעוֹלָם וָעֶד, כִּי אֵל מֶלֶךְ גָּדוֹל וְקָדוֹשׁ אָתָּה.

Ledor vador nagiyd godlecha uleneitzach netzachiym kedushatcha nakdiysh. Veshivchacha Eloheinu mipinu lo yamush le'olam va-ed. Ki Eil Melech gadol vekadosh Ata.

From generation to generation, we will tell of Your greatness and for all time we will sanctify Your holiness. O God, Your praise will never vanish from our lips, for You are a great and Holy Divine Sovereign.

We sing and praise the Holy One.

For the children and their children, (We) bless the Light.

בָּרוּךְ אַתָּה יהוה, הָאֵל [on Shabbat Shuva say הַמֶּלֶךְ] הַקָּדוֹשׁ.

Baruch Ata, Adonai ha-Eil [on Shabbat Shuva say ha-**M**elech] **hakadosh.**

A Blessing are You, Adonai, the Holy [on Shabbat Shuva say Sovereign] One.

We are seated.

🍃 Let us open ourselves to Sacredness in Shabbat.
May my heart see the world that can be,
A world of fulfillment, justice, and peace.
As we rest and celebrate on Shabbat, Your sacred day,
Lifting out voices together as one,
May we delight in our love for each other,
A foretaste of the way things can and will be!

Rabbis Marcia Prager, Mordechai and Devora Bartnoff z"l, adapted

Tefilat HaLev - Shabbat/Festivals   שבת/חג – תפלת הלב

✿ When we look at a flower, we can see You, God.
When we look at a sleeping child, You are there, too.
Your Presence is in the hugs and smiles
from friends and loved ones.
Life abounds
and we are the ones who distance ourselves.
We are the ones who hide from You.
We hide from You by hiding from ourselves
By hiding from the things we know we need to do.
Help us, God, to do what needs to be done,
To feel what needs to be felt,
To know what needs to be known,
So that we can be what we need to be.

✡ Rest is God's gift to us,
and we ask that our rest be acceptable to God.
When is our rest acceptable to God?
Our rest is acceptable when it refreshes us
in body and soul.
When we are refreshed in body and soul,
then we can do God's work with joy, devotion,
and a sense of fulfillment.
When we do that, then our rest and our actions
have meaning and purpose.
Then we have a portion in God's Torah.

🕊 Rabbi Zusya, and his brother, Rabbi Elimelich,
two students of the Magid of Mezritch,
worked hard to make Shabbat on a random weekday.
And they felt the special holiness of Shabbat
and became dismayed. Their teacher, the Magid, said:
If you prepare so diligently, Heaven responds.
Thus, Shabbat is a state of holiness to which we aspire,
and which we can reach, with proper intention.

Tefilat HaLev - Shabbat/Festivals — שבת/חג

אֱלֹהֵינוּ וֵאלֹהֵי אֲבוֹתֵינוּ וְאִמּוֹתֵינוּ, רְצֵה בִמְנוּחָתֵנוּ, קַדְּשֵׁנוּ בְּמִצְוֹתֶיךָ וְתֵן חֶלְקֵנוּ בְּתוֹרָתֶךָ, שַׂבְּעֵנוּ מִטּוּבֶךָ וְשַׂמְּחֵנוּ בִּישׁוּעָתֶךָ, ✡ וְטַהֵר לִבֵּנוּ לְעָבְדְּךָ בֶּאֱמֶת, וְהַנְחִילֵנוּ יהוה אֱלֹהֵינוּ בְּאַהֲבָה וּבְרָצוֹן שַׁבַּת קָדְשֶׁךָ, וְיָנוּחוּ בוֹ יִשְׂרָאֵל מְקַדְּשֵׁי שְׁמֶךָ. בָּרוּךְ אַתָּה יהוה, מְקַדֵּשׁ הַשַּׁבָּת:

Eloheinu velohei avoteinu ve-imoteinu, retzei vimnuchateinu, kadsheinu bemitzvotecha vetein chelkeinu betoratecha, sab'einu mituvecha vesamcheinu biyshu-atecha, ✡ **Vetaheir libeinu le-ovdecha be-emet. Vehanchileinu Adonai Eloheinu be-ahava uvratzon Shabat kodshecha, veyanuchu vo Yisra-eil mekadshei shemecha. Baruch Ata Adonai, mekadeish haShabat.**

Our God and the God of our Fathers and Mothers, who desires rest for us, who sanctifies us through mitzvot and gives us our portion in the Torah, who satisfies us with goodness and gives us joy through salvation, and who purifies our hearts to serve You truthfully. Adonai, our God, You give Your holy Shabbat to us through love and desire, that Israel and all peoples might rest therein and sanctify Your essence. A Source of Blessing are You, Adonai, who makes the Shabbat holy.

❁ Adonai, our God, let this holy time
Lift us to Your presence
In life, in peace, in leaping joy.
> *May we find rest in our rest,*
> *Holiness in our performance of mitzvot.*
> *Help us find being in Your Torah.*

Through Shabbat and Festival Days
May we, Your people Israel, find You.

Tefilat HaLev - Shabbat/Festivals שבת/חג — תפלת הלב

🍃 We Open Ourselves to Sacred Service.
We bless the One who enables us to feel deeply,
To know our needs, and the needs of our world.
May our actions flow with Your goodness, grace, love and care.
May our prayer arise and find acceptance with love.
May our lives turn always towards You,
So Your Shechinah will dwell within us always.
Rabbis Marcia Prager, Mordechai and Devora Bartnoff z"l, adapted

🔔 Shabbat is part of the ten *dibrot*, sometimes referred to as commandments, but better translated as utterances. It warrants its own prayer above and special inclusions in other prayers. It is the most important Jewish festival. The special holidays included in the *retzei* are all included in Torah. Except for Rosh Chodesh, the new month, also known as the Woman's holiday, all of these holidays are considered major holidays in the Jewish calendar, and are referred to as *chaggim*. Other holidays, such as Purim (from Esther) and Chanukah (post-biblical), are considered minor and are included in a later prayer, the *modim*.

Retzei / Receive [Our Prayers]   רצה

רְצֵה, יהוה אֱלֹהֵינוּ, בְּעַמְּךָ
יִשְׂרָאֵל, וּתְפִלָּתָם בְּאַהֲבָה
תְקַבֵּל, וּתְהִי לְרָצוֹן תָּמִיד
עֲבוֹדַת יִשְׂרָאֵל עַמֶּךָ. אֵל
קָרוֹב לְכָל קֹרְאָיו, פְּנֵה אֶל
עֲבָדֶיךָ וְחָנֵּנוּ; שְׁפוֹךְ רוּחֲךָ עָלֵינוּ,

Retzei Ado**nai** elo**hei**nu, be'am**cha** Yisra-**eil,** Utefila**tam** ba-a**ha**va teka**beil.** Utehi lerat**zon** tamid avo**dat** Yisra-**eil** a**me**cha. Eil ka**rov** le**chol** kor'**av**, pe**nei** el ava**de**cha vecha**nei**nu. She**foch** rucha**cha** a**lei**nu.

134

Tefilat HaLev - Shabbat/Festivals - שבת/חג - תפלת הלב

For Festivals:

אֱלֹהֵינוּ וֵאלֹהֵי אֲבוֹתֵינוּ, יַעֲלֶה וְיָבֹא, וְיִזָּכֵר זִכְרוֹנֵנוּ, וְזִכְרוֹן כָּל עַמְּךָ בֵּית יִשְׂרָאֵל לְפָנֶיךָ, לְטוֹבָה, לְחֵן וּלְחֶסֶד וּלְרַחֲמִים, לְחַיִּים וּלְשָׁלוֹם, בְּיוֹם

Eloheinu velohei avoteinu, ya-aleh veyavo, veyizacheir zichroneinu, vezichron kol amcha beit Yisra-eil lefanecha, letova lechein, ulechesed ulerachamiym, lechayim uleshalom, beyom

Our God and God of all ages, be mindful of Your people Israel on this

first day of the new month,

Rosh hachodesh hazeh — רֹאשׁ הַחֹדֶשׁ הַזֶּה

day of Pesach,

chag haMatzot hazeh — חַג הַמַּצּוֹת הַזֶּה

day of Shavuot,

chag haShavu-ot hazeh — חַג הַשָּׁבֻעוֹת הַזֶּה

day of Sukkot,

chag haSukot hazeh — חַג הַסֻּכּוֹת הַזֶּה

day of Shmini Atzeret,

haShmini, Chag haAtzeret hazeh — הַשְּׁמִינִי, חַג הָעֲצֶרֶת הַזֶּה

and renew in us love and compassion, goodness, life and peace.

זָכְרֵנוּ, יהוה אֱלֹהֵינוּ, בּוֹ לְטוֹבָה. אָמֵן.
Zochreinu, Adonai Eloheinu, bo letova. Amein.
This day remember us for well-being. Amen

וּפָקְדֵנוּ בוֹ לִבְרָכָה. אָמֵן.
Ufokdeinu vo livracha. Amein.
This day bless us with Your nearness. Amen.

וְהוֹשִׁיעֵנוּ בוֹ לְחַיִּים. אָמֵן.
Vehoshiyeinu vo lechayim. Amein.
This day help us to a fuller life. Amen.

Tefilat HaLev - Shabbat/Festivals — שבת/חג - תפלת הלב

וְתֶחֱזֶינָה עֵינֵינוּ בְּשׁוּבְךָ לְצִיּוֹן בְּרַחֲמִים. בָּרוּךְ אַתָּה יהוה, הַמַּחֲזִיר שְׁכִינָתוֹ לְצִיּוֹן.

**Vetechezena eyneinu beshuvecha letziyon berachamiym.
Baruch Ata Adonai, hamachazir shechinato letziyon.**

Find favor, Adonai our God, in Your people Israel and accept their prayer with love. May You always be pleased with Your people Israel's service. You are a God near to all who call to You. Turn toward us and be gracious to us, pour Your Spirit upon us. Allow our eyes to see Your return to Tzion with compassion. A Source of Blessing are You, Adonai, who returns Shechina to Tzion.

Meditation
God did not create a completed world. Rather, God gave us a purpose in life and challenges to make ourselves and the world whole.
Rabbi Sholom Silver
(1921-1974)

✡ We thank You
for the role
You have granted us
in Your creation,
for giving us tasks
that are important,
and for trusting us.
Thank You for the gift of Life and for the meaning we find in living.
Thank You for the gift of Your Love and of Hope,
Thank You for Your Loving Presence in our lives.

🍃 We Open to Gratitude.
We are thankful for all the generations that came before us,
For our parents, who brought us into this world,
For the miracles that greet us every day,
For morning, noon, and night,
For the joy of continual discovery,
For the beauty that surrounds us, and is us.
For all these things may Your Name be praised forever.

Rabbis Marcia Prager, Mordechai and Devora Bartnoff z"l, adapted

Tefilat HaLev - Shabbat/Festivals — שבת/חג — תפלת הלב

🔔 In traditional prayer books, there are two versions of the following prayer. One version is to be read aloud by the reader while the other is to be read by the congregation. At first this appears as an oddity and a bit strange. The reader's prayer does not include an ending prayer in this paragraph, the *chatima* comes later. However, the congregation's prayer is somewhat more petitionary and includes a *chatima*, a conclusion, referring to God as *Eil Hahoda-ot*, God of Gratitude, a curious title for God. This dual prayer represents two powerful opinions, two different traditions within Judaism. This format is a creative compromise to both honor the differences and the unity of our people. When we seek to resolve differences through creative unifying solutions, even when they are somewhat awkward, we help keep Judaism alive.

❀ What does it mean when we say
we are thankful to You, God, that You are our God,
and the God of our fathers?
Did we not pray earlier that each of us
experiences You in different ways?
   Indeed we did,
   and it is true that we experience You differently.
When we remember that You are still the same God,
we can still pray together, as one people.

מוֹדִים אֲנַחְנוּ לָךְ, שָׁאַתָּה הוּא יהוה
אֱלֹהֵינוּ וֵאלֹהֵי אֲבוֹתֵינוּ, (אִמּוֹתֵינוּ)
לְעוֹלָם וָעֶד צוּר חַיֵּינוּ מָגֵן יִשְׁעֵנוּ,
אַתָּה הוּא לְדוֹר וָדוֹר.

Modiym a**nach**nu lach, sha-**A**ta Hu, Ado**nai** Elo**hei**nu vei**lo**hei avo**tei**nu, (imo**tei**nu) le-o**lam** va-**ed**, tzur cha**yei**nu, ma**gein** yish'**ei**nu, **A**ta Hu le**dor** va**dor**.

We are grateful before You, that You are Adonai, our God and the God of our Fathers (Mothers) forever, the Rock of our Lives, the Shield that redeems us, You are God from generation to generation.

Tefilat HaLev - Shabbat/Festivals   שבת/חג - תפלת הלב

ON CHANUKAH AND PURIM:
We give thanks for the redeeming wonders
and the mighty deeds by which at this season
our people was saved in days of old.

Through the power of Your spirit, the weak defeated the strong,
the few prevailed over the many,
and the righteous were triumphant.

עַל הַנִּסִּים, וְעַל הַפֻּרְקָן, וְעַל הַגְּבוּרוֹת, וְעַל הַתְּשׁוּעוֹת, וְעַל הַמִּלְחָמוֹת, שֶׁעָשִׂיתָ לַאֲבוֹתֵינוּ בַּיָּמִים הָהֵם בַּזְּמַן הַזֶּה.

Al hani**siym** ve'**al** hapur**kan** ve'**al** hagvu**rot**, ve'**al** hatshu-**ot**,
ve'**al** hamilcha**mot**, she'a**si**ta la-avo**tei**nu baya**miym** ha**heim**
baz**man** ha**zeh**.

CHANUKAH

וְקָבְעוּ שְׁמוֹנַת יְמֵי חֲנֻכָּה אֵלּוּ, לְהוֹדוֹת וּלְהַלֵּל לְשִׁמְךָ הַגָּדוֹל.

Vekav'**u** shmo**nat** ye**mei** chanu**ka** ei**lu** leho**dot** ulha**leil**
leshim**cha** haga**dol**.

Then Your children returned to Your house, to purify the
sanctuary and kindle its lights. And they dedicated these days to
give thanks and praise to Your great name. We honor their
struggle and take our turn at maintaining the light.

בָּרוּךְ אַתָּה יהוה, הַטּוֹב שִׁמְךָ וּלְךָ נָאֶה לְהוֹדוֹת.

Ba**ruch** Ata Ado**nai**, ha**tov** shim**cha** ule**cha** na-**eh**
leho**dot**.

A Source of Blessing are You, Adonai, whose Essence is goodness and who is worthy of our thanks.

❀ In every community, there is work to be done. In every nation, there are wounds to heal. In every heart, there is the power to do it. Marianne Williamson

Tefilat HaLev - Shabbat/Festivals שבת/חג - תפלת הלב

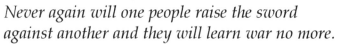

May the will come from You,
to annul wars and the shedding of blood
from the universe,
And to extend a peace, great and
wondrous, in the universe.

Never again will one people raise the sword
against another and they will learn war no more.

May we learn that if there is to be peace in this world,
it must come from us and from You.
We must draw on the Power that is You
To make peace - first within ourselves and then
between ourselves.

May we learn to seek You, not only surrounding us,
rather inside and through us.
And in that seeking may we find Your Love
in everyone we meet or see.

Dear Source of Blessing, may we see Your Love as a
Blessing of Love for all peoples.

יְבָרֶכְךָ יהוה וְיִשְׁמְרֶךָ.   כֵּן יְהִי רָצוֹן

Yevare**che**cha Adonai veyishme**re**cha.   Kein yehi ratzon.
May Adonai bless you and protect you.

יָאֵר יהוה פָּנָיו אֵלֶיךָ וִיחֻנֶּךָּ.   כֵּן יְהִי רָצוֹן

Ya-**eir** Adonai panav ei**le**cha vichu**ne**ka. Kein yehi ratzon.
May Adonai shine God's countenance on you with wisdom and grace.

יִשָּׂא יהוה פָּנָיו אֵלֶיךָ וְיָשֵׂם לְךָ שָׁלוֹם. כֵּן יְהִי רָצוֹן

Yisa Adonai panav ei**le**cha veya**seim** lecha sha**lom**.
Kein yehi ratzon.
May Adonai lift God's countenance onto you and grant you shalom, peace and wholeness.

Tefilat HaLev - Shabbat/Festivals   שבת/חג – תפלת הלב

🌸 We offer to You again, the prayer for peace:
"Peace to those near and to those far off."
> For our tradition teaches: If others are in turmoil
> and disharmony rules their lives,
> there can be no peace for us.
> When the violence of our lives
> drowns out the music
> for which we yearn,
> others likewise can find no peace.

Peace for all Israel. Peace for all humankind.
> Dear God, help us understand that we are Your hands
> and eyes that can turn our prayers into reality.

When we do that,
our prayers become more than mere words.

🍃 We Open to Wholeness, Completeness, Fulfillment, Peace.
Source of Shalom: Fulfillment and Peace
May we drink deeply from the fountain of peace,
May we know peace in ourselves,
Live in peace with our neighbors, create peace in the world.
We bless the Holy One,
Creator of Wholeness, Source of Peace.

Rabbis Marcia Prager, Mordechai and Devora Bartnoff z"l, adapted

שִׂים שָׁלוֹם טוֹבָה וּבְרָכָה, חֵן וָחֶסֶד וְרַחֲמִים,
עָלֵינוּ וְעַל כָּל יִשְׂרָאֵל עַמֶּךָ. בָּרְכֵנוּ, אָבִינוּ,
כֻּלָּנוּ כְּאֶחָד בְּאוֹר פָּנֶיךָ, כִּי בְאוֹר פָּנֶיךָ נָתַתָּ
לָנוּ, יהוה אֱלֹהֵינוּ, תּוֹרַת חַיִּים וְאַהֲבַת חֶסֶד,
וּצְדָקָה וּבְרָכָה וְרַחֲמִים וְחַיִּים וְשָׁלוֹם, וְטוֹב
בְּעֵינֶיךָ לְבָרֵךְ אֶת עַמְּךָ יִשְׂרָאֵל בְּכָל עֵת וּבְכָל
שָׁעָה בִּשְׁלוֹמֶךָ.

Tefilat HaLev - Shabbat/Festivals - שבת/חג - תפלת הלב

Sim shalom, tovah uvrachah, chein vachesed verachamiym, aleinu ve'al kol Yisra-eil amecha. Barcheinu, Avinu, kulanu ke-echad be-or panecha, ki ve-or panecha natata lanu, Adonai Eloheinu, torat chayiym ve-ahavat chesed, utzedakah uvrachah verachamiym vechayiym veshalom. Vetov be'einecha levareich et amcha Yisra-eil bechol eit uvchol sha-ah bishlomecha.

Grant peace, goodness and blessing, with grace, mercy and compassion for us and for all Your people Israel. Bless us as a parent, every one as one in the light of Your gaze. For in the light of Your gaze, You, Adonai, our God, gave us a living Torah of love and kindness and *tzedaka* and blessing and compassion, for life and peace. And You found it good in Your eyes to bless Your people Israel at every moment and in each hour with peace.

On Shabbat Shuva add

בְּסֵפֶר חַיִּים, בְּרָכָה, וְשָׁלוֹם, וּפַרְנָסָה טוֹבָה, נִזָּכֵר וְנִכָּתֵב לְפָנֶיךָ, אֲנַחְנוּ וְכָל עַמְּךָ בֵּית יִשְׂרָאֵל, לְחַיִּים טוֹבִים וּלְשָׁלוֹם.

Beseifer chayiym, beracha, veshalom, ufarnasah tovah, nizacheir venikateiv lefanecha, anachnu vechol amcha Beit Yisra-eil, lechayiym toviym ulshalom.
In the Book of Life, remember us and inscribe us for blessing and peace and good wages, us and all of Your people Israel, for a life of goodness and peace.

בָּרוּךְ אַתָּה יהוה, עוֹשֶׂה הַשָּׁלוֹם.

Baruch Ata Adonai, oseh hashalom.
Blessings are You, Adonai, Who makes peace.

[Amidah in Guided imagery is on pages 73-76.]

It is the time for our hearts and souls to have their voice as we pray silently.

Tefilat HaLev - Shabbat/Festivals

אֱלֹהַי, נְצוֹר לְשׁוֹנִי מֵרָע. וּשְׂפָתַי מִדַּבֵּר מִרְמָה: וְלִמְקַלְלַי נַפְשִׁי תִדֹּם, וְנַפְשִׁי כֶּעָפָר לַכֹּל תִּהְיֶה. פְּתַח לִבִּי בְּתוֹרָתֶךָ, וּבְמִצְוֹתֶיךָ תִּרְדּוֹף נַפְשִׁי.

Elohai netzor leshoni meira. Usfatai midabeir mirma:
Velimkalelai nafshi tidom, venafshi ke-afar lakol tihye.
Petach libiy betoratecha, uvemitzvotecha tirdof nafshi.
My God, Guard my tongue from all evil and my lips from spouting lies. May I think before I begin to speak, may my words be gentle and wise. Help me ignore those who wish me ill, help me be humble before all. Open my heart to Your Torah that I may know how to answer Your call. Juliet Spitzer

יִהְיוּ לְרָצוֹן אִמְרֵי פִי וְהֶגְיוֹן לִבִּי לְפָנֶיךָ, יהוה צוּרִי וְגוֹאֲלִי.

Yiheyu leratzon imrei fi vehegyon libi lefanecha, Adonai tzuri vego-ali.
May the words of my mouth and the meditations of my heart be acceptable before You, Adonai, my rock and my redeemer.

עֹשֶׂה שָׁלוֹם בִּמְרוֹמָיו הוּא יַעֲשֶׂה שָׁלוֹם עָלֵינוּ וְעַל כָּל יִשְׂרָאֵל, (וְעַל כָּל יוֹשְׁבֵי תֵבֵל,) וְאִמְרוּ אָמֵן:

Oseh shalom bimromav, hu ya-aseh shalom aleinu, ve'al kol Yisra-eil, (ve'al kol yoshvei teiveil,) ve-imru: amein.
May the One who makes peace in the high places, make peace for us, for Israel, and all the world, and let us say, Amen.

142

Tefilat HaLev - Shabbat/Festivals – שבת/חג תפלת הלב

Meditation

Rabbi Johanan said it in the name of Rabbi Simeon bar Yochai:
It is better for a person to cast him or herself into a fiery furnace
rather than put another person to shame in public. (B. Talmud, Brachot)

יִשְׂמְחוּ בְמַלְכוּתְךָ שׁוֹמְרֵי שַׁבָּת וְקוֹרְאֵי עֹנֶג, עַם מְקַדְּשֵׁי שְׁבִיעִי, כֻּלָּם יִשְׂבְּעוּ וְיִתְעַנְּגוּ מִטּוּבֶךָ, וּבַשְּׁבִיעִי רָצִיתָ בּוֹ וְקִדַּשְׁתּוֹ, חֶמְדַּת יָמִים אוֹתוֹ קָרָאתָ, זֵכֶר לְמַעֲשֵׂה בְרֵאשִׁית.

Yismechu vemalechutecha shomrei
Shabat vekorei oneg. Am
mekadeshei shevi-i kulam yisbe-u
veyitangu mituvecha. Uvashvi-i
ratzita bo vekidashto, chemdat
yamim oto karata, zeicher
lema-asei vereishiyt.

We delight in Divine sovereignty by guarding
our Shabbat time to make it a delight. We are a people who teach the
sanctity of the seventh day as a source of fulfillment, filled with Your
goodness. This day is Israel's festival of the spirit, sanctified and blessed
by You, the most precious of days, a symbol of the joy of creation.

Tefilat HaLev - Shabbat/Festivals – שבת/חג – תפלת הלב

Full Kaddish – קדיש שלם

יִתְגַּדַּל וְיִתְקַדַּשׁ שְׁמֵהּ רַבָּא. בְּעָלְמָא דִּי בְרָא כִרְעוּתֵיהּ, וְיַמְלִיךְ מַלְכוּתֵיהּ בְּחַיֵּיכוֹן וּבְיוֹמֵיכוֹן וּבְחַיֵּי דְכָל בֵּית יִשְׂרָאֵל. בַּעֲגָלָא וּבִזְמַן קָרִיב וְאִמְרוּ אָמֵן:

On Shabbat Shuvah, drop the italicized words and say the bracketed gray.

Yitga**dal** veyitka**dash** shi**mei** raba be'**al**ma di vra chiru**tei**, veyam**lich** malchu**tei** bechayei**chon** uveyomei**chon** uvcha**yei** dechol beit Yisra-**eil**, ba-aga**la**, uviz**man** ka**riv**, ve-imru: A**mein**.

יְהֵא שְׁמֵהּ רַבָּא מְבָרַךְ לְעָלַם וּלְעָלְמֵי עָלְמַיָּא:

Ye**hei** sh**mei** raba meva**rach** le'a**lam** ul'almei al**ma**ya.

יִתְבָּרַךְ וְיִשְׁתַּבַּח וְיִתְפָּאַר וְיִתְרוֹמַם וְיִתְנַשֵּׂא וְיִתְהַדָּר וְיִתְעַלֶּה וְיִתְהַלָּל שְׁמֵהּ דְּקֻדְשָׁא בְּרִיךְ הוּא לְעֵלָּא מִן כָּל [*לְעֵלָּא מִכָּל*] בִּרְכָתָא וְשִׁירָתָא תֻּשְׁבְּחָתָא וְנֶחֱמָתָא, דַּאֲמִירָן בְּעָלְמָא, וְאִמְרוּ אָמֵן:

Yitba**rach**, veyishta**bach**, veyitpa-**ar**, veyitro**mam**, veyitna**sei**, veyit-ha**dar**, veyit-a**leh**, veyit-ha**lal** she**mei** dekud**sha**, brich hu. Le'**eila** *min kol* [l'**eila** mi**kol**] bircha**ta** veshira**ta**, tushbecha**ta** venechema**ta** da-ami**ran** be'al**ma**, ve-imru: Amein.

תִּתְקַבֵּל צְלוֹתְהוֹן וּבָעוּתְהוֹן דְּכָל בֵּית יִשְׂרָאֵל קֳדָם אֲבוּהוֹן דִּי בִשְׁמַיָּא וְאִמְרוּ אָמֵן:

Titka**beil** tzelot-**hon** uva-ut-**hon** de**chol** Beit Yisra-**eil** ka**dam** avu**hon** di vishmaya, ve-imru: amein.

יְהֵא שְׁלָמָא רַבָּא מִן שְׁמַיָּא, וְחַיִּים עָלֵינוּ וְעַל כָּל יִשְׂרָאֵל וְאִמְרוּ אָמֵן.

Tefilat HaLev - Shabbat/Festivals — שבת/חג - תפלת הלב

Yehei shla**ma** ra**ba** min shema**ya**, vecha**yim** a**lei**nu ve'**al** kol Yisra-**eil**, ve-im**ru**: a**mein**.

יְהֵא שְׁלָמָא רַבָּא מִן שְׁמַיָּא הוּא יַעֲשֶׂה שָׁלוֹם עָלֵינוּ וְעַל כָּל יִשְׂרָאֵל, (וְעַל כָּל יוֹשְׁבֵי תֵבֵל,) וְאִמְרוּ אָמֵן:

Oseh sha**lom** bimro**mav**, hu ya-**a**seh sha**lom** a**lei**nu, ve'**al** kol Yisra-**eil**, (v'al kol yosh**vei** tei**veil**,) ve-im**ru**: a**mein**.

God's gloriousness is to be extolled, God's great Name to be hallowed in the world whose creation God willed. And may God's reign be in our day, during our life, and the life of all Israel, let us say: Amen.

Let God's great Name be praised forever and ever.

Let the Name of the Holy One, the Blessing One, be glorified, exalted, and honored, though God is beyond all the praises, songs, and adorations that we can utter, and let us say: Amen.

Receive at once the prayers and pleas of all of the House of Israel, our Parent in Heaven, and let us say: Amen.

May there be abundant peace from heaven and life for us and all Israel, and let us say: Amen.

May the One who makes peace in the high places make peace for us and for all of Israel (and all the world), and let us say: Amen.

Tefilat HaLev - Shabbat/Festivals   שבת/חג - תפלת הלב

TORAH SERVICE

**If you are comfortable doing so,
please rise when we open the ark for the Torah**

אֵין כָּמוֹךָ בָאֱלֹהִים, יהוה, וְאֵין כְּמַעֲשֶׂיךָ.
מַלְכוּתְךָ מַלְכוּת כָּל עֹלָמִים, וּמֶמְשַׁלְתְּךָ בְּכָל
דֹּר וָדֹר.

Ein ka**mo**cha va-elo**hiym**, Ado**nai**, ve-**ein** kema-a**se**cha
malchute**cha** mal**chut** kol ola**miym** umemshalte**cha**
be**chol** dor va**dor**.

There is none like You, Adonai, among those acclaimed as divine;
There are no mysteries like Yours. Your sovereignty is everlasting,
Your governance endures through all generations.

יהוה מֶלֶךְ, יהוה מָלָךְ, יהוה יִמְלֹךְ לְעֹלָם וָעֶד.
יהוה עֹז לְעַמּוֹ יִתֵּן יהוה יְבָרֵךְ אֶת עַמּוֹ בַשָּׁלוֹם.

Ado**nai me**lech Ado**nai ma**lach Ado**nai** yim**loch** le'**o**lam
va-**ed**. Ado**nai** oz le'**a**mo yi**tein** Ado**nai** yeva**reich** et
a**mo** vasha**lom**.

Adonai reigns, Adonai has reigned, Adonai will reign through all time
and space. May Adonai give strength to God's people; May Adonai
bless God's people with peace.

אַב הָרַחֲמִים, הֵיטִיבָה בִרְצוֹנְךָ אֶת צִיּוֹן, תִּבְנֶה
חוֹמוֹת יְרוּשָׁלָיִם. כִּי בְךָ לְבַד בָּטָחְנוּ, מֶלֶךְ אֵל
רָם וְנִשָּׂא, אֲדוֹן עוֹלָמִים.

Av haracha**miym** hei**ti**va virtzon**cha** et tzi**yon** tiv**neh**
cho**mot** yerusha**la**yim. Ki ve**cha** le**vad** ba**tach**nu
Melech eil ram veni**sa** adon ola**miym**.

Merciful God, favor Zion with Your goodness; Rebuild the walls of
Jerusalem. For in You alone do we trust, exalted One, Sovereign,
connector through all time and space.

Tefilat HaLev - Shabbat/Festivals — שבת/חג

We open the ark. If you are comfortable doing so, please rise.

וַיְהִי בִּנְסֹעַ הָאָרֹן וַיֹּאמֶר מֹשֶׁה: קוּמָה יהוה,
וְיָפֻצוּ אֹיְבֶיךָ, וְיָנֻסוּ מְשַׂנְאֶיךָ מִפָּנֶיךָ:

**Vayehi binso-ah ha-aron vayomer Moshe:
Kumah Adonai veyafutzu oyvecha,
veyanusu mesan-echa mipanecha.**

And it would be, as the ark set out, that Moshe would say: Arise Adonai and Your enemies will scatter and those who hate You will disperse before You.

כִּי מִצִּיּוֹן תֵּצֵא תוֹרָה, וּדְבַר יהוה מִירוּשָׁלָיִם:
בָּרוּךְ שֶׁנָּתַן תּוֹרָה לְעַמּוֹ יִשְׂרָאֵל בִּקְדֻשָּׁתוֹ:

**Ki mitziyon teitzei torah, udevar Adonai mirushalayim.
Baruch shenatan torah le'amo Yisra-eil bikdushato.**

For from Tzion, Torah goes forth and the word of Adonai from Jerusalem.
A Source of Blessing is the One who gave Torah to God's people Israel in holiness.

בֵּהּ אֲנָא רָחִיץ. וְלִשְׁמֵהּ קַדִּישָׁא יַקִּירָא אֲנָא
אֵמַר תֻּשְׁבְּחָן. יְהֵא רַעֲוָא קֳדָמָךְ דְּתִפְתַּח לִבַּאי
בְּאוֹרַיְתָא וְתַשְׁלִים מִשְׁאֲלִין דְּלִבַּאי. וְלִבָּא דְכָל
עַמָּךְ יִשְׂרָאֵל. לְטַב וּלְחַיִּין וְלִשְׁלָם:

**Bei ana rachiytz. Velishmeihh kadisha yakira ana
eimar tushbechan. Yehei ra-ava kadamach detiftach
libi beOraita vetashliym mishaliyn delibi. Veliba
dechol amach Yisra-eil. Letav ulchayin velishlam.
Amein.**

Zohar: In the One do I put my trust; to Adonai's holy, precious name do I call out in praise. Open my heart to Your Torah. Answer my heart's prayers and the heartful prayers of all Your people Israel for goodness, for life, and for peace. Amen.

Tefilat HaLev - Shabbat/Festivals — שבת/חג - תפלת הלב

(The Torah is removed from the Ark.)

CALL AND RESPONSE (first the leader, then the congregation responds)

שְׁמַע יִשְׂרָאֵל, יהוה אֱלֹהֵינוּ, יהוה אֶחָד.
Shema Yisra-eil, Adonai Eloheinu, Adonai echad!
Listen, O Israel, Adonai is our God, Adonai is One.

אֶחָד אֱלֹהֵינוּ, גָּדוֹל אֲדוֹנֵנוּ, קָדוֹשׁ שְׁמוֹ.
Echad Eloheinu gadol adoneinu kadosh Shemo.
Our God is One; Adonai is great; holy is God's Name.

Together:

גַּדְּלוּ לַיהוה אִתִּי, וּנְרוֹמְמָה שְׁמוֹ יַחְדָּו.
Gadlu laAdonai iti, uneromemah shemo yachdav.
Acknowledge Adonai's greatness with me, and let us exalt God's Essence together.

Traditionally, the leader calls out the *Sh'ma* and then the congregation responds. The same is done for the *Echad...* The congregation does the *Gadlu...* in unison with the leader, who faces the ark and bows for this blessing. The leader lifts the Torah so that it does not "bow" before God.

Tefilat HaLev - Shabbat/Festivals שבת/חג - תפלת הלב

לְךָ יהוה הַגְּדֻלָּה וְהַגְּבוּרָה וְהַתִּפְאֶרֶת וְהַנֵּצַח
וְהַהוֹד, כִּי כֹל בַּשָּׁמַיִם וּבָאָרֶץ: לְךָ יהוה
הַמַּמְלָכָה וְהַמִּתְנַשֵּׂא לְכֹל לְרֹאשׁ.

Lecha Adonai hagedula vehagevura vehatif-eret
vehaneitzach vehahod, ki chol bashamayim uva-aretz:
Lecha Adonai hamamlacha vehamitnasei lechol
lerosh.

Yours, Adonai, is the greatness, the power, the glory, the victory, and the majesty; for all that is in heaven and earth is Yours. Yours is the kingdom, Adonai, You are supreme over all.

Al Shlosha Devarim - On Three Things   עַל שְׁלֹשָׁה דְבָרִים

עַל שְׁלֹשָׁה דְבָרִים הָעוֹלָם עוֹמֵד,
עַל הַתּוֹרָה וְעַל הָעֲבוֹדָה וְעַל
גְּמִילוּת חֲסָדִים.

Al shlosha devariym, ha'olam omeid.
Al haTorah Ve'al ha-avodah, Ve'al gemilut chasadiym.

The world depends on three things: on Torah, on worship and on loving deeds.

לֹא יִשָּׂא גוֹי אֶל גּוֹי חֶרֶב
וְלֹא יִלְמְדוּ עוֹד מִלְחָמָה.

Lo yisa goy el goy cherev lo yilmedu od milchamah.

Nation shall not raise a sword against nation
Neither shall they learn war any more.

Tefilat HaLev - Shabbat/Festivals שבת/חג - תפלת הלב

Once the Torah is resting on the table, we are seated.

TORAH BLESSING (Before Reading)

בָּרְכוּ אֶת יהוה הַמְבֹרָךְ.
Barchu et Ado**nai** hamevo**rach**.
We praise Adonai, the Source of Blessing, Who blesses.

בָּרוּךְ יהוה הַמְבֹרָךְ לְעוֹלָם וָעֶד:
Baruch Ado**nai** hamevo**rach** le'o**lam** va-**ed**.
Praised be Adonai, the Source of Blessing, now and forever.

בָּרוּךְ אַתָּה יהוה אֱלֹהֵינוּ מֶלֶךְ הָעוֹלָם,
אֲשֶׁר בָּחַר בָּנוּ עִם (מִ-)כָּל הָעַמִּים
וְנָתַן לָנוּ אֶת תּוֹרָתוֹ:
בָּרוּךְ אַתָּה יהוה, נוֹתֵן הַתּוֹרָה.

Baruch Ata Ado**nai**, Elo**hei**nu **Me**lech ha-o**lam**
asher ba**char ba**nu im (mi)kol ha-a**miym**,
Vena**tan la**nu et Tora**to**.
Baruch Ata Ado**nai**, no**tein** haTo**rah**.

Blessed is Adonai, our God, Sovereign of the universe, who has chosen us with (from) all peoples and has given us Torah. A Source of Blessing is Adonai, Giver of the Torah.

Torah Blessing (After Reading)

בָּרוּךְ אַתָּה יהוה אֱלֹהֵינוּ מֶלֶךְ הָעוֹלָם, אֲשֶׁר נָתַן
לָנוּ תּוֹרַת אֱמֶת, וְחַיֵּי עוֹלָם נָטַע בְּתוֹכֵנוּ.
בָּרוּךְ אַתָּה יהוה, נוֹתֵן הַתּוֹרָה.

Baruch Ata Ado**nai** Elo**hei**nu **Me**lech ha-o**lam**, **a**sher
natan **la**nu torat **e**met, vecha**yei** olam nata beto**chei**nu.
Baruch Ata Ado**nai** no**tein** haTo**rah**.

A Source of Blessing is Adonai, our God, Sovereign of the universe, who has given us a Torah of truth, implanting it within us. A Source of Blessing is Adonai, Giver of the Torah.

Tefilat HaLev - Shabbat/Festivals   שבת/חג - תפלת הלב

Gomeil Blessing - Gift of Life   ברכת הגומל

בָּרוּךְ אַתָּה יהוה, שֶׁגְּמָלַנִי כָּל טוֹב:

Baruch **A**ta Yahh (Ado**nai**), shegma**la**ni kol tov.
Humbly I stand before You today, blessed with the gift of life.

מִי שֶׁגְּמָלְךָ כָּל טוֹב, יִגְמָלְךָ כָּל טוֹב סֶלָה: (male)

מִי שֶׁגְּמָלֵךְ כָּל טוֹב, יִגְמָלֵךְ כָּל טוֹב סֶלָה: (female)

Mi shegmal**cha** (shegma**leich**) kol tov, yigmal**cha** (yigma**leich**) kol tov **se**lah.
May the Gracious One who heard your prayers, guide your steps in peace.

© Rabbi Hanna Tiferet Seigel

Our God, God of all generations, may the sense of Your Presence never leave us; may it keep us ever faithful to Your covenant. Make us responsive to Your Teaching, that we may walk in Your ways. Fill our souls with awe, and our hearts with love, that we may return to You in truth, and with all our being.

Adonai, our God, let the strength of our longing for You help us to grow in the wise use of our powers, that through us Your power may be magnified in human life. So may it hallow this world and labor to redeem it.

Tefilat HaLev - Shabbat/Festivals — שבת/חג — תפלת הלב

Chazak

Chazak, chazak, venitchazeik. חֲזַק, חֲזַק, וְנִתְחַזֵּק.

Let us be strong, strong, and strenthen each other.

© Rabbi Hanna Tiferet Seigel

Prayer for Healing

מִי שֶׁבֵּרַךְ אֲבוֹתֵינוּ מְקוֹר הַבְּרָכָה לְאִמּוֹתֵינוּ

Mi shebeirach avoteinu mekor habracha le-imoteinu.
May the source of strength who blessed the ones before us
Help us find the courage to make our lives a blessing.
And let us say -- Amen.

מִי שֶׁבֵּרַךְ אִמּוֹתֵינוּ מְקוֹר הַבְּרָכָה לַאֲבוֹתֵינוּ

Mi shebeirach imoteinu mekor habracha la-avoteinu.
Bless those in need of healing with *refua shleima*
the renewal of body, the renewal of spirit.
And let us say -- Amen.   © Debbie Friedman

אָנָא אֵל נָא רְפָא נָא לָהּ, רְפוּאָה שְׁלֵמָה.

Ana, El na refa na lahh. Refuah Shleima.
Please God, please heal her with a full and complete healing.

Heal us Adonai, and we shall be healed.
Save us and we shall be saved.
Ana El na refa na lanu — O, God, please heal us!
Heal our bodies. Open our hearts. Awaken our minds,
Shechina / Ehyeh

וְזֹאת הַתּוֹרָה אֲשֶׁר שָׂם מֹשֶׁה לִפְנֵי
בְּנֵי יִשְׂרָאֵל עַל פִּי יהוה בְּיַד מֹשֶׁה:

Vezot haTorah asher sam Moshe lifnei benei Yisra-eil al pi Adonai beyad Moshe.
This is the Torah that Moses placed before the people of Israel, the word of Adonai.

(We are seated)

Tefilat HaLev - Shabbat/Festivals — שבת/חג – תפלת הלב

Blessing before the Reading of the Haftarah

בָּרוּךְ אַתָּה יהוה אֱלֹהֵינוּ מֶלֶךְ הָעוֹלָם, אֲשֶׁר בָּחַר בִּנְבִיאִים טוֹבִים, וְרָצָה בְדִבְרֵיהֶם הַנֶּאֱמָרִים בֶּאֱמֶת, בָּרוּךְ אַתָּה יהוה, הַבּוֹחֵר בַּתּוֹרָה וּבְמֹשֶׁה עַבְדּוֹ, וּבְיִשְׂרָאֵל עַמּוֹ, וּבִנְבִיאֵי הָאֱמֶת וָצֶדֶק.

Baruch Ata Adonai Eloheinu Melech ha-olam asher bachar bineviyiym toviym veratzah vedivreihem hane-emariym be-emet. Baruch Ata Adonai habocheir batorah uveMoshe avdo uveYisra-eil amo uvinvi-eiy ha-emet vatzedek.

A Source of Blessing are You, Adonai, our God, Sovereign of the universe, who chooses good prophets, and is pleased with their words which were spoken in truth. A Source of Blessing are You, Adonai, who chooses the Torah and Your servant Moshe, Your people Israel, and prophets of truth and righteousness.

Blessings after the Reading of the Haftarah

בָּרוּךְ אַתָּה יהוה אֱלֹהֵינוּ מֶלֶךְ הָעוֹלָם, צוּר כָּל הָעוֹלָמִים, צַדִּיק בְּכָל הַדּוֹרוֹת, הָאֵל הַנֶּאֱמָן הָאוֹמֵר וְעוֹשֶׂה, הַמְדַבֵּר וּמְקַיֵּם, שֶׁכָּל דְּבָרָיו אֱמֶת וָצֶדֶק.

Baruch Ata Adonai Eloheinu Melech ha-olam, tzur kol ha-olamiym, tzadiyk bechol hadorot, ha-Eil hane-eman, ha-omer ve-oseh, hamedabeir umekayeim, shekol devarav emet vatzedek.

A Source of Blessing are You, Adonai, our God, Sovereign of the universe, Rock of all ages, righteous in all generations, the faithful God, who says and does, who speaks and fulfills, for all Your words are truth and righteousness.

תפלת הלב – שבת/חג — Tefilat HaLev - Shabbat/Festivals

נֶאֱמָן אַתָּה הוּא יהוה אֱלֹהֵינוּ, וְנֶאֱמָנִים דְּבָרֶיךָ, וְדָבָר אֶחָד מִדְּבָרֶיךָ אָחוֹר לֹא יָשׁוּב רֵיקָם, כִּי אֵל מֶלֶךְ נֶאֱמָן וְרַחֲמָן אָתָּה. בָּרוּךְ אַתָּה יהוה, הָאֵל הַנֶּאֱמָן בְּכָל דְּבָרָיו.

Ne-eman, **A**ta Hu Ado**nai** Elo**hei**nu, vene-ema**niym** deva**re**cha, veda**var** e**chad** midva**re**cha a**chor** lo ya**shuv** rei**kam**, ki Eil **Me**lech ne-e**man** veracha**man** **A**ta. Ba**ruch** Ata Ado**nai**, ha-**Eil** hane-e**man** be**chol**-deva**rav**.

Faithful are You, Adonai, our God, and faithful are Your words, and not one of Your words returns unfulfilled, for You are a faithful and compassionate God and Sovereign. Blessings are You, Adonai, who is faithful in all words.

רַחֵם עַל צִיּוֹן כִּי הִיא בֵּית חַיֵּינוּ, וְלַעֲלוּבַת נֶפֶשׁ תּוֹשִׁיעַ בִּמְהֵרָה בְיָמֵינוּ. בָּרוּךְ אַתָּה יהוה, מְשַׂמֵּחַ צִיּוֹן בְּבָנֶיהָ.

Racheim al-Tzi**yon**, ki hi beit cha**yei**nu, vela'a**lu**vat **ne**fesh to**shi**-a bimhe**rah** veya**mei**nu. Ba**ruch** Ata Ado**nai**, mesa**mei**-ach Tzi**yon** bevane-**ah**.

Have compassion on Tzion for she is the source of our life, and lift her sad spirit speedily in our days. Blessings are You, Adonai, who makes Tzion rejoice through her children.

שַׂמְּחֵנוּ יהוה אֱלֹהֵינוּ בְּאֵלִיָּהוּ הַנָּבִיא עַבְדֶּךָ, וּבְמַלְכוּת בֵּית דָּוִד מְשִׁיחֶךָ, בִּמְהֵרָה יָבֹא וְיָגֵל לִבֵּנוּ. עַל כִּסְאוֹ לֹא יֵשֵׁב זָר וְלֹא יִנְחֲלוּ עוֹד אֲחֵרִים אֶת כְּבוֹדוֹ, כִּי בְשֵׁם קָדְשְׁךָ נִשְׁבַּעְתָּ לּוֹ, שֶׁלֹּא יִכְבֶּה נֵרוֹ לְעוֹלָם וָעֶד. בָּרוּךְ אַתָּה יהוה, מָגֵן דָּוִד.

Tefilat HaLev - Shabbat/Festivals — שבת/חג — תפלת הלב

Samcheinu, Adonai Eloheinu, be'Eliyahu hanavi avdecha, uvmalchut beit David meshichecha. Bimherah yavo veyageil libeinu, al kis'o lo yeisheiv zar, velo yinchalu od acheriym et kevodo, ki besheim kodshecha nishbata lo, shelo yichbeh nero le'olam va'ed. Baruch Ata Adonai, magein David.

Bring us joy, Adonai, our God, through Elijah, the prophet, Your servant, and through the kingdom of the house of David, Your anointed. May he soon come and gladden our hearts. Let no stranger sit upon his throne, nor let others inherit his glory; for by Your holy name, You swore to him, that his light would never be extinguished. Blessings are You, Adonai, the shield of David.

עַל הַתּוֹרָה, וְעַל הָעֲבוֹדָה, וְעַל הַנְּבִיאִים, וְעַל יוֹם הַשַּׁבָּת הַזֶּה, שֶׁנָּתַתָּ לָנוּ יהוה אֱלֹהֵינוּ, לִקְדֻשָּׁה וְלִמְנוּחָה, לְכָבוֹד וּלְתִפְאָרֶת.

Al-hatorah, ve'al ha'avodah, ve'al haneviyiym, ve'al yom haShabat hazeh, shenatata lanu, Adonai Eloheinu, likdushah velimnuchah, lechavod uletif-aret.

For the Torah, for divine service, for the prophets, for this day of Shabbat, which You, Adonai, our God, has given us for holiness and for rest, for honor and glory.

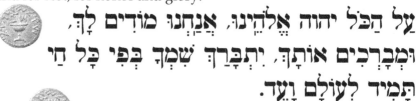

עַל הַכֹּל יהוה אֱלֹהֵינוּ, אֲנַחְנוּ מוֹדִים לָךְ, וּמְבָרְכִים אוֹתָךְ, יִתְבָּרַךְ שִׁמְךָ בְּפִי כָּל חַי תָּמִיד לְעוֹלָם וָעֶד.

בָּרוּךְ אַתָּה יהוה, מְקַדֵּשׁ הַשַּׁבָּת.

Al-hakol, Adonai Eloheinu, anachnu modiym lach umevarechiym otach, yitbarach shimcha befi kol-chai tamiyd le'olam va'ed.
Baruch Ata Adonai, mekadeish haShabat.

For all these, we thank You and bless You, Adonai, our God: May Your name be acknowledged for blessings by the mouth of every living being throughout time and space. A Source of blessings are You, Adonai, who sanctifies Shabbat.

Tefilat HaLev - Shabbat/Festivals   שבת/חג - תפלת הלב

🔔 For those who defend our nation:

Eloheinu v'Elohei avoteinu ve-imoteinu –
Our God and God of our ancestors,
Watch over those who defend our
nation. Shield them from harm and
guide them in all their pursuits.
Grant their commanders wisdom and discernment
in their time of preparation and on the battlefield.
Should battle erupt may their victory
be swift and complete.
May the loss of life for any of your creations be avoided.
Grant healing to those who are wounded
and safe redemption to those
who fall into enemy hands.
For those who have lost their lives, grant consolation
and Your presence to those who were close to them.
We also ask that you stand with our President
and all our military leaders.
Guide them in their decision making
so that Your will is implanted within their minds.
May it be Your will that world hostilities
come to a rapid end
And that those in service are returned safely
to their families.
We pray that freedom will dawn for the oppressed and
Fervently we hope that the vision of Your prophet will
come to be,
"Let nation not lift up sword against nation nor learn war anymore."
May this vision come to pass speedily and in our day,
                                                         Amen.

Rabbi Matt Friedman

Tefilat HaLev – Shabbat/Festivals שבת/חג - תפלת הלב

✡ **For Israel:**

Rock and Champion of Israel, please
bless the State of Israel, first fruit of
the flourishing of our redemption.
Guard it in the abundance of Your love.
Spread over it the shelter of Your peace.
Send forth Your light and truth to those who lead and
judge it and to those who hold elective office.
Establish in them, through Your presence, wise counsel
that they might walk
in the way of justice, freedom, and integrity.
Strengthen the hands of those who guard our Holy
Land. Let them inherit salvation and life.
And give peace to the Land
and perpetual joy to its inhabitants.
Appoint for a blessing all our kindred of the House of
Israel in all the lands of their dispersion.
Plant in their hearts a love of Zion.
And for all our people everywhere, may God be with
them, and may they have the opportunity to go up to
the Land.
Cause Your spirit's influence to emanate upon all
dwellers of our Holy Land.
Remove from their midst hatred and enmity, jealousy
and wickedness.
Plant in their hearts love and kinship, peace and
friendship. And soon fulfill the vision of Your prophet:
"Nation shall not lift up sword against nation.
Let them no longer learn ways of war."
And let us say, Amen.

Tefilat HaLev - Shabbat/Festivals שבת/חג – תפלת הלב

 For our congregation:

Eloheinu v'Elohei avoteinu ve-imoteinu – Our God and God of our ancestors, Abraham, Isaac, and Jacob, Sarah, Rebecca, Rachel, and Leah,
bless this entire congregation, along with all holy congregations:
them, their sons and daughters, their families, and all that is theirs,
along with those who unite to establish temples and synagogues for prayer and for community,

and those who enter them to pray, to educate, to learn and to experience Jewish Life.
Bless those who give funds for heat and light, refreshments for Kiddush and Havdalah,
bread to the wayfarer and charity to the poor,
teachers for our youth and adults
and all who devotedly involve themselves
with the needs of this community
and the Land of Israel.
May the Holy One Praised Be reward them,
remove sickness from them, heal them, and forgive their sins.
Please bless them by prospering all their worthy endeavors,
as well as those of the entire people Israel and all who seek peace.
And let us say: Amen.

Tefilat HaLev - Shabbat/Festivals — שבת/חג

ברכת החודש — Blessing for the New Month

מִי שֶׁעָשָׂה נִסִּים לַאֲבוֹתֵינוּ, וְגָאַל אוֹתָם מֵעַבְדוּת לְחֵרוּת, הוּא יִגְאַל אוֹתָנוּ בְּקָרוֹב, וִיקַבֵּץ נִדָּחֵינוּ מֵאַרְבַּע כַּנְפוֹת הָאָרֶץ, חֲבֵרִים כָּל יִשְׂרָאֵל, וְנֹאמַר אָמֵן.

Mi she'asa ni**sim** lavo**tei**nu, vega-al o**tam** me'av**dut** lechei**rut**, hu yi**gal** otanu beka**rov** vika**beitz** nida**chei**nu me-ar**ba** kan**fot** ha-aretz, chave**riym** kol yisraeil, veno**mar amein**.

May the One who performed miracles for our forefathers, and redeemed them from slavery into freedom, redeem us soon, and gather our dispersed ones from the four corners of the earth and may all of Israel be friends, and let us say, amen.

רֹאשׁ חֹדֶשׁ __ יִהְיֶה בְּיוֹם __ הַבָּא עָלֵינוּ וְעַל כָּל יִשְׂרָאֵל לְטוֹבָה.

Rosh cho**desh** __ yih**yeh** be**yom** __ haba aleinu ve'**al** kol Yisraeil leto**vah**.

The first of the month of ___ will be on ___ day, may it come to us and all of Israel for goodness.

יְחַדְּשֵׁהוּ הַקָּדוֹשׁ בָּרוּךְ הוּא, עָלֵינוּ וְעַל כָּל עַמּוֹ בֵּית יִשְׂרָאֵל, וְעַל כָּל יוֹשְׁבֵי תֵבֵל, לְחַיִּים וּלְשָׁלוֹם, לְשָׂשׂוֹן וּלְשִׂמְחָה, לִישׁוּעָה וּלְנֶחָמָה, וְנֹאמַר אָמֵן.

Yechad**sheihu** haKadosh Baruch Hu, aleinu ve'**al** kol amo beit Yisrael, ve'al kol yosh**vei** tei**veil**, lecha**yim** ulsha**lom**. Lesa**son** ulsim**cha**. Lishuah ulnechama. Veno**mar amein**.

May the Holy One of Blessing renew the month for us and for all of the nation Israel, and all of the earth, for life and for peace, for deliverance and for comfort, and let us say, amen.

Tefilat HaLev - Shabbat/Festivals — שבת/חג — תפלת הלב

Ashrei Yoshvei Veitecha - Joyous Are They — אשרי יושבי ביתך

אַשְׁרֵי יוֹשְׁבֵי בֵיתֶךָ, עוֹד יְהַלְלוּךָ סֶּלָה:

Ashrei yoshvei veitecha, od yehalelucha Selah.
Joyous are they who dwell in Your house, they praise You still, Selah.

אַשְׁרֵי הָעָם שֶׁכָּכָה לּוֹ, אַשְׁרֵי הָעָם שֶׁיהוה אֱלֹהָיו:

Ashrei ha-am shekachah lo, ashrei ha-am sheADONAI Elohav.
Joyous is the nation who are thus, Joyous is the nation for whom ADONAI is God.

תְּהִלָּה לְדָוִד, אֲרוֹמִמְךָ אֱלוֹהַי הַמֶּלֶךְ,
וַאֲבָרְכָה שִׁמְךָ לְעוֹלָם וָעֶד:

Tehila leDavid, Aromimcha Elohai haMelech va-avarchah Shimcha le'olam va-ed.
A Psalm for David, I extol You, my Sovereign God, I acknowledge You by Name through all time and space.

בְּכָל יוֹם אֲבָרְכֶךָּ, וַאֲהַלְלָה שִׁמְךָ לְעוֹלָם וָעֶד:

Bechol yom avarcheka, va-ahalelah Shimcha le'olam va-ed.
Every day I will acknowledge You, I will praise Your Name through all time and space.

גָּדוֹל יהוה וּמְהֻלָּל מְאֹד, וְלִגְדֻלָּתוֹ אֵין חֵקֶר:

Gadol ADONAI umhulal me-od, veligdulato ein cheiker.
ADONAI is great, is most worthy of praise, [God's] greatness is beyond questioning.

דּוֹר לְדוֹר יְשַׁבַּח מַעֲשֶׂיךָ, וּגְבוּרֹתֶיךָ יַגִּידוּ:

Dor ledor yeshabach ma-asecha, ugvurotecha yagiydu.
Generation to generation, they praise Your mysteries and they tell of Your mightiness.

הֲדַר כְּבוֹד הוֹדֶךָ, וְדִבְרֵי נִפְלְאֹתֶיךָ אָשִׂיחָה:

Hadar kevod hodecha, vedivrei niflotecha asichah.
Splendid is the impact of Your glory, we discuss the significance of Your wonders.

Tefilat HaLev - Shabbat/Festivals – שבת/חג – תפלת הלב

וֶעֱזוּז נוֹרְאוֹתֶיךָ יֹאמֵרוּ
וּגְדֻלָּתְךָ אֲסַפְּרֶנָּה:

Ve-ezuz norotecha yomeiru ugdulat-cha asaprenah.
They talk of the might of Your awesomeness, we tell of Your greatness.

זֵכֶר רַב טוּבְךָ יַבִּיעוּ, וְצִדְקָתְךָ יְרַנֵּנוּ:

Zecher rav tuvcha yabiyu, vetzidkatcha yeraneinu.
They express the greatness of Your goodness, we praise Your righteousness.

חַנּוּן וְרַחוּם יהוה, אֶרֶךְ אַפַּיִם וּגְדָל חָסֶד:

Chanun verachum ADONAI, erech apayim ugdol chased.
Gracious and compassionate is ADONAI, slow to anger with great mercy.

טוֹב יהוה לַכֹּל, וְרַחֲמָיו עַל כָּל מַעֲשָׂיו:

Tov ADONAI lakol, verachamav al kol ma-asav.
ADONAI is good to all, compassionate in all deeds/mysteries.

יוֹדוּךָ יהוה כָּל מַעֲשֶׂיךָ, וַחֲסִידֶיךָ יְבָרְכוּכָה:

Yoducha ADONAI kol ma-asecha, vachasidecha yivarchuchah.
We thank You, ADONAI, for all Your deeds/mysteries, we bless Your piety/righteousness.

כְּבוֹד מַלְכוּתְךָ יֹאמֵרוּ, וּגְבוּרָתְךָ יְדַבֵּרוּ:

Kevod malchutcha yomeiru, ugvuratcha yedabeiru.
They talk of the impact of Your sovereignty, they speak of Your mightiness.

Tefilat HaLev - Shabbat/Festivals — שבת/חג - תפלת הלב

לְהוֹדִיעַ לִבְנֵי הָאָדָם גְּבוּרֹתָיו, וּכְבוֹד הֲדַר מַלְכוּתוֹ:

Lehodiya livnei ha-adam gevurotav, uchvod hadar malchuto.

Your mightiness is known to humankind, and [so is] the impact of the splendidness of Your sovereignty.

מַלְכוּתְךָ מַלְכוּת כָּל עוֹלָמִים, וּמֶמְשַׁלְתְּךָ בְּכָל דֹּר וָדֹר:

Malchutcha malchut kol olamiym, umemshaltecha bechol dor vador.

Your sovereignty rules all the realms, Your governance is for every generation.

סוֹמֵךְ יהוה לְכָל הַנֹּפְלִים, וְזוֹקֵף לְכָל הַכְּפוּפִים:

Someich ADONAI lechol hanofliym, vezokeif lechol hakfufiym.

ADONAI is trustworthy to all who fall, lifting up all who are bent over.

עֵינֵי כֹל אֵלֶיךָ יְשַׂבֵּרוּ, וְאַתָּה נוֹתֵן לָהֶם אֶת אָכְלָם בְּעִתּוֹ:

Einei chol eilecha yisabeiru, veAta notein lahem et achlam be'ito.

The eyes of all turn to You expectantly, You give bread in its time, to all who eat.

פּוֹתֵחַ אֶת יָדֶךָ, וּמַשְׂבִּיעַ לְכָל חַי רָצוֹן:

Potei-ach et yadecha, umasbiya lechol chai ratzon.

You open up Your hand, satisfying the desires of all life.

צַדִּיק יהוה בְּכָל דְּרָכָיו, וְחָסִיד בְּכָל מַעֲשָׂיו:

Tzadik ADONAI bechol derachav, vechasiyd bechol ma-asav.

All of ADONAI's paths are righteous, pious in all deeds/mysteries.

Tefilat HaLev - Shabbat/Festivals — שבת/חג — תפלת הלב

קָרוֹב יהוה לְכָל קֹרְאָיו, לְכָל אֲשֶׁר יִקְרָאֻהוּ בֶאֱמֶת:

Karov ADONAI lechol korav, lechol asher yikra-uhu ve-emet.

ADONAI is close to all who call out, to all who call out with truth.

רְצוֹן יְרֵאָיו יַעֲשֶׂה, וְאֶת שַׁוְעָתָם יִשְׁמַע וְיוֹשִׁיעֵם:

Retzon yerei-av ya-aseh, ve-et shavatam yishma veyoshi-eim.

[ADONAI's] desires are done by those who seek/perceive; those who cry out are heard and redeemed.

שׁוֹמֵר יהוה אֶת כָּל אֹהֲבָיו, וְאֵת כָּל הָרְשָׁעִים יַשְׁמִיד:

Shomeir ADONAI et kol ohavav, ve-et kol haresha-iym yashmiyd.

ADONAI guards all who love, and destroys all wickedness.

תְּהִלַּת יהוה יְדַבֶּר פִּי, וִיבָרֵךְ כָּל בָּשָׂר שֵׁם קָדְשׁוֹ, לְעוֹלָם וָעֶד:

Tehilat ADONAI yedabeir pi, viyvarech kol basar sheim kodsho, le'olam va-ed.

My mouth speaks Your praise; let all who live acknowledge Your holy name, through all time and space.

וַאֲנַחְנוּ נְבָרֵךְ יָהּ, מֵעַתָּה וְעַד עוֹלָם, הַלְלוּיָהּ:

Va-anachnu nevarech Yahh, mei-atah ve'ad olam. HalleluYahh.

We acknowledge YAHH, from here and now and to all time and space, HalleluYahh.

Ashrei is a prayer that is traditionally recited at least three times daily in Jewish prayers during each of the three daily prayer services. The prayer is composed primarily of Psalm 145 in its entirety, with a verse each from Psalms 84 and 144 added to the beginning, and a verse from Psalm 115 added to the end. The first two verses that are added both start with the Hebrew word "ashrei" (translating to "happy", "joyous" or "praiseworthy"), hence the prayer's name.

Tefilat HaLev - Shabbat/Festivals שבת/חג - **תפלת הלב**

מִזְמוֹר לְדָוִד - Mizmor leDavid - Psalm 29

מִזְמוֹר לְדָוִד, הָבוּ לַיהוה בְּנֵי אֵלִים הָבוּ לַיהוה כָּבוֹד וָעֹז: הָבוּ לַיהוה כְּבוֹד שְׁמוֹ הִשְׁתַּחֲווּ לַיהוה בְּהַדְרַת קֹדֶשׁ:

Mizmor leDavid, Havu lAdonai benei eiliym, havu lAdonai kavod va'oz. Havu lAdonai kevod shemo, hishtachavu lAdonai behadrat kodesh.
A psalm of David. Children of the mighty, speak to Adonai's glory. Speak to Adonai's power. Speak to Adonai's glorious Name. Speak to Adonai's beauty and holiness.

קוֹל יהוה עַל הַמָּיִם אֵל הַכָּבוֹד הִרְעִים יהוה עַל מַיִם רַבִּים:

Kol Adonai al hamayim, el hakavod hir'iym, Adonai al mayim rabiym.
The voice of Adonai is on the waters. The glory of God is thundering. Adonai is on the great waters.

קוֹל יהוה בַּכֹּחַ קוֹל יהוה בֶּהָדָר: קוֹל יהוה שֹׁבֵר אֲרָזִים וַיְשַׁבֵּר יהוה אֶת אַרְזֵי הַלְּבָנוֹן,

Kol Adonai bako-ah, kol Adonai behadar. Kol Adonai shoveir araziym vayshabeir Adonai et arzei halvanon.
The voice of Adonai is powerful. The voice of Adonai is beautiful. The voice of Adonai breaks the cedar trees. Adonai breaks the cedars of Lebanon.

Tefilat HaLev - Shabbat/Festivals — שבת/חג

וַיַּרְקִידֵם כְּמוֹ עֵגֶל, לְבָנוֹן וְשִׂרְיוֹן כְּמוֹ בֶן רְאֵמִים,

Vayarkid**eim** ke**mo ei**gel, leva**non** vesir**yon** ke**mo** ven re-e**miym**.

God causes Lebanon to jump like a young cow and Sirion like a young wild animal.

קוֹל יהוה חֹצֵב לַהֲבוֹת אֵשׁ, קוֹל יהוה יָחִיל מִדְבָּר, יָחִיל יהוה מִדְבַּר קָדֵשׁ: קוֹל יהוה יְחוֹלֵל אַיָּלוֹת

Kol Ado**nai** chot**zeiv** laha**vot** eish, kol Ado**nai** ya**chiyl** mid**bar**, ya**chiyl** Ado**nai** mid**bar** ka**deish**. Kol Ado**nai** yecho**leil** aya**lot**.

The voice of Adonai makes fire in the sky. The voice of Adonai makes the desert move, Adonai makes the desert of Kadesh move. The voice of Adonai blows strongly on the trees,

וַיֶּחֱשֹׂף יְעָרוֹת וּבְהֵיכָלוֹ כֻּלּוֹ אֹמֵר כָּבוֹד:

Vayeche**sof** ye'a**rot**, uvheicha**lo** ku**lo** o**meir** ka**vod**.

and blows everything from the forest. While in God's Temple, everyone speaks respectfully.

יהוה לַמַּבּוּל יָשָׁב וַיֵּשֶׁב יהוה מֶלֶךְ לְעוֹלָם: יהוה עֹז לְעַמּוֹ יִתֵּן יהוה יְבָרֵךְ אֶת עַמּוֹ בַשָּׁלוֹם:

Ado**nai** lama**bul** ya**shav**, vayei**shev** Ado**nai** Me**lech** le'o**lam**. Ado**nai** oz le'a**mo** yi**tein**, Ado**nai** yeva**reich** et a**mo** vasha**lom**.

Adonai was sovereign at the time of the Flood. Adonai will always be sovereign. Adonai will give strength to God's people. Adonai will give God's people Shalom.

Tefilat HaLev - Shabbat/Festivals — שבת/חג - תפלת הלב

Returning the Torah to the Ark — חוזרת התורה

If you are comfortable doing so, please rise as we open the ark for returning the Torah

עֵץ חַיִּים הִיא לַמַּחֲזִיקִים בָּהּ,
וְתוֹמְכֶיהָ מְאֻשָּׁר. דְּרָכֶיהָ דַרְכֵי נֹעַם,
וְכָל נְתִיבוֹתֶיהָ שָׁלוֹם.

Eitz cha**yim** hi lamachazi**kiym** bahh,
vetom**che**-ah me-u**shar**. Dera**che**-ah
dar**chei no**-am, ve**chol** netivo**te**-ah
sha**lom**.

It is a tree of life to those who hold it fast, and all who cling to it find happiness.
Its ways are ways of pleasantness, and all its paths are peace.

הֲשִׁיבֵנוּ יהוה, אֵלֶיךָ וְנָשׁוּבָה, חַדֵּשׁ יָמֵינוּ כְּקֶדֶם.

Hashi**vei**nu Ado**nai**, ei**le**cha vena**shu**va, cha**deish** ya**mei**nu ke**ke**dem.

Help us to return to You, Adonai; then we will return.
Renew our days as in the past.

(The Ark is closed -- Please be seated)

Tefilat HaLev - Shabbat/Festivals - שבת/חג - תפלת הלב

SERMON

Ein kEiloheinu, Ein kAdoneinu, Ein keMalkeinu, Ein kemoshi'einu	אֵין כֵּאלֹהֵינוּ, אֵין כַּאדוֹנֵינוּ, אֵין כְּמַלְכֵּנוּ, אֵין כְּמוֹשִׁיעֵנוּ.
Mi chEiloheinu, Mi chAdoneinu, Mi cheMalkeinu, Mi chemoshi'einu	מִי כֵאלֹהֵינוּ, מִי כַאדוֹנֵינוּ, מִי כְמַלְכֵּנוּ, מִי כְמוֹשִׁיעֵנוּ.
Nodeh lEiloheinu, Nodeh lAdoneinu, Nodeh leMalkeinu, Nodeh lemoshi'einu	נוֹדֶה לֵאלֹהֵינוּ, נוֹדֶה לַאדוֹנֵינוּ, נוֹדֶה לְמַלְכֵּנוּ, נוֹדֶה לְמוֹשִׁיעֵנוּ.
Baruch Eiloheinu, Baruch Adoneinu, Baruch Malkeinu, Baruch moshi'einu	בָּרוּךְ אֱלֹהֵינוּ, בָּרוּךְ אֲדוֹנֵינוּ, בָּרוּךְ מַלְכֵּנוּ, בָּרוּךְ מוֹשִׁיעֵנוּ.
Ata Hu Eiloheinu, Ata Hu Adoneinu, Ata Hu Malkeinu, Ata Hu moshi'einu	אַתָּה הוּא אֱלֹהֵינוּ, אַתָּה הוּא אֲדוֹנֵינוּ, אַתָּה הוּא מַלְכֵּנוּ, אַתָּה הוּא מוֹשִׁיעֵנוּ.

This acrostic contains a message to those who might need to know that the end (of the service) is coming. The lively melodies help arouse those who might have become drowsy during any prior part of the service.

Tefilat HaLev - Shabbat/Festivals שבת/חג - תפלת הלב

In Ladino: (based on medieval Spanish, blended with Hebrew, the language of the Sephardic Jews)

Non como muestro Dio,   Non como muestro Señor,
Non como muestro Rey,   Non como muestro Salvador
Quien como muestro Dio,   Quien como muestro Señor,
Quien como muestro Rey,   Quien como muestro Salvador
Loaremos a muestro Dio,   Loaremos a muestro Señor,
Loaremos a muestro Rey,   Loaremos a muestro Salvador
Bendicho muestro Dio,   Bendicho muestro Señor,
Bendicho muestro Rey,   Bendicho muestro Salvador
Tu el muestro Dio,   Tu el muestro Señor,
Tu el muestro Rey,   Tu el muestro Salvador

There is none like our God!
There is none like our [Source of] Connection!
There is none like our Sovereign!
There is none like the One [who restores us]!
    Who is like our God?
    Who is like our [Source of] Connection?
    Who is like our Sovereign?
    Who is like the One [who restores us]?
We thank our God!
We thank our [Source of] Connection!
We thank our Sovereign!
We thank the One [who restores us]!
    Blessings flow from our God!
    Blessings flow from our [Source of] Connection!
    Blessings flow from our Sovereign!
    Blessings flow from the One [who restores us]!
You are our God!
You are our [Source of] Connection!
You are our Sovereign!
You are the One [who restores us]!

Tefilat HaLev - Shabbat/Festivals – שבת/חג – תפלת הלב

[The ARK is OPENED]

*If you are comfortable doing so,
please rise as we open the ark for the Aleinu*

Aleinu / Adoration - It Is Up to Us — עָלֵינוּ

עָלֵינוּ לְשַׁבֵּחַ לַאֲדוֹן הַכֹּל, לָתֵת גְּדֻלָּה לְיוֹצֵר
בְּרֵאשִׁית, שֶׁלֹּא עָשָׂנוּ עִם גּוֹיֵי הָאֲרָצוֹת, וְלֹא
שָׂמָנוּ עִם מִשְׁפְּחוֹת הָאֲדָמָה,
שֶׁלֹּא שָׂם חֶלְקֵנוּ עִמָּהֶם, וְגֹרָלֵנוּ עִם כָּל הָעוֹלָם
וַאֲנַחְנוּ כּוֹרְעִים וּמִשְׁתַּחֲוִים וּמוֹדִים,
לִפְנֵי מֶלֶךְ, מַלְכֵי הַמְּלָכִים, הַקָּדוֹשׁ בָּרוּךְ הוּא.

Aleinu leshabei-ach la-adon hakol, lateit gedulah
leyotzeir bereishiyt, shelo asanu iym goyei
ha-aratzot, velo samanu iym mishpechot ha-adamah,
shelo sam chelkeinu imahem, vegoraleinu iym kol
ha'olam.

Va-anachnu kor'iym umishtachaviym umodiym.
Lifnei Melech, malchei hamlachiym, haKadosh
Baruch Hu.

It is up to us to praise the Source of all, to give due
greatness to the One who created at the very beginning,
who gave us a purpose among the nations of the earth,
sending us among the families of the earth, giving us a
Divine assignment, working with all of the world.

Therefore, we bend our knees, bow, approach
and give thanks before the Ultimate Sovereign, The
Holy One, the Source of Blessing.

Tefilat HaLev - Shabbat/Festivals — שבת/חג - תפלת הלב

שֶׁהוּא נוֹטֶה שָׁמַיִם וְיֹסֵד אָרֶץ, וּמוֹשַׁב יְקָרוֹ
בַּשָּׁמַיִם מִמַּעַל, וּשְׁכִינַת עֻזּוֹ בְּגָבְהֵי מְרוֹמִים,
הוּא אֱלֹהֵינוּ אֵין עוֹד. אֱמֶת מַלְכֵּנוּ אֶפֶס זוּלָתוֹ,
כַּכָּתוּב בְּתוֹרָתוֹ: וְיָדַעְתָּ הַיּוֹם וַהֲשֵׁבֹתָ אֶל
לְבָבֶךָ, כִּי יהוה הוּא הָאֱלֹהִים בַּשָּׁמַיִם מִמַּעַל,
וְעַל הָאָרֶץ מִתָּחַת, אֵין עוֹד:

Shehu noteh shamayim ve'yoseid aretz, umoshav yekaro bashamayim mima-al, uShchinat uzo begavhei meromiym, Hu Eloheinu ein od. Emet malkeinu efes zulato, kakatuv betorato: ve'yadata hayom vehasheivota el le'vavecha, ki Adonai hu HaElohiym bashamayim mima-al, ve'al ha-aretz mitachat, ein od.

For God inclined the Heavens and established the earth, placing Divine Essence in the Heavens above; And God's Presence is a source of courage to the loftiest heights, Adonai is our God, there is nothing else. Truth is God's reign, without bounds. As it is written in Torah: "And you will know it today and return it to your heart, for Adonai is the expansive greatness in the Heavens above and on the earth below, there is nothing else.

(Ark is closed -- Please be seated)

Some day we will get it that we are all one,
that everything is God, everything is unified,
and that the more we fractionate those things,
the more we divide our own selves.

170

Tefilat HaLev - Shabbat/Festivals – שבת/חג – תפלת הלב

Let us adore the ever living God,
and render praise unto You,
who spread out the heavens and established the earth,
whose glory is revealed in the heavens above,
and whose greatness is manifest throughout the world.
You are our God, there is none else.
We bow the head in reverence and worship
HaKadosh Baruch Hu, the Holy One, Praised be God.
*Va-anachnu koriym umishtachaviym umodiym lifnei Melech
malchei hamlachiym, HaKadosh Baruch Hu,*
the Holy One, Praised be God. Amen.

May the time not be distant, O God, when Your name will be worshipped in all the earth, when unbelief will disappear and error be no more.

Fervently we pray that the day may come when all will turn to You in love, when corruption and evil will give way to integrity and goodness, when superstition will no longer enslave the mind, nor idolatry blind the eye, when all who dwell on earth will know that You alone are God. O may all, created in Your image, become one in spirit and one in friendship, forever united in Your service. Then will Your rule be established on earth, and the word of Your prophet fulfilled: the Eternal God will reign for ever and ever.

וְנֶאֱמַר, וְהָיָה יהוה לְמֶלֶךְ עַל כָּל הָאָרֶץ, בַּיּוֹם
הַהוּא יִהְיֶה יהוה אֶחָד, וּשְׁמוֹ אֶחָד:

Vene-emar, vehaya Adonai lemelech al kol ha-aretz, bayom hahu yiye Adonai echad, ushemo echad.

On that day, O God, You will be One and Your Name will be One.

171

Tefilat HaLev - Shabbat/Festivals   שבת/חג – תפלת הלב

✡ Birth is a beginning and death a destination.
And life is a journey:
   From childhood to maturity;
From innocence to awareness;
   From foolishness to discretion;
And then, perhaps, to wisdom
   And, often, back again;
From health to sickness and back,
we pray, to health again;
From offense to forgiveness, From loneliness to love,
From joy to gratitude, From pain to compassion
And grief to understanding- From fear to faith;
From defeat to defeat to defeat-
Until- looking backward or ahead,
We see that victory lies
Not at some high place along the way,
But in having made the journey, stage by stage,
   A sacred pilgrimage
   Birth is a beginning   And death a destination
   And life is a journey,   A sacred pilgrimage-
To life everlasting.

❀ When I die, please give what's left of me away
to children and the old waiting to die.
If you need to cry, cry for the one walking beside you.
When you need me, put your arms around anyone;
give them what you seek to give to me.
Look for me in those I've known or loved.
You can love me best by living life
by touching others with kindness and compassion.
You can love me best
by letting go of children that need to be free.
Love doesn't die, only people do.
So, when all that's left of me is love,
please, please, give me away.

Tefilat HaLev - Shabbat/Festivals   שבת/חג – תפלת הלב

🔔 I thought of you today, with love in my heart,
But that is nothing new.
I thought about you yesterday,
and the days before that as well.
Often I think of you in silence,
sometimes softly mouthing your name.
I still have memories and pictures, keepsakes all.
I have you in my heart.

🌴 In nature and life, God's eternal hand is felt.
When tears fill our eyes, when grief is overflowing,
it is easy to lose sight of God's Divine plan.
Our heads accept that growth and decay, life and death,
all cycles, reveal a larger purpose.
God supports us in the struggles of life,
and is the source of our hope, especially in death.
God is there for me; I shall not despair.
In God's hands are the souls of all the living
and the spirits of all flesh.
Under God's protection we abide,
and by God's love are we comforted.
O Life of our life, Soul of our soul,
cause Your light to shine into our hearts,
and fill our spirits with abiding trust in You.

🕊 Shall I wither and fall like an autumn leaf,
in deep sorrow, in painful grief?
How to continue, how to be strong?
Will anything ever again sing life's sweet song?
Grief's bitter tight sadness consumes me,
I feel the winter storm on a vast angry sea.
How can I fill my heart with hope's lovely flower?
With the love for you, still there, bringing its power.

Tefilat HaLev - Shabbat/Festivals   שבת/חג – תפלת הלב

❁ Sometimes a warm memory sheds light in the dark
And eases the pain like the song of a bird,
flitting away on silent wings. I'm alone.
I awake each morning to start a new day,
yet the pain still lingers in all that I do.
Hours pass, thoughts of you flicker and throb.
I want to call you and just hear your voice
Then I remember you are gone; my heart cries.
I want to see you again, to tell you goodbye,
To say I love you, and that I always will.
And now all my memories of you are so dear
Who now can hear me when I need to cry?
It so hard to tell you "goodbye."   I miss you.

✡ For some of us, we say Kaddish
for someone close to us that we remember,
For some of us, we say Kaddish for someone whose life
touched us in some important way,
whether we knew them in life or not.
For all whom we seek to remember and acknowledge,
we light this prayer as individuals together.
We seek to feel our grief, acknowledge our hurt,
hearing the voices of others on their similar
and unique journey.
May the souls for whom we recite Kaddish
shine in our hearts and in our lives.

🔔 We try to reconcile all the yous that you ever were.
The you I wanted, the you who was there when I needed
you, the you who understood and the you who didn't.
None of us live life with one integrated self, that meets the
world, rather a colection of selves. When someone dies,
all their selves integrate into the soul that transcends, the
essence of who we are, beyond the different faces we wear
throughout our lives.
In the Kaddish, we remember them all.

Tefilat HaLev - Shabbat/Festivals　שבת/חג - תפלת הלב

🕊 We all decide: will grief destroy me or focus me. Was the relationship all for nothing since it ended in death? Or can we recognize that in our own way, the deep meaning within each moment kept us from recognizing it at the time. So we just lived, just took life and its treasures for granted. There was sacredness then, but we see it now in our sense of being alone. It was everything, it was the why of life, every event and precious moment of it. The answer to the mystery of existence is the love shared, sometimes so imperfectly. Our loss wakes us to the sanctity and holiness, the deeper beauty of it. Yet the ache is always there, but one day not the emptiness, because to nurture the emptiness, to take refuge in it, is to disrespect the gift of life.

🌴 The *yahrzeit* of a loved one's death is particularly significant. For the first one, we see that we have done something we thought was impossible a few months earlier. We survived an entire year without someone who was as important to us as life itself. Each year after that, we are reminded of that feeling of the first *yahrzeit*.

⌛ We say Kaddish as a community to bear witness to grief, to see that the burden of loss is not placed solely upon the bereaved, with the rest of us averting our eyes, waiting for those in mourning to stop being sad, to let go, to move on, to cheer up. By saying Kaddish as a community, supporting those who grieve and mourn, we help and support them, rather than simply telling them that they need help.

📖 The days are for the living; the dead are left behind. It is disconcerting to discover how everything still continues. The sun rises and sets, the flowers bloom, the birds sing, the stars cintinue as before. We grieve, and so we remember.

Tefilat HaLev – Shabbat/Festivals — שבת/חג – תפלת הלב

Mourner's Kaddish — קדיש יתום

We now ask those of you who are in mourning or who are observing the *Yahrzeit* of a loved one to stand and let us hear and share their names with us…. Let us support you through the first paragraph and then rise with you. In this way we can link our memories with yours in the hope that we will thus draw strength and comfort from each other. Together we praise God's name.

יִתְגַּדַּל וְיִתְקַדַּשׁ שְׁמֵהּ רַבָּא. בְּעָלְמָא דִּי בְרָא כִרְעוּתֵיהּ, וְיַמְלִיךְ מַלְכוּתֵיהּ בְּחַיֵּיכוֹן וּבְיוֹמֵיכוֹן וּבְחַיֵּי דְכָל בֵּית יִשְׂרָאֵל. בַּעֲגָלָא וּבִזְמַן קָרִיב וְאִמְרוּ אָמֵן:

> On Shabbat Shuvah, drop the italicized words and say the bracketed gray.

Yitgadal veyitkadash shimei raba be'alma di vra chirutei, veyamlich malchutei bechayeichon uveyomeichon uvchayei dechol beit Yisra-eil, ba-agala, uvizman kariv, ve-imru: Amein.

יְהֵא שְׁמֵהּ רַבָּא מְבָרַךְ לְעָלַם וּלְעָלְמֵי עָלְמַיָּא:

Yehei shmei raba mevarach le'alam ul'almei almaya.

יִתְבָּרַךְ וְיִשְׁתַּבַּח וְיִתְפָּאַר וְיִתְרוֹמַם וְיִתְנַשֵּׂא וְיִתְהַדָּר וְיִתְעַלֶּה וְיִתְהַלָּל שְׁמֵהּ דְּקֻדְשָׁא בְּרִיךְ הוּא לְעֵלָּא מִן כָּל [לְעֵלָּא מִכָּל] בִּרְכָתָא וְשִׁירָתָא תֻּשְׁבְּחָתָא וְנֶחָמָתָא, דַּאֲמִירָן בְּעָלְמָא, וְאִמְרוּ אָמֵן:

Yitbarach, veyishtabach, veyitpa-ar, veyitromam, veyitnasei, veyit-hadar, veyit-aleh, veyit-halal shemei dekudsha, brich hu. Le'eila *min kol* [le'eila mikol] birchata veshirata, tushbechata venechemata da-amiran be'alma, ve-imru: Amein.

Tefilat HaLev - Shabbat/Festivals — שבת/חג - תפלת הלב

God's gloriousness is to be extolled, God's great Name to be hallowed in the world whose creation God willed. And may God's reign be in our day, during our life, and the life of all Israel, let us say: Amen.
Let God's great Name be praised forever and ever.
Let the Name of the Holy One, the Blessing One, be glorified, exalted, and honored, though God is beyond all the praises, songs, and adorations that we can utter, and let us say: Amen.

יְהֵא שְׁלָמָא רַבָּא מִן שְׁמַיָּא, וְחַיִּים עָלֵינוּ וְעַל כָּל יִשְׂרָאֵל וְאִמְרוּ אָמֵן.

Yehei shlama **raba** min shema**ya**, vecha**yim** alei**nu** ve'**al** kol Yisra-**eil**, ve-imru: a**mein**.

עֹשֶׂה שָׁלוֹם בִּמְרוֹמָיו הוּא יַעֲשֶׂה שָׁלוֹם עָלֵינוּ וְעַל כָּל יִשְׂרָאֵל, (וְעַל כָּל יוֹשְׁבֵי תֵבֵל,) וְאִמְרוּ אָמֵן:

Oseh shalom bimro**mav**, hu ya-**aseh** shalom alei**nu**, ve'**al** kol Yisra-**eil**, (ve'al kol yosh**vei** tey**veil**,) ve-imru: **amein**.

May life and a great peace from the heavens be upon us, Israel and the world, and let us say: Amen
May the One who makes peace in the heavens, make peace for us, Israel and the world, and let us say: Amen

May the Source of peace send peace to all who mourn and comfort to all who are bereaved in our midst, and let us say, Amen.

Tefilat HaLev - Shabbat/Festivals — שבת/חג — תפלת הלב

Adon Olam — אדון עולם

אֲדוֹן עוֹלָם אֲשֶׁר מָלַךְ, בְּטֶרֶם כָּל יְצִיר נִבְרָא. לְעֵת נַעֲשָׂה בְחֶפְצוֹ כֹּל, אֲזַי מֶלֶךְ שְׁמוֹ נִקְרָא.

Adon Olam, asher Malach beterem kol yetziyr nivra.
le'eit na-asah becheftzo kol azai Melech Shemo nikra.
Source of All, who was Sovereign before any forms were created.
At the time of making, it was all through the One's longings
Then, the Name was called out as Sovereign

וְאַחֲרֵי כִּכְלוֹת הַכֹּל, לְבַדּוֹ יִמְלוֹךְ נוֹרָא. וְהוּא הָיָה, וְהוּא הֹוֶה, וְהוּא יִהְיֶה, בְּתִפְאָרָה.

Ve-acharei kichlot hakol levado yimloch nora. VeHu
haya, veHu hoveh veHu yihyeh, betif-ara.
And afterwards, when all is completed,
the One will reign alone through awe
And the One was, and the One is, and the One will be, Splendorous.

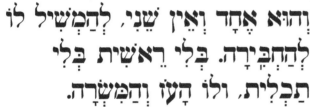 

VeHu echad ve-ein sheini lehamshiyl lo lehachbirah.
beliy reishiyt beli tachliyt veLo ha'oz vehamisrah.
And the One is one, and never changes, the One reigns, fully joined.
Without beginning, without limit, with Energy and Place.

וְהוּא אֵלִי וְחַי גֹּאֲלִי, וְצוּר חֶבְלִי בְּעֵת צָרָה. וְהוּא נִסִּי וּמָנוֹס לִי מְנָת כּוֹסִי בְּיוֹם אֶקְרָא.

VeHu Eiliy vechai go-ali vetzur chevliy be'eit tzarah.
VeHu niysiy umanos liy menat kosi beyom ekra.

Tefilat HaLev - Shabbat/Festivals — שבת/חג - תפלת הלב

And the One is my Source, redeeming my life, a Rock in my suffering when I am distressed. And the One tempers me and is my refuge, the portion in my cup on the day I am called.

בְּיָדוֹ אַפְקִיד רוּחִי, בְּעֵת אִישַׁן וְאָעִירָה.
וְעִם רוּחִי גְוִיָּתִי, יהוה לִי וְלֹא אִירָא.

Beyado afkiyd ruchiy be'eit iyshan ve-a'iyrah. Ve'im ruchiy geviyatiy Adonai liy velo iyra.

Into the One's hand I entrust my Soul at the time of sleep and arising. And with my Soul, my body, Adonai is for me, I will not fear.

RABBINIC PRAYER

Tefilat Haderech

May we be blessed as we go on our way.
May we be guided in peace.
May we be blessed with health and joy.
May this be our blessing, Amen.

Amen, Amen, may this be our blessing, Amen.

May we be sheltered by the wings of peace.
May we be kept in safety and in love.
May grace and compassion find their way to every soul.
May this be our blessing, Amen.

Amen, Amen, may this be our blessing, Amen.

© Debbie Friedman

SHABBAT SHALOM

Please join us at the *Kiddush/Motzie* table for *Kiddush* and *Motzie*.
Our tradition invites us to remember those in need through Tzedakah.

Tefilat HaLev - Shabbat/Festivals — שבת/חג - תפלת הלב

קידוש ערב שבת

Evening Kiddush

בָּרוּךְ אַתָּה יהוה אֱלֹהֵינוּ מֶלֶךְ הָעוֹלָם, בּוֹרֵא פְּרִי הַגָּפֶן. בָּרוּךְ אַתָּה יהוה אֱלֹהֵינוּ מֶלֶךְ הָעוֹלָם, אֲשֶׁר קִדְּשָׁנוּ בְּמִצְוֹתָיו וְרָצָה בָנוּ, וְשַׁבַּת קָדְשׁוֹ בְּאַהֲבָה וּבְרָצוֹן הִנְחִילָנוּ זִכָּרוֹן לְמַעֲשֵׂה בְרֵאשִׁית, כִּי הוּא יוֹם תְּחִלָּה לְמִקְרָאֵי קֹדֶשׁ, זֵכֶר לִיצִיאַת מִצְרָיִם, כִּי בָנוּ בָחַרְתָּ וְאוֹתָנוּ קִדַּשְׁתָּ עִם (מִ-)כָּל הָעַמִּים, וְשַׁבַּת קָדְשְׁךָ בְּאַהֲבָה וּבְרָצוֹן הִנְחַלְתָּנוּ. בָּרוּךְ אַתָּה יהוה, מְקַדֵּשׁ הַשַּׁבָּת.

Baruch **A**ta Ado**nai**, Elo**hei**nu **Me**lech ha-o**lam, bo**rei, **pe**ri ha**ga**fen. A**mein**.
Baruch **A**ta Ado**nai**, Elo**hei**nu **Me**lech ha-o**lam** a**sher** kid**sha**nu bemitzvo**tav** ve**ra**tza **va**nu, veSha**bat** kod**sho** b'aha**va** uvra**tzon** hinchi**la**nu zika**ron** lema-a**sei** verei**shiyt**, ki hu yom techi**la** lemikra-ei **ko**desh, **zei**cher letzi-**at** Mitz**ra**yim. Ki **va**nu va**char**ta ve-o**ta**nu ki**dash**ta im (mi-)kol ha-**amiym**, VeSha**bat** kodshe**cha**, be-aha**va** uvra**tzon**, hinchal**ta**nu.
Baruch **A**ta Ado**nai** meka**deish** haSha**bat**.

A Source of blessings is Adonai our God, Sovereign of time and space, Creator of the fruit of the vine.
A Source of blessings is Adonai our God, Sovereign of time and space, who makes us special with Mitzvot and delights in us. In God's love and favor, God made Shabbat our heritage, as a reminder of the mystery of creation. It is first among our sacred days, and a remembrance of the Exodus from Egypt. For You have chosen us among all peoples, and in love and favor have given us the Shabbat as a sacred inheritance.
A Source of Blessing is Adonai, Who makes Shabbat holy.

Tefilat HaLev - Shabbat/Festivals — שבת/חג — תפלת הלב

Daytime Kiddush — קידוש יום שבת

וְשָׁמְרוּ בְנֵי יִשְׂרָאֵל אֶת הַשַּׁבָּת, לַעֲשׂוֹת אֶת הַשַּׁבָּת לְדֹרֹתָם בְּרִית עוֹלָם: בֵּינִי וּבֵין בְּנֵי יִשְׂרָאֵל אוֹת הִיא לְעוֹלָם, כִּי שֵׁשֶׁת יָמִים עָשָׂה יהוה אֶת הַשָּׁמַיִם וְאֶת הָאָרֶץ, וּבַיּוֹם הַשְּׁבִיעִי שָׁבַת וַיִּנָּפַשׁ.

Veshamru venei Yisra-eil, et haShabat, La-asot et haShabat ledorotam, brit olam. Beini uvein benei Yisra-eil, ot hi, le-olam. Ki sheishet yamiym asa Adonai, et hashamayim ve-et ha-aretz Uvayom hashvi'i shavat vayinafash.

And the children of Israel protect the Shabbat, doing Shabbat for their generations, a covenant forever. Between Me and the children of Israel, it is a sign forever, for in six days, Adonai made the heavens and the earth and on the seventh day God rested and gave the world Soul.

עַל כֵּן, בֵּרַךְ יהוה אֶת יוֹם הַשַּׁבָּת וַיְקַדְּשֵׁהוּ.

Al kein, beirach Adonai et yom haShabat vaykadsheihu.

Therefore Adonai blessed the seventh day and made it holy.

סַבְרִי חֲבֵרִי?

Savrai cheverai?

Is the [wine/juice] suitable [for Kiddush] my friends?

בָּרוּךְ אַתָּה יהוה אֱלֹהֵינוּ מֶלֶךְ הָעוֹלָם, בּוֹרֵא פְּרִי הַגָּפֶן.

Baruch Ata Adonai, Eloheinu Melech ha-olam, borei, peri hagafen.

A Source of blessings is Adonai our God, Sovereign of time and space, Creator of the fruit of the vine.

Tefilat HaLev - Shabbat/Festivals שבת/חג – תפלת הלב

Motzie/Challah מוציא

הַמּוֹצִיא לֶחֶם מִן הָאָרֶץ.

Hamotzi lechem min ha-**a**retz.
We give thanks to God for bread.
Our voices rise in song together,
as our joyful prayer is said:

בָּרוּךְ אַתָּה יהוה אֱלֹהֵינוּ מֶלֶךְ הָעוֹלָם, הַמּוֹצִיא לֶחֶם מִן הָאָרֶץ.

Baruch **A**ta Adonai Elo**hei**nu **Me**lech ha-o**lam**, Hamo**tzi le**chem min ha-**a**retz.
A Source of blessings is Adonai our God, Sovereign of time and space, Who brings bread from the earth.

182

Tefilat HaLev - Shabbat/Festivals - שבת/חג - תפלת הלב

Intermediate Amidah Prayers for a weekday:

אַתָּה חוֹנֵן לְאָדָם דַּעַת, וּמְלַמֵּד לֶאֱנוֹשׁ בִּינָה. חָנֵּנוּ מֵאִתְּךָ דֵּעָה, בִּינָה וְהַשְׂכֵּל.
בָּרוּךְ אַתָּה יהוה, חוֹנֵן הַדָּעַת.

**Ata chonein le-adam da'at, umlameid le-enosh bina.
Chaneinu mei-itcha dei'a, bina vehaskeil.
Baruch Ata Adonai, chonein hada-at.**

Your graciousness to humankind is in knowledge, and in teaching wisdom to individuals. Be gracious to us, O Source, with knowledge, wisdom, and understanding.
Blessings are You, Adonai, who graciously bestows knowledge.

הֲשִׁיבֵנוּ אָבִינוּ לְתוֹרָתֶךָ, וְקָרְבֵנוּ מַלְכֵּנוּ לַעֲבוֹדָתֶךָ, וְהַחֲזִירֵנוּ בִּתְשׁוּבָה שְׁלֵמָה לְפָנֶיךָ.
בָּרוּךְ אַתָּה יהוה, הָרוֹצֶה בִּתְשׁוּבָה.

**Hashiveinu avinu letoratecha, vekarveinu malkeinu la'avodatecha, vehachazireinu bitshuva shleima lefanecha.
Baruch Ata Adonai, harotzeh bitshuvah.**

Return us, our Creator, to Your Torah, draw us near, O Sovereign, to Your service;
restore us to Your presence in healing repentence.
Blessings are You, Adonai, who seeks our returning.

Tefilat HaLev - Shabbat/Festivals — שבת/חג - תפלת הלב

סְלַח לָנוּ, אָבִינוּ, כִּי חָטָאנוּ, מְחַל לָנוּ, מַלְכֵּנוּ כִּי פָשָׁעְנוּ, כִּי מוֹחֵל וְסוֹלֵחַ אָתָּה.
בָּרוּךְ אַתָּה יהוה, חַנּוּן הַמַּרְבֶּה לִסְלֹחַ.

Slach **lanu**, **avinu**, ki cha**tanu**, me**chal lanu** mal**keinu** ki pasha'nu, ki mo**cheil** veso**lei**-ach **A**ta.
Baruch Ata Adonai, cha**nun** hamar**beh** lis**lo**-ach.
Forgive us, our Creator, for we have sinned; pardon us, O Sovereign, for we have transgressed;
for Your essence is pardoning and forgiving.
Blessings are You, Adonai, who forgives all graciously.

רְאֵה בְעָנְיֵנוּ, וְרִיבָה רִיבֵנוּ, וּגְאָלֵנוּ מְהֵרָה לְמַעַן שְׁמֶךָ, כִּי גּוֹאֵל חָזָק אָתָּה.
בָּרוּךְ אַתָּה יהוה, גּוֹאֵל יִשְׂרָאֵל.

Re-**ei** ve'on**yei**nu, veriva ri**vei**nu, vego-a**lei**nu mehei**ra** lema'an she**me**cha, ki go-**eil** cha**zak A**ta.
Baruch Ata Adonai, go-**eil** Yisra-**eil**.
Look at us in our neediness, as we quarrel and struggle;
free us [from these chains] quickly for the sake of Your essence, for You are a powerful redeemer.
Blessings are You, Adonai, who saves Israel.

רְפָאֵנוּ יהוה, וְנֵרָפֵא, הוֹשִׁיעֵנוּ וְנִוָּשֵׁעָה, וְהַעֲלֵה רְפוּאָה שְׁלֵמָה לְכָל מַכּוֹתֵינוּ.
בָּרוּךְ אַתָּה יהוה, רוֹפֵא חוֹלֵי.

Refa-**ei**nu Ado**nai**, vene**ira**fei, hoshi'**ei**nu venivas**hei**'a,
veha'a**lei** refu-**a** shlei**ma** le**chol** mako**tei**nu
Baruch Ata Adonai, ro**fei** cho**lei**.
Heal us, Adonai, and we will be healed; save us and we will be saved; lift us up for a full and complete healing of all our wounds. [Personal prayers may be added here.]
Blessings are You, Adonai, who heals the sick.

Tefilat HaLev - Shabbat/Festivals – שבת/חג – תפלת הלב

בָּרֵךְ עָלֵינוּ, יהוה אֱלֹהֵינוּ, אֶת הַשָּׁנָה הַזֹּאת וְאֶת כָּל מִינֵי תְבוּאָתָהּ לְטוֹבָה. וְתֵן בְּרָכָה עַל פְּנֵי הָאֲדָמָה, וְשַׂבְּעֵנוּ מִטּוּבֶךָ.
בָּרוּךְ אַתָּה יהוה, מְבָרֵךְ הַשָּׁנִים.

Bareich aleinu, Adonai Eloheinu, et hashana hazot ve-et kol minei tevu-atahh letova. Vetein beracha al penei ha-adama, vesab'einu mituvecha.
Baruch Ata Adonai, mevareich hashaniym.

Adonai, our God, bless this year for us, that its produce bring well-being. And grant blessing upon the face of the earth, for abundance and goodness for all.
Blessings are You, Adonai, who makes bountiful the year.

תְּקַע בְּשׁוֹפָר גָּדוֹל לְחֵרוּתֵנוּ, וְשָׂא נֵס לִפְדּוֹת עֲשׁוּקֵינוּ, וְקוֹל דְּרוֹר יִשָּׁמַע מֵאַרְבַּע כַּנְפוֹת הָאָרֶץ.
בָּרוּךְ אַתָּה יהוה, פּוֹדֶה עֲשׁוּקִים.

Teka beshofar gadol lecheiruteinu, vesa neis lifdot ashukeinu, vekol deror yishama me-arba kanfot ha-aretz.
Baruch Ata Adonai, podeh ashukiym.

Sound the great shofar for our freedom, and lift high the banner liberating the exploited; let the voice of freedom be heard to the four corners of the earth.
Blessings are You, Adonai, who redeems the exploited.

Tefilat HaLev - Shabbat/Festivals שבת/חג – **תפלת הלב**

עַל שׁוֹפְטֵי אֶרֶץ שְׁפוֹךְ רוּחֶךָ, וְהַדְרִיכֵם בְּמִשְׁפְּטֵי
צִדְקֶךָ, וּמְלוֹךְ עָלֵינוּ אַתָּה לְבַדֶּךָ, בְּחֶסֶד וּבְרַחֲמִים.
בָּרוּךְ אַתָּה יהוה, מֶלֶךְ אוֹהֵב צְדָקָה וּמִשְׁפָּט.

Al shof**tei** e**retz** she**foch** ru**che**cha, vehadri**cheim**
bemishpe**tei** tzid**ke**cha, um**loch** a**lei**nu A**ta** leva**de**cha,
be**che**sed uvera**cha**mim.
Baruch Ata Ado**nai**, **Me**lech o**heiv** tze**da**kah umish**pat**.

Pour Your spirit on all who rule the many lands;
guide them that they govern justly.
Then kindness and compassion will rule over us.
Blessings are You, Adonai, sovereign who loves
tzedakah and justice.

וְלָרְשָׁעָה אַל תְּהִי תִקְוָה, וְהַתּוֹעִים אֵלֶיךָ יָשׁוּבוּ,
וּמַלְכוּת זָדוֹן מְהֵרָה תְשַׁבֵּר. תַּקֵּן מַלְכוּתְךָ בְּתוֹכֵנוּ,
בְּקָרוֹב בְּיָמֵינוּ לְעוֹלָם וָעֶד.
בָּרוּךְ אַתָּה יהוה, שֹׁבֵר אֹיְבִים וּמַכְנִיעַ זֵדִים.

Velarash'a al te**hi** tik**va** vehato'**iym** ei**le**cha ya**shu**va,
umal**chut** za**don** mehei**ra** tisha**veir**. Ta**kein** malchut**cha**
beto**chei**nu, beka**rov** beya**mei**nu le'o**lam** va-ed.
Baruch Ata Ado**nai**,
sho**veir** oy**viym** umach**ni**ya' zei**diym**.

May the wicked have no expectations; may the errant
heart return to You; may the dominion of arrogance be
shattered. May Your sovereignty lead us to
righteousness, speedily, in our days, and through all
time and space.
Blessings are You, Adonai,
who uproots evil and humbles the arrogant.

Tefilat HaLev - Shabbat/Festivals – שבת/חג – תפלת הלב

עַל הַצַּדִּיקִים וְעַל הַחֲסִידִים וְעַל גֵּרֵי הַצֶּדֶק וְעָלֵינוּ,
יֶהֱמוּ נָא רַחֲמֶיךָ, יהוה אֱלֹהֵינוּ, וְתֵן שָׂכָר טוֹב לְכָל
הַבּוֹטְחִים בְּשִׁמְךָ בֶּאֱמֶת,
וְשִׂים חֶלְקֵנוּ עִמָּהֶם לְעוֹלָם.
בָּרוּךְ אַתָּה יהוה, מִשְׁעָן וּמִבְטָח לַצַּדִּיקִים.

Al hatzadi**kiym** ve'**al** hachasi**diym** ve'**al** gei**rei** hatze**dek**
ve'a**lei**nu, yehe**mu** na racha**me**cha, Adonai Elo**hei**nu,
ve**tein** sa**char** tov le**chol** habot**chiym** be-shim**cha**
be-e**met**, ve**sim** chel**kei**nu ima**hem** le'**o**lam.
Baruch Ata Adonai, mish'**an** umiv**tach** latzadi**kiym**.

For the righteous, the spiritual, the seekers of justice,
and us, show Your compassion, Adonai our God, and
reward all who sincerely put their faith in you with
goodness; may our portion always be among them.
Blessings are You, Adonai, who sustains the righteous.

שְׁכוֹן, יהוה אֱלֹהֵינוּ, בְּתוֹךְ יְרוּשָׁלַיִם עִירְךָ וִיהִי
שָׁלוֹם בִּשְׁעָרֶיהָ, וְשַׁלְוָה בְּלֵב יוֹשְׁבֶיהָ, וְתוֹרָתְךָ
מִצִּיּוֹן תֵּצֵא, וּדְבָרְךָ מִירוּשָׁלָיִם.
בָּרוּךְ אַתָּה יהוה, בּוֹנֵה יְרוּשָׁלָיִם.

She**chon**, Adonai Elo**hei**nu, be**toch** Yerusha**la**yim
ir**cha** viyhi shalom bish'are-**ah**, vesha**lva** be**leiv**
yoshve-**ah**, vetorat**cha** mitzi**yon** teit**zei**,
udvar**cha** miyrushalayim
Baruch Ata Adonai, bo**neh** Yerusha**la**yim.

Be present, Adonai our God, within Jerusalem, YOur
city; may there be peace in her gates and contentment in
the hearts of all her inhabitants. May Your Torah go
forth from Tzion and Your word from Jerusalem.
Blessings are You, Adonai, who builds Jerusalem.

Tefilat HaLev - Shabbat/Festivals — שבת/חג — תפלת הלב

אֶת צֶמַח צְדָקָה מְהֵרָה תַצְמִיחַ, וְקֶרֶן יְשׁוּעָה תָּרוּם
בִּנְאֻמֶךָ, כִּי לִישׁוּעָתְךָ קִוִּינוּ כָּל הַיּוֹם.
בָּרוּךְ אַתָּה יהוה, מַצְמִיחַ קֶרֶן יְשׁוּעָה.

Et **tze**mach tzeda**ka** mehei**ra** tatz**mi**-ach, ve**ke**ren
yeshu'a ta**rum** kin-u**me**cha,
ki lishu'at**cha** ki**vi**nu kol ha**yom**.
B**a**ruch A**ta** Ado**nai**, matz**mi**-ach **ke**ren yeshu-**ah**.

Cause the plant of righteousness to grow quickly. May the light of Your deliverance shine forth according to Your word; we wait for Your deliverance all the day.

 Blessings are You, Adonai,
who assures our deliverance.

שְׁמַע קוֹלֵנוּ, יהוה אֱלֹהֵינוּ, חוּס וְרַחֵם עָלֵינוּ,
וְתְקַבֵּל בְּרַחֲמִים וּבְרָצוֹן אֶת תְּפִלָּתֵנוּ, כִּי אֵל
שׁוֹמֵעַ תְּפִלּוֹת וְתַחֲנוּנִים אָתָּה.
בָּרוּךְ אַתָּה יהוה, שׁוֹמֵעַ תְּפִלָּה.

Shema ko**lei**nu, Ado**nai** Elo**hei**nu, chus ve ra**cheim**
a**lei**nu, veteka**beil** bera cha**miym** uvra**tzon** et tefila**tei**nu,
ki eil shome'a tefi**lot** vetachanu**niym** **A**ta.
B**a**ruch A**ta** Ado**nai**, sho**mei**ah tefi**lah**.

Hear our voice, Adonai our God. Have pity and compassionate toward us; receive our prayers with compassion, for You are a God who listens to prayer and supplication.

For the remaining prayers in the Amidah, please return to the remainder of the Amidah:
Evening: Page 63
Morning: Page 134
Guided Imagery: Page 75

Tefilat HaLev - Shabbat/Festivals - שבת/חג - תפלת הלב

Hallel הלל

Hallel is recited on holidays and on the semi-festival of the new moon (Rosh Hodesh). Many Jews also recite it on the modern festivals of Yom Ha'atzmaut (Israel Independence Day) and Yom Yerushalayim (Jerusalem Day). Although many scholars and other contemporary Jews approach Jewish liturgical texts from a literary or theological perspective, many traditional Jews use the Talmud as the primary lens through they interpret the Siddur. What are the ideas expressed in Hallel? The Gemara (the Rabbinic debates on the Mishnah) tells us that Hallel includes five major themes (Pesachim 118a):
1. The Exodus from Egypt
2. The splitting of the Reed Sea
3. The giving of the Torah
4. The revival of the dead
5. The difficulties preceding the Messianic Age

Who was the first to recite Hallel? The Gemara suggests that the prayer was originated by the Jews at the Reed Sea, Joshua defeating the kings in Canaan, or Deborah and Barak when they destroyed the army of Sisera (Pesachim 117a). Traditional Jews recite it while standing, perhaps as a second Amidah.

בָּרוּךְ אַתָּה יהוה אֱלֹהֵינוּ מֶלֶךְ הָעוֹלָם, אֲשֶׁר
קִדְּשָׁנוּ בְּמִצְוֹתָיו וְצִוָּנוּ לִקְרֹא אֶת הַהַלֵּל.

Baruch Ata Adonai Elo**he**inu **M**elech haOlam, a**sh**er kid**sh**anu bemitzvo**tav** vetzivanu lik**ro** et haHaleil.

A Source of Blessing are You, Adonai our God, Sovereign of all, who makes us special with mitzvot and instructs us to read out the Hallel.

Tefilat HaLev - Shabbat/Festivals   שבת/חג - תפלת הלב

הַלְלוּיָהּ הַלְלוּ עַבְדֵי יהוה, הַלְלוּ אֶת שֵׁם יהוה:
יְהִי שֵׁם יהוה מְבֹרָךְ מֵעַתָּה וְעַד עוֹלָם:
מִמִּזְרַח שֶׁמֶשׁ עַד מְבוֹאוֹ, מְהֻלָּל שֵׁם יהוה:
רָם עַל כָּל גּוֹיִם יהוה, עַל הַשָּׁמַיִם כְּבוֹדוֹ.
מִי כַּיהוה אֱלֹהֵינוּ הַמַּגְבִּיהִי לָשָׁבֶת:
הַמַּשְׁפִּילִי לִרְאוֹת, בַּשָּׁמַיִם וּבָאָרֶץ.
מְקִימִי מֵעָפָר דָּל, מֵאַשְׁפֹּת יָרִים אֶבְיוֹן:
לְהוֹשִׁיבִי עִם נְדִיבִים, עִם נְדִיבֵי עַמּוֹ.
מוֹשִׁיבִי עֲקֶרֶת הַבַּיִת, אֵם הַבָּנִים שְׂמֵחָה הַלְלוּיָהּ:

Hallelu-Yahh! Praise, O servants of Adonai,
praise the Name of Adonai.
Blessings in the Name of Adonai, from here and now
through all time and space.
> *From the rising of the sun to its going down,*
> *Adonai's Essence is to be praised.*
> *Adonai is high above all nations,*
> *God's glory above the heavens.*

Who is like Adonai, our God, who reaches the heights,
Who is also in the depths, embracing heaven and earth?
> *Adonai raises up the poor out of the dust*
> *and lifts up the needy from the ash heap;*
> *Setting them with princes, with the princes of our people.*

Adonai fills the spiritually barren with comfort,
making them joyful in their efforts. Hallelu-Yahh!

Betzeyt Yisrael / When Israel Went Forth   בצאת ישראל

בְּצֵאת יִשְׂרָאֵל מִמִּצְרָיִם, בֵּית יַעֲקֹב מֵעַם לֹעֵז.
הָיְתָה יְהוּדָה לְקָדְשׁוֹ, יִשְׂרָאֵל מַמְשְׁלוֹתָיו.
הַיָּם רָאָה וַיָּנֹס, הַיַּרְדֵּן יִסֹּב לְאָחוֹר:
הֶהָרִים רָקְדוּ כְאֵילִים, גְּבָעוֹת כִּבְנֵי צֹאן.

Tefilat HaLev - Shabbat/Festivals — שבת/חג — תפלת הלב

Betzeit Yisra-**eil**, miMitz**ra**yim, Beit Ya-**a**kov mey-**am** lo-**eiz**. Hai**ta** Yehu**da** lekod**sho**, Yisra-**eil** mamshelo**tav**. Ha**yam** ra-**ah** vaya**nos**, haYar**dein** yi**sov** le-a**chor**. Heha**riym** rok**du** che-ei**liym** geva-**ot** kiv**nei** tzon.

When Israel went forth out of Egypt,
the house of Jacob from a people of a foreign language;
Judah became God's sanctuary, Israel God's dominion.
The sea saw it, and fled. The Jordan was driven back.
The mountains skipped like rams,
the little hills like lambs.

Ma Lecha Hayam / What is With You, O Sea — מה לך הים

מַה לְּךָ הַיָּם כִּי תָנוּם הַיַּרְדֵּן תִּסֹּב לְאָחוֹר.
הֶהָרִים תִּרְקְדוּ כְאֵילִים, גְּבָעוֹת כִּבְנֵי צֹאן.
מִלִּפְנֵי אָדוֹן חוּלִי אָרֶץ, מִלִּפְנֵי אֱלוֹהַּ יַעֲקֹב.
הַהֹפְכִי הַצּוּר אֲגַם מָיִם, חַלָּמִישׁ לְמַעְיְנוֹ מָיִם:

Ma **le**cha ha**yam** ki ta**nus**, haYar**dein** ti**sov** le-a**chor**. Heha**riym** tirke**du** che-ei**liym** geva-**ot** kiv**nei** tzon.
Milif**nei A**don **chu**li **a**retz, milif**nei** Eh**lo**-ahh Ya-a**kov**.
Hahof**chi** hatzur **a**gam **ma**yim, chala**miysh** lema'**y**no **ma**yim.

What was it, you sea, that you fled?
You Jordan, that you turned back?
You mountains, that you skipped like rams;
you little hills, like lambs?
Tremble, you earth, before Adonai,
before the God of Jacob,
Who turned the rock into a pool of water,
the flint into a spring of waters.

Tefilat HaLev - Shabbat/Festivals – שבת/חג – תפלת הלב

Not to us, Adonai

לֹא לָנוּ יהוה לֹא לָנוּ כִּי לְשִׁמְךָ תֵּן כָּבוֹד, עַל חַסְדְּךָ עַל אֲמִתֶּךָ. לָמָּה יֹאמְרוּ הַגּוֹיִם, אַיֵּה נָא אֱלֹהֵיהֶם. וֵאלֹהֵינוּ בַשָּׁמַיִם כֹּל אֲשֶׁר חָפֵץ עָשָׂה. עֲצַבֵּיהֶם כֶּסֶף וְזָהָב, מַעֲשֵׂה יְדֵי אָדָם. פֶּה לָהֶם וְלֹא יְדַבֵּרוּ, עֵינַיִם לָהֶם וְלֹא יִרְאוּ. אָזְנַיִם לָהֶם וְלֹא יִשְׁמָעוּ, אַף לָהֶם וְלֹא יְרִיחוּן. יְדֵיהֶם וְלֹא יְמִישׁוּן, רַגְלֵיהֶם וְלֹא יְהַלֵּכוּ, לֹא יֶהְגּוּ בִּגְרוֹנָם. כְּמוֹהֶם יִהְיוּ עֹשֵׂיהֶם, כֹּל אֲשֶׁר בֹּטֵחַ בָּהֶם:

יִשְׂרָאֵל בְּטַח בַּיהוה, עֶזְרָם וּמָגִנָּם הוּא. בֵּית אַהֲרֹן בִּטְחוּ בַיהוה, עֶזְרָם וּמָגִנָּם הוּא. יִרְאֵי יהוה בִּטְחוּ בַיהוה, עֶזְרָם וּמָגִנָּם הוּא:

We do not seek glory for us,
Adonai, to Your Name is glory fitting,
for Your loving kindness, and for Your truth's sake.
> Why would other say, 'Where is their God, now?'
> For Adonai is in the heavens and everywhere else,
> as God pleases.

Idols are of silver and gold, the work of human hands.
Having mouths and speaking not.
Having eyes, and seeing not.
> Having ears, and hearing not.
> Having noses, and smelling not.
> With unfeeling hands, and feet that don't walk,
> they can not speak. Those who make them, are like them,
> when they trust in them.

Israel, trust in Adonai!
God is our help and our protection.
House of Aaron, trust in Adonai!
God is our help and our protection.
You who sense Adonai, trust in Adonai!
Adonai is our help and our protection.

Tefilat HaLev - Shabbat/Festivals — שבת/חג - תפלת הלב

Adonai Remembers Us

יהוה זְכָרָנוּ יְבָרֵךְ, יְבָרֵךְ אֶת בֵּית יִשְׂרָאֵל,
יְבָרֵךְ אֶת בֵּית אַהֲרֹן.
יְבָרֵךְ יִרְאֵי יהוה, הַקְּטַנִּים עִם הַגְּדֹלִים.
יֹסֵף יהוה עֲלֵיכֶם, עֲלֵיכֶם וְעַל בְּנֵיכֶם.
בְּרוּכִים אַתֶּם לַיהוה, עֹשֵׂה שָׁמַיִם וָאָרֶץ.
הַשָּׁמַיִם שָׁמַיִם לַיהוה, וְהָאָרֶץ נָתַן לִבְנֵי אָדָם.
לֹא הַמֵּתִים יְהַלְלוּ יָהּ, וְלֹא כָּל יֹרְדֵי דוּמָה.
וַאֲנַחְנוּ נְבָרֵךְ יָהּ, מֵעַתָּה וְעַד עוֹלָם, הַלְלוּיָהּ:

Ve-**anach**nu neva**reich** Yahh, me-**ata** ve-**ad** olam,
Hallelu-**Yahh**.

Adonai remembers us and is a source of blessing to us.
Adonai blesses Israel;
Adonai blesses the house of Aaron.
Adonai blesses those who sense Adonai,
both small and great.
> May Adonai grant you abundance,
> you and your children.
> Blessings come from Adonai,
> who made heaven and earth.
> The heavens are Adonai's;
> and the earth God gives to the children.

The dead cannot praise, nor any who keep their silence;
May we praise God,
from this time forth and forevermore. Hallelu-Yahh!"

Tefilat HaLev - Shabbat/Festivals — שבת/חג — תפלת הלב

I love Adonai

אָהַבְתִּי כִּי יִשְׁמַע יהוה, אֶת קוֹלִי תַּחֲנוּנָי. כִּי הִטָּה אָזְנוֹ לִי וּבְיָמַי אֶקְרָא: אֲפָפוּנִי חֶבְלֵי מָוֶת, וּמְצָרֵי שְׁאוֹל מְצָאוּנִי צָרָה וְיָגוֹן אֶמְצָא. וּבְשֵׁם יהוה אֶקְרָא, אָנָּה יהוה מַלְּטָה נַפְשִׁי. חַנּוּן יהוה וְצַדִּיק, וֵאלֹהֵינוּ מְרַחֵם. שֹׁמֵר פְּתָאִים יהוה דַּלּוֹתִי וְלִי יְהוֹשִׁיעַ. שׁוּבִי נַפְשִׁי לִמְנוּחָיְכִי, כִּי יהוה גָּמַל עָלָיְכִי. כִּי חִלַּצְתָּ נַפְשִׁי מִמָּוֶת אֶת עֵינִי מִן דִּמְעָה, אֶת רַגְלִי מִדֶּחִי. אֶתְהַלֵּךְ לִפְנֵי יהוה, בְּאַרְצוֹת הַחַיִּים. הֶאֱמַנְתִּי כִּי אֲדַבֵּר, אֲנִי עָנִיתִי מְאֹד. אֲנִי אָמַרְתִּי בְחָפְזִי כָּל הָאָדָם כֹּזֵב.

I love Adonai, God listens to my voice,
and my cries for mercy.
God hears me, therefore
I will call to Adonai as long as I live.
>   *The cords of death may surrounded me,*
>   *the pains of Sheol may grab me.*
>   *I have found trouble and sorrow.*

I call on the name of Adonai:
'Adonai, answer me, deliver my soul.'
Adonai is gracious and righteous.
Yes, our God is merciful.
>   *Adonai preserves the simple.*
>   *I was brought low, and God saved me.*
>   *Return to your rest, my soul,*
>   *for Adonai has dealt bountifully with you.*

For You delivered my soul from death,
my eyes from tears,
and my feet from falling.
I will walk before Adonai
in the land of the living.
I believed, therefore I said,
'I was greatly afflicted.'
I said in haste, 'All people are liars.'

Tefilat HaLev - Shabbat/Festivals - שבת/חג

What will I give to Adonai

מָה אָשִׁיב לַיהוה, כָּל תַּגְמוּלוֹהִי עָלָי. כּוֹס יְשׁוּעוֹת אֶשָּׂא,
וּבְשֵׁם יהוה אֶקְרָא. נְדָרַי לַיהוה אֲשַׁלֵּם, נֶגְדָה נָּא לְכָל עַמּוֹ.
יָקָר בְּעֵינֵי יהוה הַמָּוְתָה לַחֲסִידָיו. אָנָּה יהוה כִּי אֲנִי עַבְדֶּךָ
אֲנִי עַבְדְּךָ, בֶּן אֲמָתֶךָ פִּתַּחְתָּ לְמוֹסֵרָי. לְךָ אֶזְבַּח זֶבַח
תּוֹדָה וּבְשֵׁם יהוה אֶקְרָא. נְדָרַי לַיהוה אֲשַׁלֵּם נֶגְדָה נָּא
לְכָל עַמּוֹ. בְּחַצְרוֹת בֵּית יהוה בְּתוֹכֵכִי יְרוּשָׁלָיִם הַלְלוּיָהּ.

What can I give to Adonai
for all God's gifts toward me?
I will take the cup of salvation,
and call on the name of Adonai.
>*I will pay my debts for Adonai,*
>*yes, in the presence of all God's people.*
>*Precious in the sight of Adonai*
>*is the service of God's peoples.*

Adonai, truly I am your servant,
the child of your handmaid.
You have freed me from my chains.
I will offer to you my thanksgiving,
and will call on the name of Adonai.
>*I will pay my debts for Adonai, yes,*
>*in the presence of all God's people,*
>*in the courts of Adonai's house,*
>*in the midst of you, Jerusalem. Halleluyahh!*

Tefilat HaLev - Shabbat/Festivals — שבת/חג - תפלת הלב

Praise Adonai, all you nations!

הַלְלוּ אֶת יהוה, כָּל גּוֹיִם, שַׁבְּחוּהוּ כָּל הָאֻמִּים.
כִּי גָבַר עָלֵינוּ חַסְדּוֹ, וֶאֱמֶת יהוה לְעוֹלָם
הַלְלוּיָהּ:

Hallelu et Adonai, kol goyim, shabchuhu kol ha-umiym
Ki gavar aleinu chasdo, ve-emet Adonai leOlam
Hallelu-**Yahh**.
Praise Adonai, all you nations!
Extol God, all you peoples!
For God's loving kindness is great.
Adonai's faithfulness endures forever. Hallelu-Yahh!

Hodu l'Adonai/Give Thanks to Adonai — הודו ליהוה

הוֹדוּ לַיהוה כִּי טוֹב, כִּי לְעוֹלָם חַסְדּוֹ:
יֹאמַר נָא יִשְׂרָאֵל, כִּי לְעוֹלָם חַסְדּוֹ:
יֹאמְרוּ נָא בֵית אַהֲרֹן, כִּי לְעוֹלָם חַסְדּוֹ:
יֹאמְרוּ נָא יִרְאֵי יהוה, כִּי לְעוֹלָם חַסְדּוֹ:

Hodu laAdonai ki tov, ki leOlam chasdo.
Yomar na Yisra-eil, ki leOlam chasdo.
Yomru na Veit Aharon, ki leOlam chasdo.
Yomru na yirei Adonai, ki leOlam chasdo.
Let all who revere God's Name now say,
"Ki le'olam chasdo"
Sing praise to the One for God is good, ki le'olam chasdo.

Give thanks to Adonai for God is good and God's mercy endures forever.
Say it, please, Israel, (House of Aaron, Followers of God) for God's mercy endures forever. Ps 118:1-2

מִן הַמֵּצַר קָרָאתִי יָּהּ, עָנָנִי בַמֶּרְחָב יָהּ.

Min hameitzar karati Yahh, Anani vamerchav Yahh.
Out of my distress, I called on God. God answered me with expansive love.

Tefilat HaLev - Shabbat/Festivals — שבת/חג — תפלת הלב

Adonai is on my side.

יהוה לִי לֹא אִירָא, מַה יַּעֲשֶׂה לִי אָדָם. יהוה לִי
בְּעֹזְרָי, וַאֲנִי אֶרְאֶה בְשֹׂנְאָי. טוֹב לַחֲסוֹת בַּיהוה, מִבְּטֹחַ
בָּאָדָם. טוֹב לַחֲסוֹת בַּיהוה מִבְּטֹחַ בִּנְדִיבִים. כָּל גּוֹיִם
סְבָבוּנִי בְּשֵׁם יהוה כִּי אֲמִילַם. סַבּוּנִי גַם סְבָבוּנִי בְּשֵׁם
יהוה כִּי אֲמִילַם. סַבּוּנִי כִדְבֹרִים דֹּעֲכוּ כְּאֵשׁ קוֹצִים, בְּשֵׁם
יהוה כִּי אֲמִילַם. דָּחֹה דְחִיתַנִי לִנְפֹּל, וַיהוה עֲזָרָנִי.
עָזִּי וְזִמְרָת יָהּ, וַיְהִי לִי לִישׁוּעָה. קוֹל רִנָּה וִישׁוּעָה
בְּאָהֳלֵי צַדִּיקִים, יְמִין יהוה עֹשָׂה חָיִל. יְמִין יהוה רוֹמֵמָה,
יְמִין יהוה עֹשָׂה חָיִל. לֹא אָמוּת כִּי אֶחְיֶה, וַאֲסַפֵּר מַעֲשֵׂי יָהּ.
יַסֹּר יִסְּרַנִּי יָּהּ, וְלַמָּוֶת לֹא נְתָנָנִי.

Adonai is on my side. I am not afraid.
What can a human do to me?
Adonai is with me and those who help me,
I can face those who hate me.

> *It is better to take refuge in Adonai,*
> *than to put confidence in humans.*
> *It is better to take refuge in Adonai,*
> *than to put confidence in princes.*

All the nations surrounded me, in the name of Adonai,
I cut them off. Yes, they surrounded me.
In the name of Adonai I indeed cut them off.

> *They surrounded me like bees.*
> *They are quenched like the burning thorns.*
> *In the name of Adonai I cut them off.*

You pushed me back hard, to make me fall,
and Adonai helped me.
God is my strength and my song; God is my salvation.

> *The voice of rejoicing and salvation*
> *is in the tents of the righteous.*
> *The right hand of Adonai is valiant.*

Tefilat HaLev - Shabbat/Festivals — שבת/חג — תפלת הלב

The right hand of God is exalted!
The right hand of Adonai is valiant!
I will not die, but live, and declare God's works.
Though God may chastise me severely,
God is the source of my life.

Pitchu li / Open for me — פתחו לי

פִּתְחוּ לִי שַׁעֲרֵי צֶדֶק,
אָבֹא בָם אוֹדֶה יָהּ.
זֶה הַשַּׁעַר לַיהוה,
צַדִּיקִים יָבֹאוּ בוֹ.

**Pitchu li sha'arei tzedek,
avo vam odeh Yahh
Zeh hasha-ar la'Adonai,
tzadikiym yavo-u vo.**

Open to me the gates of righteousness.
I will enter into them. I will give thanks to God.
This is the gate of Adonai; the righteous enter by it.

Zeh hayom / This is the Day — זה היום

אוֹדְךָ כִּי עֲנִיתָנִי, וַתְּהִי לִי לִישׁוּעָה.
אֶבֶן מָאֲסוּ הַבּוֹנִים, הָיְתָה לְרֹאשׁ פִּנָּה.
מֵאֵת יהוה הָיְתָה זֹּאת, הִיא נִפְלָאת בְּעֵינֵינוּ:
זֶה הַיּוֹם עָשָׂה יהוה, נָגִילָה וְנִשְׂמְחָה בוֹ.

Zeh hayom asa Adonai, nagila venismecha vo.

I will give thanks to you, for you have answered me,
and have become my salvation.
The stone which the builders rejected
has become the cornerstone.

Tefilat HaLev - Shabbat/Festivals — שבת/חג - תפלת הלב

This is Adonai's doing. It is marvelous in our eyes.
This is the day that Adonai has made.
Let us rejoice and be glad in it!

Ana Adonai / Adonai Answer Us — אנא יהוה

Traditionally done as a call-and-response:

אָנָּא יהוה הוֹשִׁיעָה נָּא׃   אָנָּא יהוה הוֹשִׁיעָה נָּא׃
אָנָּא יהוה הַצְלִיחָה נָּא׃   אָנָּא יהוה הַצְלִיחָה נָּא׃

Ana Adonai, hosh**iyah** na;   **Ana Ado**nai, hosh**iyah** na;
Ana Adonai, hatzl**ichah** na;   **Ana Ado**nai, hatzl**ichah** na;
Adonai answer us with salvation now.
Adonai answer us with prosperity now.

Blessings to the One Who Comes

בָּרוּךְ הַבָּא בְּשֵׁם יהוה, בֵּרַכְנוּכֶם מִבֵּית יהוה.
אֵל יהוה וַיָּאֶר לָנוּ, אִסְרוּ חַג בַּעֲבֹתִים עַד קַרְנוֹת הַמִּזְבֵּחַ.
אֵלִי אַתָּה וְאוֹדֶךָּ אֱלֹהַי אֲרוֹמְמֶךָּ.
הוֹדוּ לַיהוה כִּי טוֹב, כִּי לְעוֹלָם חַסְדּוֹ׃

Hodu la'**Ado**nai ki tov, ki le**Olam** chas**do**.

Blessings to the one who comes in the name of Adonai!
Blessings from the house of Adonai.
Adonai is God, and shines upon us, .
Make the festival beautiful with myrtle,
even to the horns of the altar.
You are my God,
and I will give thanks to you.
You are my God, I will exalt you.
Give thanks to Adonai, for God is good,
God's loving kindness endures forever.

Tefilat HaLev - Shabbat/Festivals — שבת/חג - תפלת הלב

Praise Adonai, our God, who is the Source of all. Your pious and righteous do Your work in the world. And all of the House of Israel acknowledges You as the Source with joyful and glorious praise. They thank You, exalt You, ascribe sovereignty to You in Your Essence, for it is indeed good to praise You and thank you and acknowledge You and call out Your Name in song.

Praise Adonai, our God

יְהַלְלוּךָ יהוה אֱלֹהֵינוּ כָּל מַעֲשֶׂיךָ, וַחֲסִידֶיךָ צַדִּיקִים עוֹשֵׂי רְצוֹנֶךָ, וְכָל עַמְּךָ בֵּית יִשְׂרָאֵל בְּרִנָּה יוֹדוּ וִיבָרְכוּ וִישַׁבְּחוּ וִיפָאֲרוּ וִירוֹמְמוּ וְיַעֲרִיצוּ וְיַקְדִּישׁוּ וְיַמְלִיכוּ אֶת שִׁמְךָ מַלְכֵּנוּ. כִּי לְךָ טוֹב לְהוֹדוֹת וּלְשִׁמְךָ נָאֶה לְזַמֵּר,
כִּי מֵעוֹלָם וְעַד עוֹלָם אַתָּה אֵל.
בָּרוּךְ אַתָּה יהוה, מֶלֶךְ מְהֻלָּל בַּתִּשְׁבָּחוֹת.

Ki me-olam ve-ad Olam Ata Eil.
Baruch Ata Adonai, Melech mehulal batishbachot.
From realm to realm, You are God!
A Source of Blessing are You, Sovereign of all, worthy of praise.

הללויה

YIZKOR Service

Originally, Yizkor was recited only on Yom Kippur. Its primary purpose was to remember the deceased by donating *tzedakah* [righteous giving] funds so that the good deeds of the survivors would elevate the souls of the departed. The practice also contributed to personal atonement by doing *gemilut chasadim* [a deed of lovingkindness]. The Torah reading on the last day of the major *Chagim* [festivals] of Sukkot, Pesach, and Shavuot, when our ancestors made a pilgrimage to Jerusalem, mentions the importance of donations, so Yizkor has been added to these holiday services.

In medieval Germany, during the Crusades, it was the custom in each community to read a list of its martyrs [from Yizkor Books] at the Yizkor service. The practice was eventually expanded to include the names of other members of the community who had died. Today, most synagogues publish lists of those who are remembered by congregants, which are then distributed at the Yizkor services. Also, those congregations that have memorial tablets turn on all of these lights.

While some feel that those whose parents are still alive should exit from the service, there is no legal requirement to do so. In fact, many rabbis today suggest that everyone stay for Yizkor so that the entire congregation can offer the prayers for the martyrs of the Jewish people and offer moral support to friends and family who may be deeply touched by the memorial service. But, as with much of the folk religion, this custom is sure to continue in many communities. Ultimately, it is a matter of personal and family decision-making as to your practice.

Tefilat HaLev - Shabbat/Festivals שבת/חג -

Festival - YIZKOR Service

Yizkor / Remembering יזכר

יהוה, יהוה, אֵל רַחוּם וְחַנּוּן, אֶרֶךְ אַפַּיִם, וְרַב
חֶסֶד וֶאֱמֶת: נֹצֵר חֶסֶד לָאֲלָפִים, נֹשֵׂא עָוֹן וָפֶשַׁע
וְחַטָּאָה, וְנַקֵּה:

**Adonai Adonai Eil rachum vechanun, erech apayim
verav chesed ve-emet, notzeir chesed la-alafiym,
nosei avon vafesha vechata-ah venakei.**

Adonai, Adonai, God of compassion and grace, slow to anger and abounding with mercy and truth. You grant mercy to the thousands, lifting shame and inequity and sin; You are cleansing.

Four times a year we are invited by our tradition
to remember those we love who have passed on.
These times are Yom Kippur, the end of Passover,
Shavuot, and the end of Succot/Shmini Atzeret.
> *These are times when our tradition teaches*
> *that the Gates of Prayer are particularly open*
> *and we can draw most powerfully on those we remember*
> *and seek healing of the wounds from that separation.*

In the safety of our loving community,
we can expose these wounds
and give them a chance to breathe and to heal.
Healing does not mean
that we love the departed souls any less,
for love shared will never die.
> *Rather it honors their memory*
> *and shifts that memory from one of pain and hurt*
> *to one of blessing and joy*
> *of having had that bond, that connection, in the first place.*
> *If we did not love them and connect to them at a soul level,*

Tefilat HaLev - Shabbat/Festivals   שבת/חג - תפלת הלב

we would not feel hurt in our souls
for their passing from our daily routines.
Healing does not mean forgetting,
rather it means remembering,
remembering with love and joy.
And we are a remembering people.
Dear One, help us to move
from the place of pain to the place of love,
from the place of sorrow to the place of living,
from the hurt of loss to the joy of remembering.
Jewish tradition teaches us
that between the world of the living
and the world of the dead
there is a window and not a wall.
This has stood in contrast
to our culture of scientific materialism
which teaches that dead is dead,
and after death,
the channels of communication between us
and our loved ones who have died are forever ended -
a brick wall!

The rituals of *Shiva, Kaddish, Yahrzeit* and *Yizkor* open
windows to the unseen worlds of the dead.
Yizkor creates a sacred space and time
wherein we can open our hearts and minds
to the possibility of a genuine inter-connection
with beloved family members and friends
who have left behind the world of the living.
Yizkor is a window.
Prepare to open that window as...
We remember them.

Tefilat HaLev - Shabbat/Festivals — שבת/חג – תפלת הלב

Meditation

Leaves don't fall, they descend,
Longing for earth, they come winging down
In their time they'll come again.
People don't die.
Through their descendants they continue
from one generation to another,
From one life to another,
With love and trust, that -
Leaves don't fall, they descend.

23rd Psalm, a Psalm of David

א מִזְמוֹר לְדָוִד יהוה רֹעִי לֹא אֶחְסָר׃

Mizmor LeDavid: Ado**nai** ro-**i** lo ech**sar**

A Psalm of David. Adonai is my shepherd;
I will not be lacking.

ב בִּנְאוֹת דֶּשֶׁא יַרְבִּיצֵנִי עַל־מֵי מְנֻחוֹת יְנַהֲלֵנִי׃

Bin'ot deshe yarbiy**tzei**ni al mei menu**chot** yenaha**lei**ni.

God causes me to lie down [where my soul can catch its breath] in green pastures; besides the calming waters.

ג נַפְשִׁי יְשׁוֹבֵב יַנְחֵנִי בְמַעְגְּלֵי־צֶדֶק לְמַעַן שְׁמוֹ׃

Nafshi yesho**veiv** yanchei**niy** vema'**glei** tze**dek** le**ma**-an she**mo**.

God restores my soul; leading me in the ways of living righteousness for that is God's essence.

ד גַּם כִּי־אֵלֵךְ בְּגֵיא צַלְמָוֶת לֹא־אִירָא רָע כִּי־אַתָּה עִמָּדִי

Gam ki ei**leich** be**gei** tzal**ma**vet lo iy**ra** ra ki **A**ta ima**diy**.

Even though I find myself walking through the depths of the valley, feeling the very shadow of death, I will not fear evil; for you are with me;

Tefilat HaLev - Shabbat/Festivals שבת/חג - תפלת הלב

שִׁבְטְךָ וּמִשְׁעַנְתֶּךָ הֵמָּה יְנַחֲמֻנִי:

Shivtecha umish'ante**cha** hei**ma** yenachamu**niy**.
Your rod and your staff guide and comfort me.

ה תַּעֲרֹךְ לְפָנַי שֻׁלְחָן נֶגֶד צֹרְרָי דִּשַּׁנְתָּ בַשֶּׁמֶן רֹאשִׁי כּוֹסִי רְוָיָה:

Ta-aroch lefa**nai** shul**chan ne**ged tzore**rai** di**shan**ta va**she**men ro**shi** co**si** re**va**ya.
*You arrange a table before me,
even in the presence of my detractors;
you anoint my head with oil; my cup runs over.*

ו אַךְ טוֹב וָחֶסֶד יִרְדְּפוּנִי כָּל־יְמֵי חַיָּי

Ach tov va**che**sed yirdefu**niy** kol ye**mei** cha**yai**
Surely goodness and loving kindness will follow me all the days of my life;

וְשַׁבְתִּי בְּבֵית־יהוה לְאֹרֶךְ יָמִים:

Vesha**vtiy** be**veit** A**do**nai le-**o**rech ya**miym**.
*and I will live with Adonai's presence
in the house of my soul forever.*

We remember them

At the rising of the sun and at its going down, we remember them.

At the blowing of the wind and in the chill of winter, we remember them.

*At the opening of the buds and in the rebirth of spring,
we remember them.*

*At the blueness of the skies and in the warmth of summer,
we remember them.*

Tefilat HaLev - Shabbat/Festivals — שבת/חג - תפלת הלב

At the rustling of the leaves
and in the beauty of autumn, we remember them.
At the beginning of the year and when it ends,
we remember them.
> *As long as we live, they too will live:*
> *for they are now a part of us, as we remember them.*

When we are weary and in need of strength,
we remember them.
When we are lost and sick at heart, we remember them.
> *When we have joy we crave to share, we remember them.*
> *When we have decisions that are difficult to make,*
> *we remember them.*

When we have achievements that are based on theirs,
we remember them.
When we have achievements
that would make them proud, we remember them.
> *As long as we live, they too will live;*
> *for they are now a part of us, as we remember them.*

Eli, Eli / My God, My God — אֵלִי, אֵלִי

אֵלִי, אֵלִי שֶׁלֹּא יִגָּמֵר לְעוֹלָם:
הַחוֹל וְהַיָּם, רִשְׁרוּשׁ שֶׁל הַמַּיִם,
בְּרַק הַשָּׁמַיִם, תְּפִלַּת הָאָדָם.

Eli, **Eli**, she**lo** yiga**meir** le-o**lam**:
Hachol vehayam, rish**rush** shel hama**yi**m,
be**rak** hasha**may**im, tefi**lat** ha-a**dam**.
Oh God, my God,
I pray that these things never end:
the sand and the sea, the rush of the waters,
the crash of the heavens, the prayer of the heart
> © Hannah Senesh

206

Tefilat HaLev - Shabbat/Festivals   שבת/חג - תפלת הלב

Life is like a candle's flame.

Life is like a candle's flame.
It must have just the right amount of air and wick and wax to burn brightly.

If there is no air, there can be no flame.
If there is too much air, it will burn out quickly.
At any time, it is easily snuffed out.
It is beautiful while it burns brightly before us.

It must work together with other parts of its environment
to have its full beauty be appreciated.

If it gets out of control, the results
can be pure horror or wickedness
and people may be harmed by it.
Most of the time, however, the flame give us light, comfort and joy.

Each candle's flame does this,
each one is special when we look at it.
The shape and appearance of the flame
changes with every moment as we look at it,
it is never static.

A single candle flame can pierce the darkest space.
With the light of a single candle, the dark place is no longer completely dark.
The light of a single candle
can guide us through the darkness.

One candle's flame can light another candle
and both will shine brightly
without diminishing the other.
One candle flame can light many candles,
turning their potential into reality.

Tefilat HaLev - Shabbat/Festivals שבת/חג – תפלת הלב

The light from a single candle
can spread throughout the world,
each candle flame lighting another's,
each burning with their own special glow
and in their own unique way.

They can join together and raise a flame
that is larger than the sum of the parts
and they can separate without either losing its flame.

   The flame of the candle is like our souls.
          © *Rabbi Shafir Lobb*

In moments like this, I realize once more
how much I miss those I loved.
Time has brought some healing,
and the pain I felt when they died has abated.
   Thank God I realize in new and unexpected ways
   how deeply they are still a part of me.

All that we shared together-the joy and the pain,
the misunderstandings and the reconciliations-
all that and more have shaped me profoundly
in ways I only dimly comprehend.
You all live on in me.
   Not all my memories are pleasant and easy to embrace.
   There are also some things, more than a few, that I regret:
   words I spoke or failed to speak, actions taken or avoided,
   silences endured, pain inflicted.

Tefilat HaLev - Shabbat/Festivals   שבת/חג - תפלת הלב

I ask myself why I could not have been more loving,
more understanding and patient,
and on this Day of Reconciliation,
I ask your forgiveness.

> *As I grow older,*
> *I have learned pain and loneliness are the inescapable price*
> *I must pay for having loved.*
> *May I find the strength to accept my sorrow*
> *and bear it with dignity.*

In silence now, as part of this vast Jewish family
that gathers to remember its dead,
I turn inward.

Tefilat HaLev - Shabbat/Festivals שבת/חג – תפלת הלב

The Five Stages of Grief

The night I lost you someone pointed me towards the
Five Stages of Grief.
   Go that way, they said, it's easy,
   like learning to climb stairs after amputation.
   And so I climbed.
                    Denial was first.
I sat down at breakfast
carefully setting the table for two.
I passed you the toast - you sat there.
I passed you the paper - you hid behind it.
   Anger seemed more familiar.
   I burned the toast, snatched the paper,
   and read the headlines myself.
   But they mentioned your departure and
   so I moved on to
                    Bargaining.
What could I exchange for you?
The silence after storms? My typing fingers?
Before I could decide,
                    Depression
   came puffing up, a poor relation,
   its suitcase tied together with string.
   In the suitcase were bandages for the eyes
   and bottles of sleep.
   I slid all the way down the stairs feeling nothing.
   And all the time
                    Hope
flashed on and off in defective neon.
Hope was a signpost pointing straight in the air.
Hope was my uncle's middle name, he died of it.

Tefilat HaLev - Shabbat/Festivals שבת/חג - תפלת הלב

After a year I am still climbing,
though my feet slip on your stone face.
The treeline has long since disappeared;
green is a color I have forgotten.
But now I see what I am climbing towards:
>Acceptance

written in capital letters, a special headline: Acceptance.
Its name is in lights.
I struggle on, waving and shouting.
Below, my whole life spreads its surf,
all the landscape I've ever known or dreamed of.
Below a fish jumps: the pulse in your neck.
>Acceptance.

I finally reach it.
>But something is wrong.
>>Grief is a circular staircase.
>>>I have lost you.

© Linda Pastan, PM/AM: New and Selected Poems.

YIZKOR RITUAL

Tefilat HaLev – Shabbat/Festivals — תפלת הלב – שבת/חג

For a father

יִזְכֹּר אֱלֹהִים נִשְׁמַת אָבִי מוֹרִי ___ בֶּן ___ שֶׁהָלַךְ לְעוֹלָמוֹ, בַּעֲבוּר שֶׁבְּלִי נֶדֶר אֶתֵּן צְדָקָה בַּעֲדוֹ. בִּשְׂכַר נַפְשׁוֹ צְרוּרָה בִּצְרוֹר הַחַיִּים עִם נִשְׁמוֹת אַבְרָהָם יִצְחָק וְיַעֲקֹב, שָׂרָה רִבְקָה רָחֵל וְלֵאָה, וְעִם שְׁאָר צַדִּיקִים וְצִדְקָנִיּוֹת שֶׁבְּגַן עֵדֶן, וְנֹאמַר אָמֵן.

Yizkor Elohiym nishmat avi mori ____ ben ____ shehalach le-olamo, ba-avur shebli neder etein tzedakah ba-ado. Bischar nafsho tzerura bitzror hachayim im nishmot Avraham Yitzchak veYa-akov Sara Rivka Racheil veLei-ah, ve-im she-ar tzadiykim vetzidkaniyot shebegGan Eiden, venomar amein.

May the memory of my father and teacher _____ son of ____, who returned to You, the Source of All, be sanctified in me. May I be led to acts of Tzedakah in his memory, for the sake of blessing. Dear Holy One, may his Soul be bound up with those of our ancestors, Abraham, Isaac, Jacob, Sarah, Rebeccah, Rachel and Leah and with those pious Souls that are in Gan Eden. And let us say, Amen.

Tefilat HaLev - Shabbat/Festivals – שבת/חג – תפלת הלב

For a mother

יִזְכֹּר אֱלֹהִים נִשְׁמַת אִמִּי מוֹרָתִי ___ בַּת ___ שֶׁהָלְכָה לְעוֹלָמָהּ, בַּעֲבוּר שֶׁבְּלִי נֶדֶר אֶתֵּן צְדָקָה בַּעֲדָהּ. בִּשְׂכַר נַפְשָׁהּ צְרוּרָה בִּצְרוֹר הַחַיִּים עִם נִשְׁמוֹת אַבְרָהָם יִצְחָק וְיַעֲקֹב, שָׂרָה רִבְקָה רָחֵל וְלֵאָה, וְעִם שְׁאָר צַדִּיקִים וְצִדְקָנִיּוֹת שֶׁבְּגַן עֵדֶן, וְנֹאמַר אָמֵן.

Yizkor Elo**hiy**m nish**mat** imi morati ___ bat ___ shehal**cha** le-ola**mahh**, ba-avur shebli neder e**tein** tzeda**kah** ba-a**dahh**. Bis**char** naf**shahh** tzeru**ra** bitz**ror** hacha**yim** im nish**mot** Avraham Yitzchak veYa-akov Sara Rivka Ra**cheil** veLei-ah, ve-im she-ar tzadiy**kim** vetzidkani**yot** shebeg**Gan Ei**den, ven**omar amein.**

May the memory of my mother and teacher ____ daughter of ____, who returned to You, the Source of All, be sanctified in me. May I be led to acts of Tzedakah in her memory, for the sake of blessing. Dear Holy One, may her Soul be bound up with those of our ancestors, Abraham, Isaac, Jacob, Sarah, Rebeccah, Rachel and Leah and with those pious Souls that are in Gan Eden. And let us say, Amen.

Tefilat HaLev - Shabbat/Festivals — שבת/חג – תפלת הלב

For a male spouse or partner

יִזְכֹּר אֱלֹהִים נִשְׁמַת אִישִׁי מוֹרִי __ בֶּן __ שֶׁהָלַךְ לְעוֹלָמוֹ, בַּעֲבוּר שֶׁבְּלִי נֶדֶר אֶתֵּן צְדָקָה בַּעֲדוֹ. בִּשְׂכַר נַפְשׁוֹ צְרוּרָה בִּצְרוֹר הַחַיִּים עִם נִשְׁמוֹת אַבְרָהָם יִצְחָק וְיַעֲקֹב, שָׂרָה רִבְקָה רָחֵל וְלֵאָה, וְעִם שְׁאָר צַדִּיקִים וְצִדְקָנִיּוֹת שֶׁבְּגַן עֵדֶן, וְנֹאמַר אָמֵן.

Yizkor Elo**hiym** nish**mat** i**shi** mori ____ ben ____ sheha**lach** le-o**lamo**, ba-a**vur** she**bli ne**der e**tein** tzeda**kah** ba-a**do**. Bis**char** naf**sho** tzeru**ra** bitz**ror** hacha**yim** im nish**mot** Avra**ham** Yitz**chak** veYa-a**kov** Sara Riv**ka** Ra**cheil** veLei-**ah**, ve-**im** she-**ar** tzadiy**kim** vetzidkani**yot** shebeg**Gan Ei**den, veno**mar amein**.

May the memory of my (spouse or partner) and teacher ___ son of ___, who returned to You, the Source of All, be sanctified in me. May I be led to acts of Tzedakah in his memory, for the sake of blessing. Dear Holy One, may his Soul be bound up with those of our ancestors, Abraham, Isaac, Jacob, Sarah, Rebeccah, Rachel and Leah and with those pious Souls that are in Gan Eden. And let us say, Amen.

Tefilat HaLev – Shabbat/Festivals – שבת/חג – תפלת הלב

For a female spouse or partner

יִזְכֹּר אֱלֹהִים נִשְׁמַת אִשְׁתִּי מוֹרָתִי __ בַּת __ שֶׁהָלְכָה לְעוֹלָמָהּ, בַּעֲבוּר שֶׁבְּלִי נֶדֶר אֶתֵּן צְדָקָה בַּעֲדָהּ. בִּשְׂכַר נַפְשָׁהּ צְרוּרָה בִּצְרוֹר הַחַיִּים עִם נִשְׁמוֹת אַבְרָהָם יִצְחָק וְיַעֲקֹב, שָׂרָה רִבְקָה רָחֵל וְלֵאָה, וְעִם שְׁאָר צַדִּיקִים וְצִדְקָנִיּוֹת שֶׁבְּגַן עֵדֶן, וְנֹאמַר אָמֵן.

Yizkor Elohiym nishmat ishti morati __ bat __ shehalcha le-olamahh, ba-avur shebli neder etein tzedakah ba-adahh. Bischar nafshahh tzerura bitzror hachayim im nishmot Avraham Yitzchak veYa-akov Sara Rivka Racheil veLei-ah, ve-im she-ar tzadiykim vetzidkaniyot shebegGan Eiden, venomar amein.

May the memory of my (spouse or partner) and teacher __ daughter of __, who returned to You, the Source of All, be sanctified in me. May I be led to acts of Tzedakah in her memory, for the sake of blessing. Dear Holy One, may her Soul be bound up with those of our ancestors, Abraham, Isaac, Jacob, Sarah, Rebeccah, Rachel and Leah and with those pious Souls that are in Gan Eden. And let us say, Amen.

Tefilat HaLev - Shabbat/Festivals — שבת/חג

For a son

יִזְכֹּר אֱלֹהִים נִשְׁמַת בְּנִי ____ בֶּן ____ שֶׁהָלַךְ לְעוֹלָמוֹ, בַּעֲבוּר שֶׁבְּלִי נֶדֶר אֶתֵּן צְדָקָה בַּעֲדוֹ. בִּשְׂכַר נַפְשׁוֹ צְרוּרָה בִּצְרוֹר הַחַיִּים עִם נִשְׁמוֹת אַבְרָהָם יִצְחָק וְיַעֲקֹב, שָׂרָה רִבְקָה רָחֵל וְלֵאָה, וְעִם שְׁאָר צַדִּיקִים וְצִדְקָנִיּוֹת שֶׁבְּגַן עֵדֶן, וְנֹאמַר אָמֵן.

Yizkor Elohiym nishmat beni ____ ben ____ shehalach le-olamo, ba-avur shebli neder etein tzedakah ba-ado. Bischar nafsho tzerura bitzror hachayim im nishmot Avraham Yitzchak veYa-akov Sara Rivka Racheil veLei-ah, ve-im she-ar tzadiykim vetzidkaniyot shebegGan Eiden, venomar amein.

May the memory of my son _____ son of _____, who returned to You, the Source of All, be sanctified in me. May I be led to acts of Tzedakah in his memory, for the sake of blessing. Dear Holy One, may his Soul be bound up with those of our ancestors, Abraham, Isaac, Jacob, Sarah, Rebeccah, Rachel and Leah and with those pious Souls that are in Gan Eden. And let us say, Amen.

Tefilat HaLev - Shabbat/Festivals — שבת/חג - תפלת הלב

For a daughter

יִזְכֹּר אֱלֹהִים נִשְׁמַת בִּתִּי ‗‗ בַּת ‗‗ שֶׁהָלְכָה לְעוֹלָמָהּ, בַּעֲבוּר שֶׁבְּלִי נֶדֶר אֶתֵּן צְדָקָה בַּעֲדָהּ. בִּשְׂכַר נַפְשָׁהּ צְרוּרָה בִּצְרוֹר הַחַיִּים עִם נִשְׁמוֹת אַבְרָהָם יִצְחָק וְיַעֲקֹב, שָׂרָה רִבְקָה רָחֵל וְלֵאָה, וְעִם שְׁאָר צַדִּיקִים וְצִדְקָנִיּוֹת שֶׁבְּגַן עֵדֶן, וְנֹאמַר אָמֵן.

Yizkor Elohiym nish**mat** bi**ti** ___ bat ___ shehal**cha** le-ola**mahh**, ba-a**vur** she**bli** **neder** e**tein** tze**dakah** ba-a**dahh**. Bis**char** naf**shahh** tze**rura** bitz**ror** ha**cha**yim im nish**mot** Avra**ham** Yitz**chak** veYa-a**kov** Sara Rivka Ra**cheil** veLei-**ah**, ve-**im** she-**ar** tzadiy**kim** vetzidkani**yot** shebeg**Gan Ei**den, veno**mar amein**.

May the memory of my daughter _____ daughter of _____, who returned to You, the Source of All, be sanctified in me. May I be led to acts of Tzedakah in her memory, for the sake of blessing. Dear Holy One, may her Soul be bound up with those of our ancestors, Abraham, Isaac, Jacob, Sarah, Rebeccah, Rachel and Leah and with those pious Souls that are in Gan Eden. And let us say, Amen.

Tefilat HaLev - Shabbat/Festivals — שבת/חג — תפלת הלב

For a male

יִזְכֹּר אֱלֹהִים נִשְׁמַת יָקִירִי ＿ בֶּן ＿ שֶׁהָלַךְ לְעוֹלָמוֹ, בַּעֲבוּר שֶׁבְּלִי נֶדֶר אֶתֵּן צְדָקָה בַּעֲדוֹ. בִּשְׂכַר נַפְשׁוֹ צְרוּרָה בִּצְרוֹר הַחַיִּים עִם נִשְׁמוֹת אַבְרָהָם יִצְחָק וְיַעֲקֹב, שָׂרָה רִבְקָה רָחֵל וְלֵאָה, וְעִם שְׁאָר צַדִּיקִים וְצִדְקָנִיּוֹת שֶׁבְּגַן עֵדֶן, וְנֹאמַר אָמֵן.

Yizkor Elohiym nishmat yakiri ____ ben ____ shehalach le-olamo, ba-avur shebli neder etein tzedakah ba-ado. Bischar nafsho tzerura bitzror hachayim im nishmot Avraham Yitzchak veYa-akov Sara Rivka Racheil veLei-ah, ve-im she-ar tzadiykim vetzidkaniyot shebegGan Eiden, venomar amein.

May the memory of my dear _____ son of ____, who returned to You, the Source of All, be sanctified in me. May I be led to acts of Tzedakah in his memory, for the sake of blessing. Dear Holy One, may his Soul be bound up with those of our ancestors, Abraham, Isaac, Jacob, Sarah, Rebeccah, Rachel and Leah and with those pious Souls that are in Gan Eden. And let us say, Amen.

Tefilat HaLev - Shabbat/Festivals — שבת/חג — תפלת הלב

For a female

יִזְכֹּר אֱלֹהִים נִשְׁמַת יָקִירִי __ בַּת __ שֶׁהָלְכָה לְעוֹלָמָהּ, בַּעֲבוּר שֶׁבְּלִי נֶדֶר אֶתֵּן צְדָקָה בַּעֲדָהּ. בִּשְׂכַר נַפְשָׁהּ צְרוּרָה בִּצְרוֹר הַחַיִּים עִם נִשְׁמוֹת אַבְרָהָם יִצְחָק וְיַעֲקֹב, שָׂרָה רִבְקָה רָחֵל וְלֵאָה, וְעִם שְׁאָר צַדִּיקִים וְצִדְקָנִיּוֹת שֶׁבְּגַן עֵדֶן, וְנֹאמַר אָמֵן.

Yiz**kor** Elo**hiym** nish**mat** yakiri __ bat __ shehal**cha** le-ola**mahh**, ba-**avur** shebli **neder** etein tzedakah ba-a**dahh**. Bis**char** naf**shahh** tzerura bitz**ror** hacha**yim** im nish**mot** Avra**ham** Yitz**chak** veYa-a**kov** Sara Rivka Ra**cheil** veLei-**ah**, ve-**im** she-**ar** tzadi**ykim** vetzidkani**yot** shebeg**Gan** Eiden, veno**mar** amein.

May the memory of my dear ____ daughter of ____, who returned to You, the Source of All, be sanctified in me. May I be led to acts of Tzedakah in her memory, for the sake of blessing. Dear Holy One, may her Soul be bound up with those of our ancestors, Abraham, Isaac, Jacob, Sarah, Rebeccah, Rachel and Leah and with those pious Souls that are in Gan Eden. And let us say, Amen.

Tefilat HaLev - Shabbat/Festivals — שבת/חג — תפלת הלב

Eil Malei / God of Compassion — אל מלא

אֵל מָלֵא רַחֲמִים שׁוֹכֵן בַּמְּרוֹמִים. הַמְצֵא מְנוּחָה נְכוֹנָה תַּחַת כַּנְפֵי הַשְּׁכִינָה. בְּמַעֲלוֹת קְדוֹשִׁים וּטְהוֹרִים כְּזֹהַר הָרָקִיעַ מַזְהִירִים אֶת נִשְׁמוֹת כָּל אֵלֶה שֶׁהָלְכוּ לְעוֹלָמָם בַּעֲבוּר שֶׁבְּלִי נֶדֶר אֶתֵּן צְדָקָה בְּעַד הַזְכָּרַת נִשְׁמָתָם, בְּגַן עֵדֶן תְּהֵא מְנוּחָתָם. לָכֵן בַּעַל הָרַחֲמִים יַסְתִּירֵם בְּסֵתֶר כְּנָפָיו לְעוֹלָמִים. וְיִצְרוֹר בִּצְרוֹר הַחַיִּים אֶת נִשְׁמָתָם. יהוה הוּא נַחֲלָתָם. וְיָנוּחוּ בְשָׁלוֹם עַל מִשְׁכָּבָם. וְנֹאמַר אָמֵן:

El malei rachamiym shochein bamromiym. Hamtzei menuchah nechonah tachat kanfei haShechinah. Bema-alot kedushiym ut-horiym kezohar harakiyah mazhiriym et nishmot kol eileh shehalchu le-olamam, Ba-avur shebli neder, etein tzedakah be-ad hazkarat nishmatam. BeGan Eiden tehei menuchatam. Lachein ba-al harachamiym yastireim beseiter kenafav le-olamiym. Veyitzror bitzror hachayim et nishmatam. Adonai Hu nachalatam. Veyanuchu beshalom al mishkavam. Venomar Amein.

O compassionate God, who dwells in the high places, grant complete repose to these souls who have gone to Your realm. May it be under the wings of the Shechina in the heavens, where this holy and pure soul, that sparkles as the bright lights of the firmament, can rest. For the sake of these souls, we pledge to give tzedaka for the memory of these souls. May the Garden of Eden be their resting place. May their souls be treasured and protected under Your wings to all the realms. May these souls be gathered and bound with the other treasured and immortal souls for eternal life. Adonai, may You treasure them and may they rest in peace. And let us say, Amen.

Tefilat HaLev - Shabbat/Festivals — שבת/חג - תפלת הלב

MAY YOU FIND COMFORT
AND
MAY THEIR MEMORIES
BE EVERLASTING
BLESSINGS!

TEFILAT HADERECH

May we be blessed as we go on our way.
May we be guided in peace.
May we be blessed with health and joy.
May this be our blessing, Amen.

Amen, Amen, may this be our blessing, Amen.

May we be sheltered by the wings of peace.
May we be kept in safety and in love.
May grace and compassion find their way to every soul.
May this be our blessing, Amen.

Amen, Amen, may this be our blessing, Amen.
© Debbie Friedman

Tefilat HaLev - Shabbat/Festivals שבת/חג - תפלת הלב

Havdalah הבדלה

The separation between Shabbat and the new week starts again tonight.

When Adonai began the creation of heaven and earth,
the earth was chaos, without form.
Darkness blanketed the deep
and God's Divine breath hovered over the waters.

Adonai spoke: "Let there be light!"
..... And light was.

Adonai saw the goodness in the light,
that it separated itself from the darkness.
Adonai called to the light "Day"
and to the darkness Adonai called "Night".

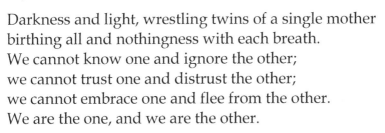

There was evening, there was morning;
day one.

Darkness and light, wrestling twins of a single mother
birthing all and nothingness with each breath.
We cannot know one and ignore the other;
we cannot trust one and distrust the other;
we cannot embrace one and flee from the other.
We are the one, and we are the other.

Light and dark, in and out, up and down, male and female,
good and evil, right and wrong;
each is known only from the other, each is incomprehensible
without the other.

There are no singularities, no lonely bits of drifting log
afloat in a cosmic sea.
There is only the on/off pulsating rhythms of life,
beating first one then another,
an infinite series of clangs and drums and whispers,
each singing the magic of creation.

There are no opposites, only polarities,
only the inter-relatedness of things,
only the inter-dependence of the Many and the One.

Tefilat HaLev - Shabbat/Festivals שבת/חג - תפלת הלב

Havdalah is a reminder of polarity,
of the two-ness of things
that is the outer form of an inner unity.
Havdalah is a moment of reflection and differentiation
that affirms the Many even as it confirms the One.

*Havdalah moves us from Shabbat to Week, from rest to labor,
from eternity to time, from Moment to Moment.*

Havdalah is a soft tug pulling our shirt sleeve,
gaining our attention for an instant's revelation:

Adonai is the Unity beyond the One and the Many.
Adonai is the imageless Zero that sustains all diversity.
*Adonai is the Sameness that makes us one family, one planet,
one universe.*
*Adonai is the Difference that fashions
our uniqueness and individuality.*
*Adonai is the Power that makes for freedom, justice,
creativity and truth.*

Ritual is but the outward expression of an inner process.
The magic of ritual is not that anything new happens,
but that we take the time to notice
that anything is happening at all.

*We rush through life
as if there were a prize awaiting us at the end.
Certainly there is an end, but the prize is questionable.
In all our hurrying here and there
in hopes of glimpsing something really special,
we rarely appreciate the magic of the ordinary.*

Ritual was created to remind us of the ordinary.
For all its formality,
ritual is, in fact,
the simplest of things crying out
the simplest of messages:
pay attention to the moment,
it is all we ever have,
it is all we ever have.

Tefilat HaLev - Shabbat/Festivals – שבת/חג

הִנֵּה אֵל יְשׁוּעָתִי, אֶבְטַח וְלֹא אֶפְחָד,

Hi**nei** Eil yeshu'**ati**, ev**tach** velo efchad.

כִּי עָזִּי וְזִמְרָת יָהּ יהוה, וַיְהִי לִי לִישׁוּעָה:

Kiy **azi** vezim**rat** Yahh Adonai, vay**hi** liy liyshu'**ah**.

וּשְׁאַבְתֶּם מַיִם בְּשָׂשׂוֹן מִמַּעַיְנֵי הַיְשׁוּעָה:

Ushav**tem ma**yim besa**son** mima'ai**nei** hayeshu'**ah**.

לַיהוה הַיְשׁוּעָה עַל עַמְּךָ בִרְכָתֶךָ סֶּלָה:

La-Adonai hayeshu'**ah** al am**cha** virchate**cha** **Se**lah.

יהוה צְבָאוֹת עִמָּנוּ מִשְׂגָּב לָנוּ אֱלֹהֵי יַעֲקֹב סֶלָה:

Ado**nai** tzva-**ot** i**ma**nu mis**gav** lanu Elo**hei** Ya'**akov** **Se**lah.

יהוה צְבָאוֹת אַשְׁרֵי אָדָם בֹּטֵחַ בָּךְ:

Ado**nai** tzva-**ot** ash**rei** a**dam** bo**tei**-ach bach.

Behold, God is my Deliverer;
my assurance so that I can release fear.
For Adonai sustains me and is my Stronghold,
the Source of my deliverance.

We will draw water from the wells of salvation with joy.
Adonai is the source of deliverance and blessing to God's people.

Adonai Tzva-ot is with us,
the God of Jacob surrounds us like a warm comforter.
Adonai Tzva-ot, happy is the one who feels your Presence
and trusts in You!

יהוה הוֹשִׁיעָה הַמֶּלֶךְ יַעֲנֵנוּ בְיוֹם קָרְאֵנוּ:

Adonai hos**hi**yah haMelech ya-a**nei**nu veyom ko**rei**nu.

לַיְּהוּדִים הָיְתָה אוֹרָה וְשִׂמְחָה וְשָׂשֹׂן וִיקָר:

Laihu**diym** hai**ta** o**rah** vesim**chah** vesa**son** viy**kar**.

כֵּן תִּהְיֶה לָּנוּ, כּוֹס יְשׁוּעוֹת אֶשָּׂא. וּבְשֵׁם יהוה אֶקְרָא:

Kein ti**yeh** lanu, kos yeshu'**ot** esah. Uv**sheim** Ado**nai** ekra.

Adonai is our Deliverer,
the Sovereign that answers us when we call out.

God has been Israel's source of Light and Joy and rejoicing,
Judah's precious gift.

Tefilat HaLev - Shabbat/Festivals - שבת/חג - תפלת הלב

So it is for us, the cup of Deliverance from which we drink and the Essence upon which we call.

The wine cup is raised, but no drink taken.

בָּרוּךְ אַתָּה יהוה אֱלֹהֵינוּ מֶלֶךְ הָעוֹלָם, בּוֹרֵא פְּרִי הַגָּפֶן.

Baruch Ata Adonai, Eloheinu Melech haOlam, borei pri hagafen.

A Source of Blessing are You, Adonai our God, Sovereign of all, creator of the fruit of the vine.

בָּרוּךְ אַתָּה יהוה אֱלֹהֵינוּ מֶלֶךְ הָעוֹלָם, בּוֹרֵא מִינֵי בְשָׂמִים.

Baruch Ata Adonai, Eloheinu Melech haOlam, borei minei besamim.

A Source of Blessing are You, Adonai our God, Sovereign of all, creator of different spices.

The spices are sniffed.

בָּרוּךְ אַתָּה יהוה אֱלֹהֵינוּ מֶלֶךְ הָעוֹלָם, בּוֹרֵא מְאוֹרֵי הָאֵשׁ.

Baruch Ata Adonai, Eloheinu Melech haOlam, borei me-orei ha-eish.

A Source of Blessing are You, Adonai our God, Sovereign of all, creator of the light of fire.

The light of the candles are reflected off the fingernails.

בָּרוּךְ אַתָּה יהוה, אֱלֹהֵינוּ מֶלֶךְ הָעוֹלָם, הַמַּבְדִּיל בֵּין קֹדֶשׁ לְחוֹל,

Baruch Ata Adonai, Eloheinu Melech haOlam, hamavdiyl bein kodesh lechol,

A Source of Blessing are You, Adonai our God, Sovereign of all, who separates holiness from potential,

בֵּין אוֹר לְחֹשֶׁךְ, בֵּין יִשְׂרָאֵל לָעַמִּים.

Bein or lechoshech, bein Yisra-eil le'amim.

Who separates light from darkness, the House of Israel to the nations,

Tefilat HaLev - Shabbat/Festivals — שבת/חג — *תפלת הלב*

בֵּין יוֹם הַשְּׁבִיעִי, לְשֵׁשֶׁת יְמֵי הַמַּעֲשֶׂה:

Bein yom hashvi-**iy**, le**shei**shet ye**mei** hama'**aseh**;
Who separates the seventh day from the six days of creation;

בָּרוּךְ אַתָּה יהוה הַמַּבְדִּיל בֵּין קֹדֶשׁ לְחוֹל.

Baruch Ata Adonai, hamav**diy**l bein **ko**desh le**chol**.
A Source of Blessing are You, Adonai our God, who separates holiness from potential.

The wine is sipped and the candle is extinguished

אליהו הנביא / מרים הנביאה

Eliyahu HaNavi, Miriam HaNevi'a

אֵלִיָּהוּ הַנָּבִיא, אֵלִיָּהוּ הַתִּשְׁבִּי,
אֵלִיָּהוּ, אֵלִיָּהוּ, אֵלִיָּהוּ הַגִּלְעָדִי.
בִּמְהֵרָה בְיָמֵינוּ, יָבֹא אֵלֵינוּ,
עִם מָשִׁיחַ בֶּן דָּוִד. (2)

מִרְיָם הַנְּבִיאָה עֹז וְזִמְרָה בְּיָדָהּ
מִרְיָם תִּרְקֹד אִתָּנוּ לְתַקֵּן אֶת הָעוֹלָם.
בִּמְהֵרָה בְיָמֵינוּ הִיא תְּבִיאֵנוּ
אֶל מֵי הַיְשׁוּעָה, (2)

Eli**ya**hu haNa**vi**; Eliyahu haTish**bi**,
Eliyahu, (3x) haGila**di**.
Bimheira veyamei**nu**, yavo eilei**nu**
im moshi-**ach** ben David. (2x)
Miriam haNevi'**a**, oz vezim**ra** beya**dah**.
Miriam tir**kod** i**tanu**
leta**kein** et ha'o**lam**.
Bim**hei**ra veyamei**nu**,
hee tevi-**ei**nu
el mei ha-ye**shua**. (2x)
Rabbi Leila Gal Berner (2nd verse)

Eliyahu the prophet, Eliyahu the Tishbite, Eliyahu the Gileadi. Quickly, in our time, come to us, Bringing Moshiach, ben David

Miriam the Prophet, strength and song are in her hand. Miriam will dance with us to heal the world. Quickly, in our time, she will lead us to the waters of salvation.

Tefilat HaLev - Shabbat/Festivals – שבת/חג

לכבוד חמדת לבבי Lichevod Chemda levavi / May my heart cleave to God

הַמַּבְדִּיל בֵּין קֹדֶשׁ לְחוֹל חַטֹּאתֵינוּ הוּא יִמְחוֹל
זַרְעֵנוּ וְכַסְפֵּנוּ יַרְבֶּה כַּחוֹל וְכַכּוֹכָבִים בַּלַּיְלָה
לִכְבוֹד חֶמְדָּת לְבָבִי, אֵלִיָּהוּ הַנָּבִיא

Hamav**dil** bein **ko**desh le**chol** Chato**tei**nu, hu yim**chol**
Zareinu vechas**pei**nu, yar**beh** cha**chol** vekakocha**vim** ba**lai**la
Liche**vod** chem**dat** le**va**vi, Eli**ya**hu hana**vi**,

A la derecha Michael Y la Isierda y Gavriel
Y sovre la cabeza Shechinat el dio
Un cada el Dio, un cada el noche
Liche**vod** chem**dat** le**va**vi, Eli**ya**hu hana**vi**.

Ladino Havdalah favorite

לכבוד חמדת לבבי Lichevod Chemda levavi / May my heart cleave to God

לִכְבוֹד חֶמְדָּת לְבָבִי, אֵלִיָּהוּ הַנָּבִיא
לִכְבוֹד חֶמְדָּת לְבָבִי, מִרְיָם הַנְּבִיאָה

Liche**vod** chem**dat** le**va**vi, Eli**ya**hu hana**vi**,
Liche**vod** chem**dat** le**va**vi, Miriam haNevi'a

May my heart cleave to God [in order to bring] Eliyahu HaNavi
May my heart cleave to God [in order to bring] Miriam HaNevi'a

227

Tefilat HaLev - Shabbat/Festivals שבת/חג – תפלת הלב

SHABBAT SHALOM!
AND WELCOME TO THE APPENDIX

This section of our Siddur (prayer book) includes explanations and other additional information about prayers and sections in our service. This section helps provide some of the Kavannah (intention) that accompanies and enhances the Keva (form) of our service.

Kavannah is not easy to define. Kavannah is the creative thought, word or movement that adds meaning to the Keva.

This Kabbalat Shabbat Siddur (prayer book) presents the Keva as it should be…and in this section of our book, we offer a Kavannah or explanation that reflects the spiritual journey of our members. Other kavannot are for us to add.

In many instances the original dates of creation of the prayers are unknown. Myriad explanations exist as to their meaning and purpose. For every explanation in this section (or elsewhere), there are dozens and even hundreds of other opinions, translations and points of view. We admit that and invite you to continue where we have ended, in your own quest for greater understanding and appreciation of the liturgy of the Jewish people.

Many of us have heard these prayers chanted for our entire lives without knowing their purpose or the meanings of their lines and verses. We may know the words or we may have forgotten them completely. Others of us, in one way or another new to Judaism, may be in the dark from word one. We hope that this siddur will make our time in worship services more meaningful for all of us.

Tefilat HaLev - Shabbat/Festivals שבת/חג – תפלת הלב

Nigun

A nigun is a wordless melody, often described as a mystical musical prayer or a spiritual language beyond words. It is believed by some that every soul possesses its own melody before it is born into this world, but existance on earth covers up this essential song of each of us with many layers of noise, and so it is lost. Perhaps, then, part of life should be a search by each of us to rediscover our own original melody.

Nigunim (the plural of nigun) originated with the Hassidic movement in the 1700's, in which it was thought that personal piety and experience would add greater value to Jewish life than intellectual study by itself. Singing a nigun is an effort to move beyond words and rational thought and into the realm of the soul.

The sources of the melodies are wide-ranging; many groups chant the nigunim that have been created by their rabbis while others have taken well-known songs ("La Marseillaise," for example) and converted them into nigunim of their own in an effort to take them "...from spiritual exile" as they exist in their secular form and "...raise holy sparks" in their newer form. The original sources of the music are less important than the *kavanah*, the intent of the heart, in reaching an understanding of a nigun.

So, in place of words we find multiple syllables with no apparent meaning such as "li, li, li" or "di, di, di" sung with dramatic inflections in the manner of cantorial music (often called *krekhts*, in Yiddish, connoting a moaning, sighing or sobbing style). Sometimes, a nigun is used at the start of a service to transport the congregation, figuratively speaking, from the sidewalk to a spiritual level within the sanctuary.

In the words of a sage, a nigun is "...the pen of the soul".

Tefilat HaLev - Shabbat/Festivals שבת/חג – תפלת הלב

Lighting Shabbat Candles

Just as creation began with the words "Let there be light," so does the celebration of the creation week begin with the kindling of Shabbat candles. Often the candles are lit by the woman of the household, but the lighting may also be done by a man. Some feel that lighting the candles should be done eighteen minutes before sunset each Friday evening, while others are less particular about the timing, focusing instead on the experience of coming together as a community.

After the candles have been lit, the lighter stretches her/his hands towards them and moves the hands in a circular motion three times. After the third time, the lighter covers her/his eyes with the hands and recites the blessing.

Why do we wave our hands in circular motions after lighting the candles? There are many explanations. We welcome in the Sabbath Queen, we draw the light into ourselves and spread the light to those in need, or we may lift our hands over the flames six times to bring all six days into Shabbat. Why do we close our eyes? To complete the blessing before enjoying the light and to remember to use the light to look in as well as out.

From early Talmudic sources we learn that lighting candles is an essential preparation for the Sabbath. As soon as the candles have been lit, Shabbat has begun for the person who lit them. Therefore the person might not extinguish the match, but rather should place it on a safe surface so that it burns itself out.

As a rule, two candles are lit. Some say they represent the two important biblical references to Shabbat: "Remember the Sabbath" (Exodus 20:8) and "Observe the Sabbath" (Deuteronomy 5:12). It is customary in some circles for the candle lighter to add a silent prayer after the blessing has been said...perhaps for the health and welfare of her (or his) family.

230

Tefilat HaLev - Shabbat/Festivals - שבת/חג - תפלת הלב

Yedid Nefesh

The original poem that comprises this prayer is ascribed to Rabbi Eliezer Azikri, a 16th century Kabbalist from Safed (Tzfat, Israel), although he never took credit for it. Deeply Kabbalistic in tone and structure, this love poem speaks of the intense yearning between the human soul and its Godly source. In its original form, its intensity is quite evident:

> My soul longs in pain with love for You;
> O God, I beg you please heal it
> By showing it the sweetness of
> Your splendor; then it will be
> Invigorated and healed,
> Experiencing everlasting joy.

There is a popular traditional melody written by the Magid (a lecturer) of Terchovitza in the early 1800s, who wrote it as a gift to the Bretzlav community. The complexity and depth of this melody betray a deep musical understanding, not to mention a profound sense of the poetry as it was originally written. In the ancient village of Tzfat, Israel, the mystics left the synagogue as Sabbath arrived and walked slowly in the fields, chanting this poem to express their longing for Shechina, the female in-dwelling aspect of God to be found in creation.

Tefilat HaLev - Shabbat/Festivals שבת/חג – תפלת הלב

Shalom Aleichem

Inspired by Talmudic legend and believed to have been written in the seventeenth century, Shalom Aleichem is one of the hymns meant to welcome in the Sabbath. Originally intended to be chanted before the Shabbat meal, as the family comes to the table, it recounts how each Shabbat eve two ministering angels accompany a person home from synagogue. The opening lines greet and wish peace on the angels:

> **Sha**lom alei**chem**, malaa**chei** hasha**ret**, malaa**chei** el**yon**
> Peace upon you, O ministering angels,
> angels of the Exalted One

The prayer is about peace…peace to the accompanying angels as indicated above, and peace to the supplicant:

> Bo-a**chem** lesha**lom**, malaa**chei** hasha**lom**,
> malaa**chei** el**yon**
> Bless me for peace, O angels of peace,
> angels of the Exalted One

The ending is of the same theme, as the person singing the prayer hopes for peace for the departing angels:

> Tzeit**chem** lesha**lom**, malaa**chei** hasha**lom**,
> malaa**chei** el**yon**
> May your departure be with peace, O angels of peace,
> angels of the Exalted One

Why bid the ministering angels such a hasty farewell? One source suggests that it is because it would be in poor taste to partake of a meal in front of those who will not, or cannot, eat. In other traditions, it is felt appropriate to wait until *after* Shabbat to sing the final verse and bid farewell to the angels.

Tefilat HaLev - Shabbat/Festivals שבת/חג – תפלת הלב

Shabbat Psalms

"The Psalms of David, in sublimity, beauty, pathos and originality, or in one word, poetry, are superior to all the odes, hymns and songs in any language."

John Adams in a letter to Thomas Jefferson

Psalms (Tehillim) -- there are 150 of them in the Book of Psalms -- are intended to praise God, instruct, entreat, reflect, recount and even chastise. They look back to creation and ahead to the time a deliverer might come. They are used extensively in Jewish liturgy and in Christian liturgy as well. Although the Book of Psalms contains only 150 psalms, in fact many more were written.

We sing Psalms in Hebrew because of their beautiful poetry. The primary poetic device of the Psalms is parallelism, a sort of rhyme in which an idea is expressed by use of repetitions: "Adonai is my light and my salvation, whom shall I fear? Adonai is the stronghold of my life; of whom shall I be afraid?" (Psalm 27:1). Another form of parallelism found in Psalms is antithetic parallelism, in which the sentences express opposite points: "Adonai watches over the way of the righteous, but the way of the wicked will perish" (Psalm 1:6).

Psalms are used throughout Jewish worship and for a multitude of purposes, although some are specific to a certain holiday. Psalms 95-99, 29 and 92 (the Sabbath Psalm), and 93, have become a centerpiece of Kabbalat Shabbat. Congregations usually select one to three of them in any given week. We can also create modern Psalms, with words from our hearts, and such a Psalm is included in many Shabbat services. The poet/songwriter Leonard Cohen is a master at modern Psalms, as are others who have put their own words to his music.

Tefilat HaLev - Shabbat/Festivals שבת/חג - תפלת הלב

Lecha Dodi

This poem initiates the Raza, the Secret, of Shabbat that bestirs in us the ancient memory of shalom, of wholeness that preceded separation and alienation. Like the earlier prayer, Yedid Nefesh, this poem was sung as the sun was setting. The famous Kabbalist Rabbi Isaac Luria and his disciples, dressed in white, would actually lead their congregations outside to chant it overlooking the fields and valleys surrounding Tzfat as they received the presence of Shabbat, which some imagine as the Sabbath Bride or Queen. Inspired by imagery of union and integration, it invites us to call to that which will make us whole. The reference to the Shabbat "bride" or "queen" conveys a sense of beauty or radiance. In kabbalistic thought, the Shabbat bride is called "Shechina," the female in-dwelling aspect of God, who enters the sanctuary and unites with Jewish people on Shabbat. The text was written in the sixteenth century by Rabbi Shlomo Halevi Alkabetz, a Kabbalist of Tzfat.

The refrain between stanzas states:
Lechah dodi likrat kalah, penei Shabat nekablah
Come, my beloved, to greet the bride,
the Sabbath presence let us welcome.

The poem, called an acrostic, is arranged so that the first letters of each of the nine stanzas spells out the name of the author, a practice quite common among liturgical poets. Actually, only the first two and the last stanzas relate to the Shabbat; the rest of the phraseology is largely borrowed from the Hebrew Bible and alludes to the desire for ultimate redemption. In most congregations, only 4 of the 9 verses are sung (typically verses 1, 2, 5 and 9).

Tefilat HaLev - Shabbat/Festivals שבת/חג – תפלת הלב

Verse two is interesting in that the last lines indicate that although God created the universe before there was a Sabbath, it had been preordained that there would be a Sabbath:

> **Likrat Shabat lechu veneilchah ki hi mekor habrachah**
> **Meirosh mikedem nesuchah sof ma'aseh bemachashavah techilah.**
> To greet Shabbat let us go,
> let us travel for she is the wellspring of blessing
> From the start, from ancient times she was chosen,
> Last made, but first planned.

As the final verse is sung, the congregation rises and turns towards the door, hoping to glimpse the "Bride of Sabbath."

Lecha Dodi has been described as perhaps one of the finest pieces of religious poetry in existence.

Tefilat HaLev - Shabbat/Festivals שבת/חג - תפלת הלב

Kaddish

The Kaddish is largely an Aramaic prayer of praise about the Source of Life we call God. The central verse of the Kaddish is: *Yehei sh'mei raba m'varach l'alam ul'almei almaya.* "Let God's great name be praised forever and ever," which is an Aramaic translation of Psalm 113:2. The Kaddish is essentially a declaration of belief in the holiness and greatness of God, a prayer that God's name (Essence) be made Holy in this world. It is a recognition that even that which humankind cannot understand is a consequence of God's will. To highlight this symbolism, it is often traditional for the reader to recite the Kaddish and for the congregation to affirm it by answering Amen after each verse.

The Kaddish has several variations, each of which may indicate a section of the service. One variant is the Chatzi Kaddish, or Reader's Kaddish. This form is the short or half-Kaddish (chatzi means half). The full Kaddish is called Kaddish Shalem (shalem means complete). There is also a special Kaddish d'Rabanan (Teacher's or Rabbi's Kaddish) which has a special section in it that talks about learning, teachers and their students, and the students of their students. Kaddish Yatom is known as the Mourner's Kaddish. It is the same as the full version, a prayer of praise. There is no reference to death to distinguish this Kaddish from the others. Persons who have lost a dear one or are making a Yahrzeit recite this version, which occurs at the end of services. Additionally, there are four Yizkor services during the year at which the Mourner's Kaddish is said: the last days of the festivals of Pesach, Shavu'ot and Sukkot; and also on the Day of Atonement, Yom Kippur.

The Kaddish is recited in the presence of a Minyan, since, like the Kedusha prayer, it praises God's name. There are several customs as to who stands for the Kaddish. When one recites the Kaddish, one traditionally stands. Therefore,

Tefilat HaLev - Shabbat/Festivals שבת/חג – תפלת הלב

mourners rise when they recite the prayer. Some people will stand when they hear the Kaddish being recited. Thus, you may see several people stand when the Kaddish is recited, be it the half or full version. At some congregations, the entire congregation stands part-way through, and participates in the recitation of the prayer after standing. Each community develops its traditions in this area, which may change over time. God does not change, but our perceptions and understanding of God and God's worship change over time.

Tefilat HaLev - Shabbat/Festivals שבת/חג – תפלת הלב

Bar'chu!

Bar**chu** et Ado**nai** hamevo**rach**.
Praise Adonai to whom praise is due forever

These are the words of the Bar'chu, the traditional call to Jewish prayer. They are chanted by the leader of the service and the congregation acknowledges its readiness to participate by responding with very nearly the same words:

Ba**ruch** Ado**nai** hamevo**rach** le'**olam** va'**ed**.
Praised be to Adonai to whom our praise is due
now and forever.

Blessing God may seem odd; after all, why does God need our blessing? Jewish thought understands that God and creation are deeply interwoven and interconnected, so when we bless, we return the Divine flow to the Godhead, allowing it to flow back down to us. We play an integral part in the recycling of spiritual energy!

This is the prayer which begins the main body of our Sabbath evening service, following Kabbalat Shabbat, the welcoming of the Sabbath. Just as those in heaven above unite into Oneness, so the Sabbath on earth below joins the mystery of Oneness. This is the secret of Shabbat: Shabbat is attached to the secret of Oneness, Oneness that descends through the Shabbat evening prayer. When the Sabbath arrives, all manner of strife is kept from her; she remains in union with the holy light. All tyranny and affliction flee from her and vanish. There is no higher realm in the entire universe. Her face is illuminated with a higher light. On earth, she is crowned by holy people who are endowed with new souls. This prayer blesses her with joy and the light of rapture. The secret is: our prayer inspires the union. This is the deep secret of Shabbat, called "raza deShabbat."

Tefilat HaLev - Shabbat/Festivals שבת/חג – תפלת הלב

In some Chasidic traditions, the five words of the response correspond to five levels of the soul, which become fully integrated by the reciting of the blessing. The "Barchu" occupies a similar place in other services, always leading up to the "Shema," which follows shortly after it. In many congregations, to bring added Kavanah -- intention -- to the prayer, we add one of the English poems/chants to the traditional "Bar'chu."

When responding to the "Barchu," one should face east, in the direction of Jerusalem.

Tefilat HaLev - Shabbat/Festivals שבת/חג – תפלת הלב

Ma'ariv (Evening) Service

Once we are called to prayer, we continue with the Ma'ariv (evening) service, with the Shema at its center. The blessings before and after the Shema are in brilliant order. First we marvel at the wisdom of creation, Ma'ariv Aravim. Then we acknowledge that we are loved unconditionally, Ahavat Olam. With the Shema, we proclaim the unity of all things emanating from the Source. For the Shema, we may cover our eyes with a hand (forming the Hebrew letter "Shin" with our fingers), sensing that we are part of a greater whole. Knowing that we are loved, we are able and willing to love back and are told how to do so in the Ve-ahavta. But the final section of the Ve-ahavta, Vehaya Im Shemoa, contains a collective warning that is most appropriate for our time. If we do not care for all life, we will surely perish. The Shema and Her Blessings part of the service concludes with two blessings of redemption, Mi Chamochah and Hashkiveinu. The world, we remind ourselves, moves from the way things are to the way they ought to be. Surely, repair of the heart and repair of the world are possible.

The prayer Ma'ariv Aravim - praising God for creation - begins with the words: "Who brings on the evening with his word . . ." With the first chapter of Genesis in mind, our prayer accentuates the uniqueness of God's use of language to create worlds. We humans do that morally, but God does so in a physical sense as well.

Progressive Judaism sees no conflict between God as creator and evolutionary science.

A great musician was once asked, "How do you play the notes so perfectly?" The artist replied, "The notes can be played by anyone; it is the pause between the notes that gives them their beauty and meaning." On this Shabbat, may we all learn to pause.

Tefilat HaLev - Shabbat/Festivals שבת/חג - תפלת הלב

Ahavat Olam

Ahavat olam beit Yisraeil ame**cha ahav**ta,
tora umitz**vot**, chu**kim** umishpa**tiym**, otanu li**ma**deta.
With unlimited/everlasting love You have loved Your people, Israel (the God-wrestlers); Torah, mitzvot, guiding principles and laws You have taught us.

The theme of this prayer is that God is love in good times and bad. For Jews, a tangible sign of that love is the fact that God revealed Godself to the Hebrew people in the act of revealing the Torah. As a result we dedicate ourselves joyously to its study, a labor of love.

God's love for us is often misunderstood because our reference point is human love. But God's love is so unconditional that there can be no comparison.

Ahavat Olam, which immediately precedes the Shema during evening services, parallels another prayer -- Ahavat Rabbah ("Great Love") -- which is recited during morning services. The sages of the Talmud were divided regarding a preference for either prayer so the compromise of using each during different services was reached. The Ahavat Rabbah is the longer and more complex of the two but both basically tell that the gift of the Torah showed God's love for Israel/ God-wrestlers.

Tefilat HaLev - Shabbat/Festivals שבת/חג – תפלת הלב

The Shema

The Shema, Deuteronomy 6:4, is a call between God and Israel, from each one of us to the other. The second verse is a response, whispered in humble acceptance of the connectedness of all creation. Whispering the verse is a rabbinic practice; the verse is said aloud only on Yom Kippur, recalling the custom of the High Priest in the ancient Temple. More than any other prayer, the Shema is THE prayer of the Jewish people. Often, it is translated: "Hear, O Israel! Adonai is our God! Adonai is One!", but it can also be rendered as "Hear, O Israel! Adonai is our God-Adonai alone" (there is nothing other than God).

The "Shema" is included in both the morning and evening services, and is also a bed-time prayer. It has been sanctified over the ages as the last words of many Jews, both those dying peacefully and those as they were martyred. The Talmud teaches that when Jacob was about to die, he gathered his children around him and asked whether they would remain faithful to the spiritual values he had taught them. They responded, "*Shema Yisrael, Adonai Eloheinu, Adonai Echad!* (Listen Israel [Jacob], the One God is our God.)' To which Jacob replied with his last breath, "*Baruch Shem kevod...*" thanking God for his children's commitment to carry on the tradition.

In 1945, Rabbi Eliezer Silver was sent from the United States to Europe to help reclaim Jewish children who had been hidden with non-Jewish families during the Holocaust. Many of the young ones had been only infants when they were separated from their parents and had no idea of their religious heritage. The rabbi went where children were gathered and loudly say: "Shema Yisrael...". He would look at the faces of the children to see who might have tears of remembrance in their eyes...those who might have had a distant memory of their mothers putting them to bed and saying the "Shema."

Tefilat HaLev - Shabbat/Festivals שבת/חג - תפלת הלב

Jewish tradition instructs that the first line of the "Shema" be intoned with the utmost concentration. Sometimes each word is elongated to allow deep concentration on each word. Some worshippers will close or cover their eyes as they say the prayer and emphasize the last word -- Echad (oneness) -- by prolonging it. In the Torah itself and in the siddurs (prayer books), the last letter of the first and last words of the Shema are written in larger print. These two letters form the word "eid" (witness) to remind Jews of their responsibility to be witnesses to God's sovereignty by leading exemplary lives.

Shema Yisra-eil: Adonai Eloheinu, Adonai Echad!

These six simple words have reverberated through the ages, speaking of the mysterious unity of all things, infinitely full of wonder and awe.

Ve-ahavta eit Adonai Elohecha; bechol levavcha uvechol nafshecha uvechol me-odecha.
Love Adonai, your God, with all your heart,
with all your soul, with all your being-ness.

And these words which I command you this day shall be taken to your heart. Teach them diligently to your children and talk of them when you sit in your house, when you walk on the road, when you lie down and when you rise up. Bind them for a sign upon your hand and for the frontlets between your eyes. Write them on the doorposts of your house and on your gates.

This prayer is the first passage of the continuation of the "Shema." It teaches that remembering God's presence is not enough; the teachings must be lived and taught.
Kavanah: The word emet literally means truth. In rabbinic practice, it is added directly to the end of the Shema as an immediate affirmation of its truth for us.

תפלת הלב – שבת/חג Tefilat HaLev - Shabbat/Festivals

Mi Chamocha

Tradition calls us to remember Yetsiat Mitzrayim - our going out from Egypt -- in every service. We remember that we were slaves and affirm that until all people are free, not one of us is completely free. Though we mourn for the suffering of the Egyptians and know that the journey ahead is long and difficult, we join together in celebration of this precious moment of freedom. The wisdom of celebrating that moment has carried us through times of deep despair when a glimmer of hope came from remembering the miracle at the shores of the sea when, according to the Torah (Exodus 15), Miriam the prophetess took her timbrel in her hand and together with Moses led the people in song and dance.

> Mi cha**mo**cha ba-ei**lim**, Ado**nai**?
> Mi ka**mo**cha, ne**dar** ba**ko**desh, **no**ra tehi**lot**, **o**sei **fe**leh?
> Who is like You, Adonai,
> among the gods that are worshipped
> Who is like You, awesome in splendor,
> working wonders.

The prayer follows the Shema and Ve-ahavta and acknowledges the great power of God, in particular the astounding miracles which allowed our people to survive and escape the slavery imposed upon them in Egypt. While this prayer, like many others, extols the power and wonder of God, it also makes us aware of the importance of this power in our freedom to be who we are. Its importance is supported by the many musical settings to which it has been put over the ages.

244

Tefilat HaLev - Shabbat/Festivals שבת/חג - תפלת הלב

Hashkiveinu

This is the last prayer in the Shema and Her Blessings. It is only said in the evening. We ask that a shelter of peace be spread over us that we may have a moment of Shabbat rest under the gentle wings of the Shechina and the safety of our community. To pray for a sukkat shalom is to pray for a full house, a shelter that reflects creation in its glorious diversity.

This ancient prayer dates back to the Talmudic period when the center of Jewish life was found in Babylonia. Almost lullaby-like, the Hashkiveinu begs God:

> Hashki**vei**nu, Ado**nai** Elo**hei**nu, lesha**lom**,
> veha'ami**dei**nu mal**kei**nu lechayy**iym** ...
> U**fros** a**lei**nu, su**kat** sho**me**cha.
> Lay us down to sleep, Adonai, our God, in peace;
> and raise us up, our Sovereign, to renewed life ...
> and spread over us the shelter of your peace.

The night, in those times, was fraught with dangers both real and imagined. Would the soul, which was believed to be returned to heaven while one slept, be returned when morning came? Would morning come at all? The security of the all-encompassing protection of God was something to be desired. Picture the imagery and the comfort:

> Veha**gein** ba-a**dei**nu, veha**seir** mei'a**lei**nu, o**yeiv**, **dever**,
> ve**che**rev, vera-**av**, veya**gon**. Uv**tzeil** kena**fe**cha tasti**rei**nu
> Shield us, remove from us foe, plague, sword, famine, and woe. And in the shadow of your wings shelter us.

Is there relevance to be found in this prayer in the world today? Perhaps so, since some forty million Americans are believed to suffer from sleep problems and since our times are filled with twenty-first century nightmares such as terrorism, divorce, racism, economic woes and the like. There very well may be serenity to be found in:

Tefilat HaLev - Shabbat/Festivals שבת/חג – תפלת הלב

Ushmor tzei**te**inu uvo-**ei**nu lechay**yiy**m ulesha**lom**,
mei-a**tah** ve'ad o**lam.** U**fros** a**lei**nu su**kat** sha**lom**.
Safeguard our going and coming-for life and peace from now to eternity. And spread over us the shelter of peace.

As we pray this prayer, we are asked to continue the holy work of uprooting the brokenness within our homes, and in all communities. We look forward to the time when our Jewish family will embrace all those who wrestle with God. Then, our Sukkat Shalom will become the shelter of peace it was always intended to be.

Tefilat HaLev - Shabbat/Festivals - שבת/חג – תפלת הלב

VeShamru

"...And they shall keep the Sabbath." VeShamru is a welcoming prayer of Shabbat, taken from Exodus 31:16-17. Just as God rested on the seventh day, Shabbat is created to give us rest and restore the soul. "Vayinafash," the last word of the prayer and referring to resting, is derived from the Hebrew "nefesh" or soul. Shabbat is the promise of a time of peace for all. As God guards us, we are charged with guarding (keeping) the Sabbath.

**Veshamru venei Yisra-eil, et haShabat,
La-asot et haShabat ledorotam, brit olam.**
And the Children of Israel shall keep the Sabbath,
to make the Sabbath an eternal covenant
for their generations.

**Beini uvein benei Yisra-eil, ot hi, le-olam.
Ki sheishet yamiym asa Adonai, et hashamayim ve-et ha-aretz. Uvayom hashvi'i shavat vayinafash.**
Between Me and the Children of Israel it is a sign forever that in six days God made heaven and earth and on the seventh day God rested and was refreshed"

Sung every Friday evening, the prayer follows the Shema, after the congregation has had the opportunity to unite itself and begin to move as one through the rest of the service. The custom to recite the biblical passage at this point in the service has its origins in the Lurianic Kabbalah, and does not appear before the sixteenth century. It is absent in traditions and prayer books less influenced by Kabbalah (such as the Yemenite Baladi tradition) or in those that opposed adding additional readings to the siddur based upon Kabbalah, such as that of the Vilna Gaon.

Tefilat HaLev - Shabbat/Festivals שבת/חג – תפלת הלב

The Shabbat Amidah

The Shabbat Amidah has seven blessings, seven opportunities for laying bare our most vulnerable private self before the One Self with whom pretense is useless. This is one of the most powerful meditations in Jewish spiritual practice. The Hebrew text, when memorized and softly chanted (or davvened), is an hypnotic mantra enabling the "davven-er" to use its images as aids to deep inner work. Seven is the number of Shabbat: creation completed, creation's purpose fulfilled. To aid your journey, three versions of the Amidah are here: A Hebrew Amidah, an interpretive Amidah for English davvenen', and an image-oriented Amidah using visualizations. Of course, Amidah time can also be used for the personal silent meditation of your heart.

The Tefilah or Amidah is the core of all Jewish services. It is known as "The Standing Prayer" (because it is said standing for those able to stand), "The Prayer" ("Ha Tefilah"), and "The Eighteen Blessings" ("Shemoneh Esrei"). (It originally consisted of 18 blessings, although there are now 19). In ancient times, this was the time for the spontaneous prayers of the congregation. The more popular prayers were preserved. These became keva. The kavannot, our own personal blessings and hopes, are for us to add. In the 19 blessings, which became traditional, the worshipper begins with three prayers of praise, followed by petitions, and concludes with three prayers of thanksgiving/peace. On Shabbat however, the middle petitioning section is omitted and is replaced by a blessing which celebrates the holiness of Shabbat, the receiving of the Ten Commandments and the giving of Shabbat. So, on Shabbat there are a total of seven blessings - three of praise, one about Sabbath, and three of thanksgiving/peace.

Tefilat HaLev - Shabbat/Festivals שבת/חג - תפלת הלב

This Amidah should be said while standing (for those able to stand) with feet together and preferably facing Jerusalem, it should be said with complete concentration, and without external interruptions. The guideline derives from Hannah's behavior during prayer, when she prayed in the Temple for the ability to bear a child. She prayed "speaking upon her heart..."

There are different customs as to when and whether the Amidah is said silently, aloud, or sometimes both (first silently, then repeated aloud). Some congregations may say the Amidah silently routinely or occaisionally (especially on Friday evening), and sometimes aloud. If said silently, one's voice should be audible only to one's self. The custom of standing with feet together is done to imitate the angels, whom Ezekiel perceived as "...having one straight leg."

The first three prayers of the first section ("Praise") of the Amidah relate to Avot (our ancestors), Gevurot (powers or might of God), and Kedushat ha-Shem (sanctification of the Name). The core blessing describes angels in heaven singing God's blessings:

> Holy, holy, holy is Adonai Tzeva-ot; the whole world is filled with Divine glory.

The first blessing of the final section is "Avodah" (Service), asking God to restore us as holy Temples. This is followed by Hoda'ah (Thanksgiving), thanking God for our lives, our souls and the miracles that are with us daily. For some, this prayer begins and ends with a bow from the hips symbolizing our gratitude. And, finally, Shalom Rav (Peace) where we ask God for peace, goodness, justice and mercy for the world.

It is customary to take three steps back and three steps forward before and after reciting the Amidah. The steps back represent the withdrawal of one from the material

Tefilat HaLev - Shabbat/Festivals שבת/חג – תפלת הלב

world and the steps forward are symbolic of approaching Adonai.

Our siddur offers several alternative amidah choices: the traditional amidah, an English Amidah to be read or chanted (the option with the 🍃 is designed to be chanted if you include the final prayer, the chatima), as well as an amidah in guided imagery (pp. 73-76). The reader is encouraged to select any one during this time of prayer. If none of these options work, the reader, of course, may substitute the prayers of his/her heart.

250

Tefilat HaLev - Shabbat/Festivals שבת/חג - תפלת הלב

Oseh Shalom

Oseh shalom bimromav, hu ya-**aseh** shalom a**lei**nu,
ve'**al** kol Yisra-**eil**, ve'al kol yoshvei tei**veil** ve-im**ru**: a**mein**.
May the One who makes peace in high places,
make peace for us, for Israel, and for all the earth,
and let us say, Amen.

Reference to the phrase "oseh shalom" is found in the Book of Job 25:2, which reads "Dominion and awe are with [God]; who makes peace in the high places." The origin of the prayer is unknown, but it is probably one of the more modern of the chants in the liturgy. It is often sung at the end of the Amidah, when each individual has an opportunity to say a few private words to God. Perhaps that is an appropriate place for a wish for peace for one's family, one's country, the State of Israel and the world as a whole.

Ve-imru: a**mein**.

Tefilat HaLev - Shabbat/Festivals שבת/חג – תפלת הלב

Aleinu

"Aleinu" is a prayer which along with the Mourner's Kaddish closes the Shabbat and Holy Day services. It is also recited at the end of each of the three daily services. It is among our oldest prayers, originally dating back, in the Rosh Hashanah liturgy, to the third century; and was perhaps first included at the end of the three daily services in the thirteenth century.

"Aleinu" means "it is upon us." In other words, at the end of the day, after all of our prayers, it is upon us to leave the sanctuary and continue our praise for God by how we live. Real prayer begins when we leave the synagogue and re-enter our lives. As we conclude the service, Aleinu offers thanks and praise for the creation of heaven and earth:

> **A**lei**n**u lesha**bei**-ach la-**a**don ha**kol**,
> la**teit** gedu**lah** leyo**tzeir** berei**shiyt**.
> It is upon us to praise the Master of all
> To ascribe greatness to the Author of creation.

In its praise of creation, it directs us to bow...

> **Va-a**nach**n**u kor'**iym** umishtacha**viym** umo**diym**.
> Lif**nei** **M**elech, mal**chei** hamla**chiym**.
> in awe and thankfulness, before the Sovereign,
> the Sovereign of Sovereigns.

This prayer is said while standing because the first and last letters of the prayer, ayin and dalet, spell the Hebrew word for witness (Eid), and it is appropriate for a witness to stand while testifying. Finally, the prayer expresses a hope for the time when the world will be united in pursuit of its ethical goals.

Tefilat HaLev - Shabbat/Festivals שבת/חג – תפלת הלב

Adon Olam

There is no consensus as to when this piyut—liturgical poem—was originally written. Perhaps it originated in the tenth or eleventh centuries and ultimately found its way into the liturgy during the fifteenth century. While most other prayers and hymns speak to our relationship to God as a group or nation, "Adon Olam" is very personal. This is especially illustrated in the last verse, which reads:

> Into your hands I entrust my spirit,
> When I sleep and when I wake,
> And with my spirit, my body also,
> *You are with me and I shall not fear.*

Perhaps that is why this most familiar of hymns is sung at the end of the Shabbat service, at the end of the Kol Nidre service of atonement, sometimes at night before going to bed and sometimes in the presence of an individual near death. It is our reminder to ourselves that there is a greater presence than ourselves, and that our relationship with that greater presence provides meaning to our lives and the comfort of knowing that there is no cause to fear.

Tefilat HaLev - Shabbat/Festivals שבת/חג – תפלת הלב

SONGS

Alphabetical Listing of Songs

Adon Olam / Master of All..178
Adonai, Adonai..202
Adonai Eloheichem Emet / Adonai is True................264
Adonai Sefatai / Open My Lips...................................49
Ahavah Rabah / With a Great Love............................108
Ahavat Olam / With an Eternal Love..........................33
Al Hanisiym / For the Miracles...................................138
Alef Bet...265
All Shlosha Devarim / On Three Things....................149
America, The Beautiful...263
Ana Becho-ach / Please, with Strength......................2
Ana, El Na / Heal Us, God..152
Ani Noladeti / I was born..262
And Then..260
Anim Zemirot / The Song in My Heart.......................88
As We Bless...27
Ashrei / Joyous are They...160
Barchi Nafshi / Bless, my Soul...................................82
Barchu, Dear One..80
Baruch She-amar / Blessed is He..............................80
Baruch She-amar / Blessings.....................................90
Bei Ana Racheitz / In the One....................................147
Beini Uvein / Let it be a Sign.....................................260
Beshem Adonai / In the Name of God.......................5
Betzeit Yisra-eil / When Israel Went Out...................190
Birkat Hamazon / Blessings After the Meal..............266
Chazak / Strength..152
Come Let Us Light...9
David, Melech Yisra-eil / David, King of Israel..........260
Ein Keloheinu / None Like Our God..........................167
Ein Keloheinu - Ladino...168
Eileh Chamdah Libi / These my Heart Desired.........259
Eitz Chayim Hi / It is a Tree of Life............................166
Eli, Eli / Oh God, My God...206
Eliyahu Hanavi / Elijah the Prophet............................226
Elohai Neshama / My God, the Life...........................86
Elohai Netzor / My God..77
Eilu, Ve-eilu, / These and These................................264
Emet / True..118
Esa Einai / I Lift Up My Eyes.....................................261
Evening the Evening..29
Gomeil / Benefactor...151
Hallelu et Adonai / Praise Adonai..............................196

254

Tefilat HaLev - Shabbat/Festivals שבת/חג - תפלת הלב

SONGS

Alphabetical Listing of Songs - Continued

HaleluYahh (traditional)	95
Hallelujah (broken)	96
Hamavdil / Separation	227
Hashiveinu / Return Us	166
Hashkiveinu / May We Lie Down	43
Hatikva / The Hope (Israeli National Anthem)	257
Hinei Mah Tov / Behold How Good	4
Hodu LaAdonai / Give Thanks to Adonai (Morning)	92
Hodu LaAdonai (Hallel) / Let All Who Revere	196
Ivdu et HaShem / Serve the One	259
Kedusha / Holiness	128
Ki Eshmera Shabbat / As I Guard Shabbat	257
Ki MeOlam / From Realm	200
Ki Mitziyon / For From Zion	147
Kol Ha'olam kulo / The Whole World	260
Laihudiym Haita / To the Jews	224
Lecha Adonai / To You, Adonai	149
Lecha Dodi / Come My Beloved	13
Lechi Lach / Go for Yourself	1
Ledor Vador / Generation to Generation	131
Let Us Adore	171
Lichevod Chemda levavi / May my heart cleave	227
Lo Yisa Goy / Nation Shall not Lift Up	149
Love Depends on Me	264
Mah Godlu / How Great	21
Mah Lecha Hayam / What is with You, O Sea	191
Mah Tovu / O How Good	7
Mah Tovu / Blessing Flow	80
Mah Yafeh Hayom/ How lovely is this day	260
Mi Chamocha / You is Like You (evening)	42
Mi Chamocha / You is Like You (morning)	120
Mi Shebeirach / Healing	152
Min Hameitzar / Out of My Distress	196
Mizmor LeDavid / A Psalm of David	164
Mizmor LeDavid / 23rd Psalm	204
Modeh(ah) Ani / I am Grateful	79
Modiym / We are Grateful	67
Nishmat / The Breath	97
Nishmati / O My Soul	1
Od Yavo Shalom / Peace will Yet Come	70
Open to Me	33
Oseh Shalom / Maker of Peace	78

Tefilat HaLev - Shabbat/Festivals שבת/חג – תפלת הלב

SONGS

Alphabetical Listing of Songs - Continued

Ozi vezimrat Yahh / My strength and song of God..............261
Pitchu Li / Open for Me..............198
Powerful Sun..............23
Praise the One..............27
Return Again..............22
Retzei / Recieve..............63
Romemu / Exalt..............23
Sanctuary (Shaker Hymn)..............265
Se-u She-ariym / Lift Up You Gates..............261
Shalom Aleichem / Peace to You..............6
Shalom Rav / A Great Peace..............71
Shiru LaAdonai / Sing to God..............23
Shochein / You Dwell..............98
Shomeir Yisrael / Guardian of Israel..............259
Sim Shalom / Grant Peace..............140
Star Spangled Banner, The..............263
Tefilat Haderech / Prayer of the Road..............179
Tov Lehodot / It is Good to Give Thanks..............20
Tzadik Catamar / The Righteous will flourish..............21
Ufros Aleinu / Spread Over Us..............44
Ushavetem Mayim / Draw Water..............224
Va-ani Tefilati / I am my prayer..............7
Ve-ahavta / And You Shall Teach..............35
Va-anachnu Nevarech / And We Bless..............79
Veha-eir Eineinu / Enlighten Our Eyes..............109
Veshamru / And You Shall Protect..............46
Vetaheir Libeinu / Purify Our Hearts..............60
Vezot HaTorah / This is the Torah..............152
We are Walking / Zulu Hymn..............265
When I Sing..............22
Yad Elohiym Bakol / God's Hands are in Everything..............263
Yedid Nefesh / Lover of My Soul..............257
Yehuda Le'olam / Judah Persists..............265
Yiheyu Leratzon / May the Words..............77
Yigdal / Magnified..............258
Yismechu Vemalechutcha / O You who Rejoice..............47
Yismechu Hashamayim / Rejoice O Heavens..............23
Zochreinu / Remember Us..............52

Tefilat HaLev - Shabbat/Festivals - תפלת הלב - שבת/חג

Hatikva / The Hope (Israeli National Anthem) — התקוה

Kol od balei**vav** peni**ma**
Nefesh Yehu**di** homi**ya**,
Ulfa-**atei** miz**rach** kadi**ma**
Ayin leTzi**yon** tzofi**ya**.

Od lo av**da** tikva**tei**nu,
Hatik**va** bat shnot alpa**yim**,
Li**hyot** am chof**shi**
be-artz**ei**nu
Eretz Tzi**yon** virushalayim.

כָּל עוֹד בַּלֵּבָב פְּנִימָה
נֶפֶשׁ יְהוּדִי הוֹמִיָּה,
וּלְפַאֲתֵי מִזְרָח, קָדִימָה,
עַיִן לְצִיּוֹן צוֹפִיָּה.

עוֹד לֹא אָבְדָה תִּקְוָתֵנוּ
הַתִּקְוָה בַּת שְׁנוֹת אַלְפַּיִם
לִהְיוֹת עַם חָפְשִׁי בְּאַרְצֵנוּ,
אֶרֶץ צִיּוֹן וִירוּשָׁלַיִם.

As long as in the heart, within, a Jewish soul still yearns, and onward, towards the ends of the east, an eye still gazes toward Zion. Our hope is not yet lost, the hope of two thousand years, to be a free people in our land, the land of Zion and Jerusalem.

Yedid Nefesh / Lover of My Soul — ידיד נפש

Yedid nefesh av haracha**man**,
me**shoch** avde**cha** el
retzo**ne**cha.
Yarutz avde**cha** kemo **a**yal,
yishtacha**ve** el mul hada**re**cha.

יְדִיד נֶפֶשׁ, אָב הָרַחֲמָן,
מְשׁוֹךְ עַבְדְּךָ אֶל רְצוֹנֶךָ.
יָרוּץ עַבְדְּךָ כְּמוֹ אַיָּל,
יִשְׁתַּחֲוֶה אֶל מוּל הֲדָרֶךָ.

Lover of my soul, merciful God, bring Your servant close to Your will. Your servant will run like a gazelle, to prostrate before Your glory.

See Appendix for more on Yedid Nefesh

Ki Eshmera Shabbat / As I Guard Shabbat — כי אשמרה שבת

כִּי אֶשְׁמְרָה שַׁבָּת, אֵל יִשְׁמְרֵנִי,
אוֹת הִיא לְעוֹלְמֵי עַד בֵּינוֹ וּבֵינִי.

Ki Eshme**ra** Shab**bat**, Eil Yishm**rei**ni,
ot he le'o**le**mei ad **bei**no uvei**ni**.

As I guard Shabbat, God guards me. It is a sign forever between God and me.

Tefilat HaLev - Shabbat/Festivals – שבת/חג – תפלת הלב

יגדל — Yigdal / Magnified

Yigdal Elohim chai veyishtabach,	יִגְדַּל אֱלֹהִים חַי וְיִשְׁתַּבַּח,
nimtza ve-ein eit el metziyuto.	נִמְצָא, וְאֵין עֵת אֶל מְצִיאוּתוֹ:
Echad ve-ein yachid keyichudo,	אֶחָד וְאֵין יָחִיד כְּיִחוּדוֹ,
ne'elam vegam ein sof le-achduto.	נֶעְלָם, וְגַם אֵין סוֹף לְאַחְדּוּתוֹ:
Ein lo demut haguf ve-eino guf, lo	אֵין לוֹ דְּמוּת הַגּוּף וְאֵינוֹ גוּף,
na'aroch eilav kedushato.	לֹא נַעֲרוֹךְ אֵלָיו קְדֻשָּׁתוֹ:
Kadmon lechol davar asher nivra,	קַדְמוֹן לְכָל דָּבָר אֲשֶׁר נִבְרָא,
rishon ve-ein reishiyt lereishito.	רִאשׁוֹן וְאֵין רֵאשִׁית לְרֵאשִׁיתוֹ:
Hino adon olam lechol notzar,	הִנּוֹ אֲדוֹן עוֹלָם, לְכָל נוֹצָר.
yoreh gedulato umalchuto.	יוֹרֶה גְדֻלָּתוֹ וּמַלְכוּתוֹ:
Shefa nevuato netano,	שֶׁפַע נְבוּאָתוֹ נְתָנוֹ,
el anshei segulato vetif-arto.	אֶל אַנְשֵׁי סְגֻלָּתוֹ וְתִפְאַרְתּוֹ:
Lo kam beYisra-eil keMoshe od	לֹא קָם בְּיִשְׂרָאֵל כְּמֹשֶׁה עוֹד,
navi umabiyt et temunato.	נָבִיא וּמַבִּיט אֶת תְּמוּנָתוֹ:
Torat emet natan le'amo el,	תּוֹרַת אֱמֶת נָתַן לְעַמּוֹ אֵל,
al yad neviyo ne-eman beito.	עַל יַד נְבִיאוֹ נֶאֱמַן בֵּיתוֹ:
Lo yachaliyf ha-eil velo yamiyr	לֹא יַחֲלִיף הָאֵל וְלֹא יָמִיר דָּתוֹ,
dato, le'olamiym, lezulato.	לְעוֹלָמִים, לְזוּלָתוֹ:
Tzofeh veyodei-a setareinu,	צוֹפֶה וְיוֹדֵעַ סְתָרֵינוּ,
mabiyt lesof davar bekadmato.	מַבִּיט לְסוֹף דָּבָר בְּקַדְמָתוֹ:
Gomeil le-ish chesed kemif-alo,	גּוֹמֵל לְאִישׁ חֶסֶד כְּמִפְעָלוֹ,
notein lerasha ra kerish'ato.	נוֹתֵן לְרָשָׁע רָע כְּרִשְׁעָתוֹ:
Yishlach lekeitz yamiyn meshicheinu,	יִשְׁלַח לְקֵץ הַיָּמִין מְשִׁיחֵנוּ,
lifdot mechakei keitz yeshu'ato.	לִפְדּוֹת מְחַכֵּי קֵץ יְשׁוּעָתוֹ:
Metiym yechayeh El berov chasdo,	מֵתִים יְחַיֶּה אֵל בְּרוֹב חַסְדּוֹ,
Baruch adei ad shem tehilato.	בָּרוּךְ עֲדֵי עַד שֵׁם תְּהִלָּתוֹ:

Magnified and praised be the living God, who is, and without limit in time unto being. Who is One, and there is no unity alike; inconceivable, and unending in unity. Without bodily form or substance, who can compare in holiness? Who was before anything was created; the first, without beginning. Behold the master of the universe, who teaches greatness and sovereignty to every creature. The rich gift of prophecy to those chosen in glory. There has never arisen again in Israel a prophet like Moses, who beheld God. A Torah of truth, God gave to us, by the hand of the faithful prophet. God will not alter nor change to everlasting. Who watches and knows our secret thoughts; who sees the end before something is. Who bestows lovingkindness according to effort; who gives to the wicked according to their wickedness. Who will send our anointed at the end of days, to redeem those who wait for salvation. In the abundance of lovingkindness, God will quicken the dead. Blessed for evermore be God's glorious name.

Tefilat HaLev - Shabbat/Festivals – שבת/חג – תפלת הלב

Eileh chamdah libi / These my Heart Desired — אלה חמדה ליבי

Eileh chamdah libi
chusa na ve-al na tit'aleim.

אֵלֶּה חָמְדָה לִיבִּי
חוּסָה נָא וְאַל נָא תִּתְעַלָּם.

These my heart desired. Have mercy on me and do not hide yourself.

Shomeir Yisra-eil / Guardian of Israel — שומר ישראל

שׁוֹמֵר יִשְׂרָאֵל. שְׁמוֹר שְׁאֵרִית יִשְׂרָאֵל. וְאַל יֹאבַד יִשְׂרָאֵל. הָאוֹמְרִים שְׁמַע יִשְׂרָאֵל:
שׁוֹמֵר גּוֹי אֶחָד. שְׁמוֹר שְׁאֵרִית עַם אֶחָד. וְאַל יֹאבַד גּוֹי אֶחָד. הַמְיַחֲדִים שִׁמְךָ יהוה אֱלֹהֵינוּ יהוה אֶחָד:
שׁוֹמֵר גּוֹי קָדוֹשׁ. שְׁמוֹר שְׁאֵרִית עַם קָדוֹשׁ. וְאַל יֹאבַד גּוֹי קָדוֹשׁ. הַמְשַׁלְּשִׁים בְּשָׁלֹשׁ קְדֻשּׁוֹת לְקָדוֹשׁ:

Shomeir Yisra-eil, shemor she-eiriyt Yisra-eil,
Ve'al yovad Yisra-eil, ha-omriym, shema Yisra-eil
  Shomeir goy echad, shemor she-eiriyt am echad
  Ve'al yovad goy echad, hamyachadiym shimcha
  Adonai eloheinu Adonai echad.
Shomeir goy kadosh, shemor she-eiriyt am kadosh
Ve'al yovad goy kadosh, hamshalshiym beshalosh
Kedushot lekadosh.

Guardian of Israel, protect the remnant of Israel,
Don't let Israel be destroyed, Those who say "Shma Yisrael."
  Guardian of the one nation, Protect the remnant of the one people
  Don't let the one nation be destroyed, Those who proclaim the
  oneness of your name; "Adonai is our God, Adonai is One."
Guardian of the holy nation, Protect the remnant of the holy people,
Don't let the holy nation be destroyed, Those who proclaim three-fold,
Sanctifications to the Holy One.

Ivdu et HaShem / Serve the One — עבדו את־יהוה

עִבְדוּ אֶת־יהוה בְּשִׂמְחָה בֹּאוּ לְפָנָיו בִּרְנָנָה:

Ivdu et HaShem besimcha, bo-u lefanav birnana.
Serve the One with joy, Come before God with joyous song. (Ps 100:2)

תפלת הלב - Tefilat HaLev - Shabbat/Festivals שבת/חג

Mah Yafeh Hayom / How lovely is this day מה יפה היום

מָה יָפֶה הַיּוֹם, שַׁבָּת שָׁלוֹם.

Ma yafeh hayom, Shabbat Shalom.
How lovely is this day, Shabbat Shalom.

Beini Uvein / Between You and Me ביני ובין

בֵּינִי וּבֵין בְּנֵי יִשְׂרָאֵל אוֹת הִיא לְעוֹלָם,
כִּי שֵׁשֶׁת יָמִים עָשָׂה יהוה אֶת הַשָּׁמַיִם וְאֶת הָאָרֶץ,
וּבַיּוֹם הַשְּׁבִיעִי שָׁבַת וַיִּנָּפַשׁ.

**Beini uvein benei Yisra-eil, ot hi, le-olam.
Ki sheishet yamiym asa Adonai, et hashamayim ve-et
ha-aretz. Uvayom hashvi'i shavat vayinafash.**
Let it be a sign between us forever,
for in six days I made everything
and on the seventh day I made Shabbat.
I made Shabbat for My soul.   © R. Shefa Gold

Kol Ha'olam kulo / The whole world כל העולם כלו

כָּל הָעוֹלָם כֻּלּוֹ גֶּשֶׁר צַר מְאֹד וְהָעִקָּר לֹא לְפַחֵד כְּלָל

**Kol Ha'olam kulo Gesher Tzar me'od
Veha'ikar lo lefached klal.**
The whole world is a very narrow bridge,
And the main thing to recall is not to be afraid at all.

David, Melech Yisra-eil / David, King of Israel דוד מלך ישראל

דָּוִד מֶלֶךְ יִשְׂרָאֵל חַי חַי וְקַיָּם.

David, Melech Yisra-eil, chai vekayam.
David, King of Israel, lives and endures.

And Then

And then, both men and women will be gentle,
And then, both women and men will be strong,
And then, all will be so varied, rich and free,
And then, everywhere will be called Eden once again.
© Judy Chicago (adapted)

260

Tefilat HaLev - Shabbat/Festivals — שבת/חג

Esa Einai / I Lift Up My Eyes — אשא עיני

אֶשָּׂא עֵינַי אֶל־הֶהָרִים מֵאַיִן יָבֹא עֶזְרִי:
עֶזְרִי מֵעִם יהוה עֹשֵׂה שָׁמַיִם וָאָרֶץ:

Esa einai el heharim mei-ayin yavo ezri?
Ezri mei-iym Adonai osei shamayim va-aretz.

I lift up my eyes to the mountains. From whence will my help come?
My help will come from the Source of all,
the power that fashions heavens and earth,
the power that sustains Life even in the midst of death. (Ps 121:1-2)

Se-u She-ariym / Lift Up You Gates — שאו שערים

שְׂאוּ שְׁעָרִים רָאשֵׁיכֶם וְהִנָּשְׂאוּ פִּתְחֵי עוֹלָם וְיָבוֹא
מֶלֶךְ הַכָּבוֹד: מִי הוּא זֶה מֶלֶךְ הַכָּבוֹד? יהוה
צְבָאוֹת, הוּא מֶלֶךְ הַכָּבוֹד. סֶלָה.

Se-u she-ariym rasheichem, vehinas-u pitchei olam, Veyavo melech hakavod. Mi hu zeh melech hakavod: Adonai tzeva-ot, Hu Melech hakavod. Selah.

Lift up your heads, O gates. Lift yourselves up, oh ancient doors. Let the Sovereign of Glory enter. Who is this Sovereign of Glory? Adonai Tz'va-ot, the Sovereign of Glory!

Tefilat Haderech / Prayer of the Road

May we be blessed as we go on our way.
May we be guided in peace.
May we be blessed with health and joy.
May this be our blessing, Amen.
Amen, Amen, may this be our blessing, Amen.
May we be sheltered by the wings of peace.
May we be kept in safety and in love.
May grace and compassion find their way to every soul.
May this be our blessing, Amen.
Amen, Amen, may this be our blessing, Amen.

© Debbie Friedman

עָזִּי וְזִמְרָת יָהּ, וַיְהִי לִי לִישׁוּעָה.

Ozi vezimrat Yahh, vayehi li lishua.
My strength and song of God, be for me my deliverance.

Tefilat HaLev - Shabbat/Festivals — שבת/חג — תפלת הלב

Ani Noladeti / I was born — אני נולדתי

אֲנִי נוֹלַדְתִּי אֶל הַמַּנְגִּינוֹת
וְאֶל הַשִּׁירִים שֶׁל כָּל הַמְּדִינוֹת.
נוֹלַדְתִּי לַלָּשׁוֹן וְגַם לַמָּקוֹם,
לַמְעַט, לֶהָמוֹן, שֶׁיּוֹשִׁיט יָד לַשָּׁלוֹם.
אֲנִי נוֹלַדְתִּי לַשָּׁלוֹם שֶׁרַק יַגִּיעַ.
אֲנִי נוֹלַדְתִּי לַשָּׁלוֹם שֶׁרַק יָבוֹא.
אֲנִי נוֹלַדְתִּי לַשָּׁלוֹם שֶׁרַק יוֹפִיעַ
אֲנִי רוֹצָה, אֲנִי רוֹצָה לִהְיוֹת כְּבָר בּוֹ!
אֲנִי נוֹלַדְתִּי אֶל הַחֲלוֹם
וּבוֹ אֲנִי רוֹאָה שֶׁיָּבוֹא הַשָּׁלוֹם
נוֹלַדְתִּי לָרָצוֹן וְלָאֱמוּנָה
שֶׁהִנֵּה הוּא יָבוֹא אַחֲרֵי שְׁלוֹשִׁים שָׁנָה.
אֲנִי נוֹלַדְתִּי לַשָּׁלוֹם שֶׁרַק יַגִּיעַ...
נוֹלַדְתִּי לְאֻמָּה וְלָהּ שָׁנִים אַלְפַּיִם
שְׁמוּרָה לָהּ אֲדָמָה וְלָהּ חֶלְקַת שָׁמַיִם
וְהִיא רוֹאָה צוֹפָה הִנֵּה עוֹלֶה הַיּוֹם
וְהַשָּׁעָה יָפָה זוֹהִי שְׁעַת שָׁלוֹם.
אֲנִי נוֹלַדְתִּי לַשָּׁלוֹם שֶׁרַק יַגִּיעַ...

Ani noladeti el hamanginot ve-el
hashirim shel kol hamedinot
noladeti lalashon vegam lamakom
lame'at lehamon sheyoshiyt yad lashalom.
Ani noladeti el hachalom
uvo ani ro-e/ro-ah sheyavo hashalom
noladeti laratzon vela'emunah
shehinei hu yavo acharei shloshim shanah.
CHORUS: Ani noladeti lashalom
  sherak yagi'a
  Ani noladeti lashalom
  sherak yavo
  Ani noladeti lashalom
  sherak yofi'a
  Ani rotzah, lihyot kvar bo.
Ani noladeti el hachalom
uvo ani ro'e/ro'ah sheyavo hashalom
noladeti laratzon vela'emunah.
shehinei hu yavo acharei shloshim shanah.
noladeti la'umah velah
shanim alpayim
shmurah lah adamah velah
chelkat shamayim
vehi ro-ah, tzofah, hinei
oleh hayom vehasha'ah yafah
zohi sha'at shalom.
Ani noladeti lashalom

I was born to the melodies and to the songs of all countries
I was born to the language and the place too
to the few and many who will give peace a hand. Ah - ah - ah - ah -
  I was born to peace - let it arrive. I was born to peace - let it come.
  I was born to peace - let it appear. I want, I want to be in it already.
I was born to the dream and in it I see that peace will come
I was born to the desire and the belief that it will come after thirty years.
  Chorus...
I was born to a people two thousand years old that have a land and it has a piece of heaven and it sees, watches the day unfold and it's a beautiful moment, moment of peace. Ah - ah - ah - Chorus...

© Uzi Hitman

Tefilat HaLev - Shabbat/Festivals - שבת/חג - תפלת הלב

The Star Spangled Banner

Oh, say can you see by the dawn's early light
What so proudly we hailed at the twilight's last gleaming?
Whose broad stripes and bright stars thru the perilous fight,
O'er the ramparts we watched were so gallantly streaming?
And the rocket's red glare, the bombs bursting in air,
Gave proof through the night that our flag was still there.
Oh, say does that star-spangled banner yet wave
O'er the land of the free and the home of the brave?

Francis Scott Key 1814

America, The Beautiful

O beautiful for spacious skies, For amber waves of grain,
For purple mountain majesties above the fruited plain!
America! America! God shed His grace on thee,
And crown thy good with brotherhood,
From sea to shining sea!

O beautiful for pilgrim feet, Whose stern impassion'd stress
A thoroughfare for freedom beat across the wilderness!
America! America! God mend thine ev'ry flaw,
Confirm thy soul in self-control, Thy liberty in law!

O beautiful for heroes proved In liberating strife,
Who more than self their country loved,
and mercy more than life!
America! America! May God thy gold refine
Till all success be nobleness, And ev'ry gain divine!

O Beautiful for patriot dream that sees beyond the years
Thine alabaster cities gleam, undimmed by human tears!
America! America! God shed His grace on thee,
And crown thy good with brotherhood from sea to shining sea!

Katharine Lee Bates - 1913

Yad Elohiym Bakol / God's Hands are in Everything יד אלהים בכל

Yad Elohiym, Elohiym Bakol יָד אֱלֹהִים, אֱלֹהִים בַּכֹּל

Yad Elohiym Bakol יָד אֱלֹהִים בַּכֹּל

God's hands are in everything. © Eli Lester

Tefilat HaLev - Shabbat/Festivals – שבת/חג – תפלת הלב

Love Depends on Me

Chorus: I will do what I can, to repair the world we live in.
I will give of myself, and help bring harmony.
I will open my heart, to my sisters and my brothers,
Because I depend on love, and love depends on me

I don't need to be a hero. I don't need to understand.
Alone, I can not fix the world, but to help is in my hands.
Chorus:

I can't stand by, remaining silent, allowing evil to prevail.
I will raise my voice in chorus, for together we can't fail.
Chorus:

I will give of my highest self, holy essence, from within.
With my love, and true compassion, healing can begin.
Chorus: © Eli Lester & Phil Bell

Eilu, Ve-eilu, / These and These   אלו ואלו

אֵלוּ וְאֵלוּ דִבְרֵי אֱלֹהִים חַיִים

Eilu, Ve-**eilu**, di**vrei** Elo**hiym** Cha**yim**
These words, and these words, are the words of the Living God
These things, and these things, are the things of the Living God
(Eruvin 13b)   © Eli Lester

Adonai Eloheichem Emet / Adonai is True   יהוה אלהיכם אמת

Adonai Elo**hei**chem e**met.**   יְהוָה אֱלֹהֵיכֶם אֱמֶת

יְהוָה שְׁכִינָה אֱלֹהֵינוּ שָׁלוֹם

Ado**nai** Shechi**na** Elo**hei**nu shalom.

הַקָּדוֹשׁ בָּרוּךְ הוּא הָאֱמֶת

HaKa**dosh** Ba**ruch** Hu ha-e**met.**

Ado**nai** (Ado**nai**) Elo**hei**- (Elo**hei**-) chem e**met**. (2x)
Ado**nai** (Ado**nai**) Shechi**na** (Shechi**na**) Elo**hei**nu shalom (shalom)
HaKa**dosh** (HaKa**dosh**) Ba**ruch** Hu (Ba**ruch** Hu) ha-e**met**
Ado**nai** Elo**hei**chem e**met**.
Adonai is a true God. Adonai, Shechina, Our God of Peace,
Holy One of Blessing, One of truth. Adonai is a true God.
       © Eli Lester

Tefilat HaLev - Shabbat/Festivals - שבת/חג - תפלת הלב

Sanctuary (Shaker Hymn)

וְעָשׂוּ לִי מִקְדָּשׁ וְשָׁכַנְתִּי בְּתוֹכָם:
וַאֲנַחְנוּ נְבָרֵךְ יָהּ, מֵעַתָּה וְעַד עוֹלָם:

Ve'asu li Mikdash, **vesho**chanti beto**cham.**
Va-anachnu neva**rech** Yahh, mei-**atah** ve'**ad olam.**

Make a Holy space for me, and I will dwell within. (Ex 25:8)
We acknowledge YAHH, from here and now and to all time and space.

God, prepare me to be a sanctuary
Pure and holy, tried and true
With thanksgiving I'll be a living Sanctuary for You!

We are walking (Zulu Hymn)

We are walking in the Light of God (4)
We are walking (2)
We are walking in the Light of God (4)

Yehudah Le'olam Tosheiv - Judah Lives Forever (Joel 4:20)

וִיהוּדָה לְעוֹלָם תֵּשֵׁב וִירוּשָׁלַם לְדוֹר וָדוֹר:

Viyhuda le'**olam** tei**sheiv** (2x); ViYerusha**lam** le**dor vador.** (2x)

Alef Bet

Alef א, Bet בּ, Vet ב;

Gimel ג, Dalet ד, Hei ה;

Vav ו, Zayin ז, Chet ח, Tet ט;

Yud י, Kaf כּ, Chaf כ;

Lamed ל, Mem מ, Nun נ;

Samech ס, Ayin ע, Pei פּ, Fei פ;

Tzadi צ, Kuf ק, Reish ר;

Shin שׁ; Sin שׂ; Tav ת.

Tefilat HaLev - Shabbat/Festiv

Birkat Hamazon -

Ve-achalta - We Ate

(Deut 8:10) וְאָכַלְתָּ וְשָׂבָעְתָּ וּבֵרַכְתָּ

Refrain: **Ve-achalta, vesavata, uveyrachta** (2x)

We ate when we were hungry
And now we're satisfied
We thank the Source of Blessing
For all that S/He provides. Refrain:

Hunger is a yearning
In body and soul
Earth, Air, Fire, Water
And Spirit make us whole. Refrain:

Giving and Receiving
We open up our hands
From Seedtime through Harvest
We're partners with the Land. Refrain:

We share in a vision
Of wholeness and release
Where every child is nourished
And we all live in peace. Refrain

For Shabbat: We've eaten together
Rejoicing as we sing
We cling to Your Torah
To open to our being.

© Rabbi Hanna Tiferet Seigel (Shabbat verse added)

(Ps 145:16) פּוֹתֵחַ אֶת יָדֶךָ, וּמַשְׂבִּיעַ לְכָל חַי רָצוֹן:

Potei-ach et yadecha, umasbiya lechol chai ratzon.

You Open Your hand; I open my heart;
To this abundance (2x)
And all life, All will, is satisfied (2x)

© Rabbi Shefa Gold

בְּרִיךְ רַחֲמָנָא מַלְכָּא דְעָלְמָא מָרֵיהּ דְהַאי פִּתָּא.

Brich rachamana malka d'alma ma'rei dehai pita. Brachot 40b

You are the Source of Life for all that is
And Your blessings flow through me.

© Rabbi Shefa Gold